Services Trade in the
Western Hemisphere

Services Trade in the Western Hemisphere

Liberalization, Integration, and Reform

Sherry M. Stephenson
Editor

ORGANIZATION OF AMERICAN STATES

BROOKINGS INSTITUTION PRESS
Washington, D.C.

The Brookings Institution is a private nonprofit organization devoted to research, education, and publication on important issues of domestic and foreign policy. Its principal purpose is to bring knowledge to bear on current and emerging policy problems. The Institution maintains a position of neutrality on issues of public policy. Interpretations or conclusions in Brookings publications should be understood to be solely those of the authors.

Library of Congress Cataloging-in-Publication Data

Services trade in the Western Hemisphere : liberalization, integration, and reform /
Sherry M. Stephenson, editor.
    p. cm.
Includes bibliographical references and index.
    ISBN 0-8157-8147-4 (alk. paper)
    1. Service industries--Government policy—Western Hemisphere. 2. International business enterprises—Western Hemisphere. 3. Free trade—Western Hemisphere. 4. International trade. 5. General Agreement on Trade in Services (1994) I. Stephenson, Sherry. II. Title.

HD9985.A2 S47 2000   00-010085
382'.45--dc21   CIP

                              9 8 7 6 5 4 3 2 1

The paper used in this publication meets minimum requirements of the American National Standard for Information Sciences—Permanence of Paper for Printed Library Materials: ANSI Z39.48-1992.

Typeset in
Times New Roman

Composition by
AlphaWebTech
Mechanicsville, Maryland

Printed by
R. R. Donnelly and Sons
Harrisonburg, Virginia

To my parents

Contents

Foreword

OVER THE LAST FIVE YEARS the Organization of American States (OAS), through its Trade Unit, has been deeply involved in trade and economic integration issues and processes in the Western Hemisphere, particularly in supporting the negotiation of the Free Trade Area of the Americas (FTAA) since that initiative was launched at the first Summit of the Americas in December 1994.

The work of the OAS in the area of trade includes technical and analytical support for the FTAA negotiating process as well as trade-related technical assistance and training to countries and subregions. In the fulfillment of its mission in recent years the Trade Unit team of experts, reflecting on its own experience, has produced an important stream of contributions to the analysis of trade and integration issues, which includes several books and numerous working papers.

This is the second volume produced in partnership with the Brookings Institution Press. The first was *Trade Rules in the Making: Challenges in Regional and Multilateral Negotiations*, published in 1999. Edited by Miguel Rodriguez, Patrick Low, and Barbara Kotschwar, that volume contains a series of papers by OAS Trade Unit staff and other leading trade experts on the GATT/WTO-consistency of regional trade agreements, particularly the FTAA.

This volume, edited by Sherry Stephenson, deputy director of the OAS Trade Unit, focuses on the challenges of liberalization, integration, and reform of trade in services in the Western Hemisphere. This is a timely and useful publication for at least three reasons. First, for the first time in history all of the countries of the Western Hemisphere are engaged in simultaneous negotiations to liberalize trade in services at the multilateral, regional, and subregional levels. While much has been written about services negotiations at the multilateral level, this volume represents a pioneering effort by services experts to discuss the articulation and linkages among these three different levels of services negotiations.

Second, it has become increasingly clear to governments, the private sector, and trade analysts that the quality and competitiveness of the services sector are essential to economic growth and development. From banking and financial services to telecommunications and transportation, along with tourism and professional services, services are now among the most critical elements for continued economic dynamism for the countries of the Americas. Services account on average for 60 percent of the Western Hemisphere's gross domestic product. In trade terms, services are even more important for the smaller economies of Central America and the Caribbean, for many of which services exports are the largest foreign exchange earner and the largest source of employment. For those economies, investment in services could well prove to be one of the main engines of growth in future years.

A third reason why this volume is timely and of interest is related to the fact that over the past decade trade negotiations have undergone a decisive shift in focus from negative prescription to positive rule-making. Before the Uruguay Round the basic trade policy model was exemplified by an interlocking set of negative prescriptions by which governments would discipline their ability to impose trade barriers at the border or to discriminate among domestic or imported goods or among their trading partners. Today, trade agreements require governments not only to live up to the traditional disciplines by reducing trade barriers at the border, but also to adopt and implement specific policies, practices, and procedures that reach well behind national borders. This new focus of trade rules constitutes a major paradigm shift with profound implications in the relationship between trade rules and domestic regulations and governance, as well as in the political management of trade rules and trade negotiations and in the balance of economic benefits derived from trade rules. In few areas of trade negotiations is this shift to positive rule-making as apparent as it is in services. How best to remove discrimination against foreign services providers, how to deal with nondiscriminatory domestic regulations that have the effect of restricting trade, and how to design rules that enhance transparency, ensure stability, and help improve the liberalizing character of any given services agreement are among the key "new paradigm" issues analyzed in this volume.

Many of the chapters in this volume were presented at the conference "Services Trade and the Western Hemisphere," held in San José, Costa Rica, in July

1999, which was organized by the OAS Trade Unit in partnership with the International Development Bank–Institute for the Integration of Latin America and the Caribbean (IDB-INTAL) and the Ministry of Foreign Trade of Costa Rica. The conference constituted the contribution by the OAS to a series of events leading up to the initiation of multilateral negotiations under the WTO General Agreement on Trade in Services (GATS), the WTO Ministerial Meeting in Seattle in December 1999, and the first World Services Congress in Atlanta in November 1999. The San José conference was particularly motivated by the fact that in the Americas countries had launched regional negotiations on services in April 1998 as part of the process of creating the FTAA.

We would like to thank the IDB-INTAL and the Ministry of Foreign Trade of Costa Rica for joining the OAS/Inter-American Council for Integral Development (CIDI) and the OAS Trade Unit in sponsoring and organizing this event. We would also like to recognize the role of the Coalition of Services Industries of the United States (CSI), in particular its executive director, Robert Vastine, for his vision and motivation in supporting the series of events leading up to the World Services Congress.

Sherry Stephenson is uniquely positioned to edit this book. As the senior Trade Unit specialist in services she has been the key person providing technical support to the Hemispheric FTAA Working Group on Services since its creation in 1996 during the FTAA preparatory stage, and more recently to the FTAA Negotiating Group on Services. She has also been engaged in numerous technical assistance activities to OAS member countries in the services area and has written extensively on services negotiation issues. We express our recognition of her efforts and those of her collaborators in the Trade Unit for putting together this volume in an efficient and timely manner.

Finally, special thanks are due to all of the authors of this volume. Their high-quality contributions are the best guarantee that this book will be a useful resource for the countries of the Western Hemisphere as they move toward the goal of greater competitiveness and liberalization in the services sectors of their economies.

César Gaviria
Secretary General
Organization of American States

José M. Salazar-Xirinachs
Chief Trade Adviser
Organization of American States

Acknowledgments

A BOOK IN ITS FINISHED form never entirely conveys the amount of effort and hard work that goes into it during its preparation. This book in particular is the culmination of the collaboration and efforts of many trade analysts and trade officials in the Western Hemisphere who believe in the cause of free trade and in the liberalization of services markets and who work tirelessly for this cause.

First and foremost, however, the book is the result of the extremely devoted and professional efforts of my two collaborators over the past year, Soonhwa Yi and Anne-Lise Georges. The conference "Services Trade in the Western Hemisphere" held in San José, Costa Rica, in July 1999, would never have happened without the work carried out for the preparation of the conference by Anne-Lise Georges, who put the final organizing glue on all of the details that go into such an ambitious project. Her friendly manner also helped to place the conference participants at ease for the sessions and discussion. The present volume, a product of the papers presented at the conference and of subsequent further contributions, would never have materialized without the work of Soonhwa Yi, who was responsible for coordinating the editing of the papers and for putting them in final form. She also checked substance and provided several helpful comments and suggestions. Her cheerful messages to the authors probably account for this volume going to press on time!

I would also like to thank the chief trade adviser of the Organization of American States (OAS), José Manuel Salazar, for supporting the idea to hold a conference on services when I proposed it, and for doing his maximum to ensure that the conference was a success. Likewise, I would like to acknowledge the enthusiasm for the services conference and book on the part of Maryse Robert at the OAS Trade Unit, who also provided useful comments on some of the papers. The efforts of Francisco Coves of the OAS Trade Unit for the administration of the project are also very much appreciated. Donald Mackay, as always, provided support and inspiration for me in this project as in so many other areas.

Thanks must especially go to the many services negotiators throughout the Western Hemisphere who agreed to take time from their busy schedules to write a chapter for this book. Their efforts are truly appreciated, and their contributions have made the volume a much richer and more authentic one.

Gratitude is also due to the Ministry of Foreign Trade in Costa Rica (COMEX) for hosting the conference in San José, and for proving to be a very efficient interlocutor for the execution of this project. In particular, thanks must be expressed to Anabel González, the vice minister of trade of Costa Rica, for obtaining the support and joint sponsorship of COMEX for this effort, and to Fernando Ocampo, who coordinated the organization of the conference in Costa Rica in a most professional manner. I would also like to thank Janet Mowery for doing a thorough and conscientious job with the copy editing of the manuscript for the Brookings Institution Press, and Christopher Kelaher and Janet Walker for their patience and efficiency in managing the editing process for Brookings.

Financial support from the Committee on Integral and Sustainable Development (CIDI) of the OAS and from the Institute for the Integration of Latin America and the Caribbean (INTAL) made it possible for the conference speakers as well as the services negotiators from the countries participating in the Free Trade Area of the Americas (FTAA) negotiations to attend the conference. OAS-CIDI funds also permitted the publication of this volume.

None of the sponsors or any of the persons mentioned above, however, is accountable for any errors, omissions, or statements made in the book. The authors of each chapter and I, as the editor, take full responsibility for its content.

Finally, I am grateful to my two children, Matthew and Corinne, who have grown to share my enthusiasm for the cause of trade liberalization, and for their patience in allowing my time and their lives to be intertwined with this goal.

S.M.S.
May 2000

Overview: Services Issues for the Western Hemphisphere

SHERRY M. STEPHENSON

INTEREST IN THE LIBERALIZATION of services trade in the Western Hemisphere has been running high since the mid-1990s, and all of the countries of the region are participating in liberalization efforts, often on various fronts simultaneously. The majority of chapters in this volume were presented at the conference "Services Trade and the Western Hemisphere," in San José, Costa Rica, in July 1999. This conference was one of the key events leading up to the first World Services Congress in Atlanta in November 1999, and to the negotiations under the WTO General Agreement on Trade in Services (GATS) in January 2000. One inspiration for the conference was the fact that in the Western Hemisphere countries had already launched regional negotiations on services in April 1998 as part of the effort to create a Free Trade Area of the Americas (FTAA). In addition, since 1994 all of the countries in the hemisphere have also concluded one or more subregional integration agreements to cover trade in services or are in the process of doing so.

Thus, efforts to negotiate the liberalization of services trade are currently under way at three levels in the Western Hemisphere: the multilateral level, the regional or hemispheric level, and the subregional level. These efforts make it imperative both to understand what is being discussed and implemented and to articulate the linkages and relationships between the different agreements and the disciplines and obligations they contain. A great deal has been written about services at the multilateral level under GATS, but no one volume addresses the subregional and regional efforts to liberalize services in the Western Hemi-

1

sphere. This book fills that gap and explores the link between the ongoing regional, subregional, and multilateral negotiations on services.

Part One deals with the main issues relevant to services liberalization at the multilateral and regional levels, including options to improve the GATS architecture; the scope of regulatory reform; the treatment of investment; and the clarification of WTO requirements for countries to engage in an economic integration agreement. Part Two examines regional agreements on trade in services concluded by several economic integration groups—including NAFTA, the Andean Community, MERCOSUR, and CARICOM—as well as several bilateral free trade agreements covering services, especially those signed by Mexico. These agreements are examined in depth by regional trade experts, who also evaluate the degree of market opening and regulatory reform such agreements have achieved. Also discussed is the way these agreements might best contribute to ongoing services liberalization.

What lies behind the recent activity and interest in negotiating liberalization of services trade by countries of the Western Hemisphere? Interest in this area was heightened by the fact that services were brought under multilateral disciplines for the first time with the coming into force of the World Trade Organization in January 1995. Countries first negotiated on services during the Uruguay Round, from 1986 to 1994, becoming familiar with the concepts. The Uruguay Round translated to the policy level a phenomenon that had been occurring for some time at the practical level as trade in services increased in importance in world trade. By the middle of the 1990s, services trade constituted more than one-fifth of world exports and imports of goods and services. The conclusion of NAFTA and its implementation in January 1994 proved to be an equally strong catalyst for the countries of the hemisphere, inciting them by example to incorporate services into their subregional arrangements. In particular, Mexico extended the liberalization of services to other Latin American countries in the hemisphere through a series of NAFTA-type free trade agreements.

The economic importance of trade in services has been increasing steadily in the Western Hemisphere over the past few decades and has become one of the most critical elements of economic growth for the region. The region has a slight comparative advantage in services trade, accounting for 25 percent of world services exports in 1998, as compared with around 21 percent of world merchandise exports. However, trade in services achieved only sluggish growth during the 1990s, compared with the dynamism of trade in goods in the Western Hemisphere. According to the WTO annual report of 1999, services exports of the Western Hemisphere grew 7 percent over the 1990 to 1998 period. This compares with 9 percent for merchandise trade over the same period. This situation suggests that considerable barriers to trade in services remain within the region, in contrast to tariffs, which have been lowered by more than two-thirds since the mid-1980s (from an average of over 40 percent for the region in 1986 to around 12 percent in 1999).

Among countries within the region, the importance of services varies considerably. Although as a percentage of GDP the U.S. service sector is the largest, with service activities constituting 75 percent of output, for the region as a whole the figure is over 60 percent on average. In terms of trade, however, services are more important by far for the smaller countries of the Caribbean and Central America; in 1994 the specialization ratio for traded services (that is, the percentage derived by dividing the value of services exports by that of merchandise exports) was over 100 percent for twelve countries of the hemisphere and between 30 and 100 percent for another six countries. Thus for the smaller and even medium-sized countries of Latin America and the Caribbean, commercial services exports constitute the largest foreign exchange earner, and services represent the largest source of employment for their economies. For these countries the importance of services can hardly be overstated. The bulk of commercial service activity at present is primarily in tourism, financial services, and transport. However, exports of other services, helped by evolving technological developments such as the Internet, are rapidly increasing in importance as well (health care services, data processing, and educational services, in particular).

Thus all countries in the Western Hemisphere have a strong interest in improving the quality and competitiveness of their service sector and in expanding the growth of their services exports. One of the best ways to reach this objective is by engaging in market-opening and rule-setting negotiations. However, attempting to do this at several levels simultaneously is both challenging and complex for policymakers, although the fundamental issues to be addressed contain many similarities. These include the threefold challenge of how best to remove discrimination against foreign service providers, how to deal with non-discriminatory regulations that have the effect of restricting trade, and how to design rules that enhance transparency, ensure stability, and help to optimize the liberalizing character of any given services agreement. The chapters in this volume attempt to answer these questions, examining services issues and developments for countries in the Western Hemisphere on all three levels—multilateral, regional, and subregional—as well as their interrelationship.

Part One: Crosscutting Services Issues

In the first section of the book, which deals with crosscutting services issues, the chapter by Geza Feketekuty evaluates the principal existing GATS provisions and their application and suggests how they could be improved in the coming round of multilateral services negotiations. The author emphasizes the threefold challenge faced by negotiators in designing GATS, namely the removal of discrimination against foreign service providers, the problem of nondiscriminatory regulations having the effect of restricting trade, and the four different ways or modes through which services can be traded. Several of the deficiencies encountered by GATS in its first five years of operation stemmed from the fact that many of its concepts and terminology were adapted from the GATT system and do not fit comfortably in their application to services trade. This is due to the nature of restrictions affecting trade in services, which are present in the form of different regulatory regimes and discriminatory laws or decrees. The author suggests that most of the present shortcomings in GATS do not require a fundamental overhaul of the system but could be remedied through specific improvements in the GATS structure. These would include: clarifying the scheduling procedures; separating the commitments on discriminatory and nondiscriminatory quantitative restraints into two separate categories; obliging greater precision in specifying how a particular law violates national treatment or imposes quantitative barriers; adopting negotiating targets or formulas in order to expand both the number of commitments in GATS schedules and the number of service sectors covered; and establishing conditions under which countries would be prepared to eliminate existing MFN reservations. The author also suggests that it would make sense to begin thinking about integrating GATT and GATS into a single instrument for liberalizing trade in goods and services because the distinction between the two should become less important in the future.

The chapter by Joel Trachtman and Kalypso Nicolaïdis stresses the importance of having regulatory reform and the development of regulatory disciplines to accompany services liberalization in critical, regulated sectors so that service providers are assured of their ability to effectively gain access to foreign markets. Although most attention with respect to services has been focused on *discriminatory* barriers to trade in services, the authors underline that *nondiscriminatory* regulatory diversity also poses a substantial barrier to international trade in services. They explore options for developing regulatory principles and fostering recognition agreements for service industries under GATS and the subregional agreements, including an assessment of the kind of criteria that should guide the fundamental trade-off between trade liberalization objectives and legitimate domestic constraints. The authors point out the choice to be made between elaboration of more general principles for regulatory practices, which would require interpretation and clarification through disputes and panel rulings, and agreement on more specific rules, which would mandate recognition or harmonization through political agreement. For such a choice to be made, it is critical for governments to decide how to allocate regulatory jurisdiction. It is also critical to determine the appropriate regulatory structure by service sector and the institutional framework within which to implement this structure.

GATS has only recently begun to address the issue of regulatory barriers to services, which should be one of the major areas of focus during the coming round of multilateral service negotiations. Provisions on domestic regulation and recognition are also included in the various integration agreements in the Western Hemisphere. The choice made by members of these agreements, to adopt general standards or specific rules to develop regulatory principles and promote recognition agreements, will depend upon the institutional setting in which such a choice takes place. Because the circumstances for a small number of states in a regional arrangement may differ from those of a larger and more disparate membership, different groupings of states will have different preferences and affinities. The authors provide arguments in favor of and against the alternative approaches and recommend that governments choose a standard that maximizes the level of liberalization, that rules and standards be combined whenever possible, and that an evolutionary approach to rule-making be adopted.

The question of what governments should do about the growing links between services trade and investment is considered by Pierre Sauvé in his chapter. The central tenet of the paper is that although the time appears not yet ripe for the development of a generic set of investment disciplines at the multilateral level, the FTAA process offers countries of the Western Hemisphere a unique opportunity to consolidate the liberalization they have already been carrying out in the investment and services area at the regional level, and to explore new avenues of liberalization and rule-making through novel solutions to what have become emotionally charged problems. The author underlines the heightened sensitivities over possible international investment rules resulting from the failure of the negotiations on a Multilateral Agreement on Investment at the OECD in 1998 and the failure of the Seattle WTO ministerial meeting of December 1999. He states that the development of multilateral investment rules at the WTO will most likely be a slow, incremental process, given the lack of a compelling rationale in support of a multilateral set of investment protection disciplines. In fact, it is through the services negotiations under GATS (mode 3 of service supply) that discriminatory regulations inhibiting foreign direct investment in service activities might best be rolled back. The author proposes several ways to enhance the "investment-friendliness" of the agreement.

This situation at the multilateral level contrasts sharply with the decision of the countries in the Western Hemisphere to negotiate generic investment disciplines in the context of the FTAA process. Such negotiations are already well advanced, and a broad consensus exists on what an investment agreement at the regional level should include, borrowing heavily from those disciplines contained in the many existing bilateral investment treaties. The author thus urges the countries of the hemisphere to go forward in the FTAA context and incorporate investment into a broad hemispheric free trade agreement; this would give much greater commercial value and political legitimacy to previous uni-lateral liberalization efforts by providing a floor of juridical security along with procedural and regulatory transparency. Countries in the Western Hemisphere are in a position to innovate in the design of rules and disciplines and to make the interface between services and investment an effective one.

The only link between WTO multilateral disciplines on services and regional integration efforts to liberalize services trade is found in GATS Article V, the equivalent for services of GATT Article XXIV for goods, covering customs unions and free trade areas. All regional integration arrangements incorporat-ing provisions on services trade must meet the requirements set out in GATS Article V in order to be deemed compatible with the multilateral trading system and to be considered as contributing to trade liberalization overall. In her chap-ter, Sherry Stephenson argues that GATS Article V is extremely important be-cause it should provide the underpinning for members of regional agreements to set their objectives for liberalization and integration as high as possible. However, at this writing, GATS Article V is not functioning well for two basic reasons, one of a systemic nature and the other of a practical but ultimately political nature. The systemic problem is a lack of clarity in its provisions, the concepts of which have largely been taken from GATT Article XXIV but which cannot be easily applied to services trade. Unlike reductions in tariff barriers, reductions in barriers to service providers are difficult to measure quantita-tively because they are found in the form of national laws, regulations, and administrative requirements. Moreover, the degree of liberalization in services trade that a regional integration arrangement is expected to achieve among its members (in order to qualify for the removal of "substantially all discrimina-tion" under Article V) is not uniformly understood, nor is the interpretation of what is meant by "substantially all trade" in terms of encompassing the four modes of service supply and various service sectors. The second problem is that parties to regional integration agreements covering trade in services, par-ticularly those with membership of developing countries, have not chosen to notify such agreements to the WTO. This situation is resulting in a low degree of transparency over the provisions and disciplines of regional integration agree-ments in the Western Hemisphere and elsewhere. The author argues that if this article is not strengthened in the current round of services negotiations under

GATS it may undermine the trading system in the future, given the proliferation of regional efforts to liberalize services.

Very little has been written on the dispute-settlement process involving services. The chapter by Hector A. Millán Smitmans fills this gap. In particular,
the author discusses whether the existing rules and procedures set up originally
to deal with trade in goods and now extended to services under the WTO Understanding on Rules and Procedures Governing the Settlement of Disputes
(DSU) are adequate, or whether they should be amended to deal with the particularities of services trade. His analysis focuses on those WTO dispute-settlement cases in which the provisions of GATS have been invoked. Within the
five years that the DSU has been operational, no fewer than twelve cases have
been brought to the WTO in which services issues have been involved and
provisions of the GATS have been invoked, including Articles I, II, III, VI,
XVI, XVII, XXI, and XXVIII. These disputes have involved complaints by
Ecuador, Guatemala, Honduras, Mexico, and the United States over the regime
of the European Communities for the importation, sale, and distribution of bananas, involving wholesale and distribution services and the definition of these
as well as subsequent related complaints over the implementation of the panel's
report and the recommendations of the Dispute Settlement Body (DSB); the
United States against Japan on measures affecting distribution services; the
European Communities against Canada on measures affecting film distribution
services; the United States against Canada on certain measures concerning the
tax treatment of "split-run" periodicals; the European Communities against
Korea regarding its laws, regulations, and practices in the telecommunications
procurement sector; and the United States against Japan concerning its laws,
regulations, and requirements affecting the distribution and internal sale of
photographic film and paper.

The author points out that WTO DSU rules and procedures may only be
invoked for disputes concerning the general obligations of GATS and with
regard to the specific commitments set out in the national GATS schedules.
Given the history of the services disputes to date and the tendency of the various panels and the Appellate Body to interpret the definition of services involved in the disputes in a broad rather than a narrow manner, this may have
implications for the willingness of participants in future GATS negotiations to
take on additional, wide-ranging market-access commitments. The author writes
that there is a risk that the DSB will be called upon to examine increasingly
complex issues in the services sector where a simple extrapolation of existing
provisions may not be adequate without prior agreement on the rules and principles that must be observed. It is also notable that several of the disputes con-

sidered by the WTO touching on services involve members of regional groupings who have chosen to have these adjudicated at the multilateral rather than
the regional level, although both options are available through the dispute-settlement mechanisms of the various regional integration agreements. This is also
an issue that may need to be considered in future negotiations.

Part Two: Services Liberalization at the Regional Level

Services have been the object of considerable liberalizing zeal at the regional level in the Western Hemisphere, and several agreements were signed or
extended during the 1990s to promote the liberalization of services trade. The
forerunner of such efforts is NAFTA (January 1994) among Canada, Mexico,
and the United States. In his chapter, Carlos Piñera discusses the provisions and
disciplines contained in the NAFTA treaty and its innovations in the area of
trade in services. These include, in particular: the liberalization of services trade
in all covered sectors without restriction, except in the case of those measures
otherwise specified and set out in lists of reservations or nonconforming measures; the binding of national laws affecting services suppliers in order to consolidate the degree of liberalization existing upon entry into force of the agreement; the inclusion of a "ratchet" clause to lock in future liberalization; the
absence of a safeguard clause; the elimination of the residency requirement for
professional service providers within a two-year period; and the existence of
separate chapters on investment and government procurement covering both
goods and services and integral to the agreement. The author explains how the
NAFTA approach to services liberalization has been extended by Mexico to
six other countries throughout Central and South America (Bolivia, Chile, Colombia, Costa Rica, Nicaragua, and Venezuela) in five subsequent free trade
agreements negotiated since 1994, such that the member countries of these
agreements (both NAFTA and the NAFTA-type agreements) now account for
over 85 percent of trade in services in the Western Hemisphere.

In the agreements negotiated by Mexico subsequent to NAFTA, the sectoral
emphasis and coverage of the various agreements varies somewhat, but the
basic principles of national treatment, most-favored-nation treatment, and nonobligatory local presence represent the cornerstone of disciplines on trade in
services in all. The author points out that certain of the subsequent agreements
go further than and improve upon NAFTA through the incorporation of a built-
in dynamic to foster future trade liberalization. In several of the agreements
(Mexico-Bolivia; Mexico–Costa Rica; Mexico-Nicaragua), a provision binds
both parties to carry out periodic negotiations at least every two years, with a
view to removing substantially all of the remaining nonconforming measures

contained in the lists of reservations. The agreements also contain an obligation to carry out periodic future negotiations to remove remaining nondiscriminatory quantitative restrictions. The author concludes that Mexico's extensive efforts to carry out services liberalization since 1994 through the conclusion of the various free trade agreements described in the chapter have resulted in an improvement of efficiency in Mexico's service sector and in the provision of higher-quality services to the domestic market at internationally competitive prices.

Members of MERCOSUR (Argentina, Brazil, Paraguay, and Uruguay) signed the Protocol on Services of Montevideo in December 1997 in order to extend the coverage of the MERCOSUR agreement (March 1991) to services trade. The chapter by María-Angelica Peña examines the provisions of this protocol, pointing out the characteristics that distinguish its approach to the liberalization of services trade. The author points out that, inspired by the GATS model and closely modeled after its main provisions, the MERCOSUR services agreement is based upon the same principles that have guided the MERCOSUR integration process from its beginning, namely gradual and progressive liberalization and pragmatism. Like the GATS participants, MERCOSUR members have chosen to carry out services liberalization through the establishment of lists of commitments covering all service sectors, improving upon their multilateral commitments, and to do this by means of annual rounds of negotiations.

The MERCOSUR agreement on services differs from GATS, however, in at least three very important ways. The first difference is found in the unconditional form of the most-favored-nation principle (which cannot be qualified by MERCOSUR members among themselves). The second is found in the final objective of liberalization. MERCOSUR members have agreed to remove all restrictions to services trade among themselves within a ten-year period, once the Protocol of Montevideo has come into effect and has been ratified by three of the four governments. The third difference is the lack of a provision on safeguard action such that no liberalization, once extended among MERCOSUR members, can be modified, once the transition period of ten years for the liberalization process is completed. In the MERCOSUR Protocol, four sectors are singled out for special consideration and rules—namely financial services, maritime transport, land transport, and the movement of natural persons. The author points out that the latter area is an important one for MERCOSUR members, who are also trying to promote this form of services trade by encouraging the professional associations of the member countries to develop agreed requirements and standards for the recognition of diplomas and the right to practice. A challenge for MERCOSUR members in the future will be to articulate the linkages between services-related areas such as competition policy, investment, subsidies, and government procurement (some of which are already covered in separate protocols, some of which are being elaborated) and services themselves under the Montevideo Protocol, so as to ensure that the treatment of these issues is coherent and compatible.

In the early 1990s, the transformation of the Andean Group into the Andean Community and a modern and outward-looking trade agreement has included the extension of the agreement to encompass liberalization of services as well as goods. Andean Decision 439 of June 1998 provides a framework of principles and disciplines for the liberalization of services trade within the subregion. The decision has already been put into effect and incorporated into the national law of the five member states (Bolivia, Colombia, Ecuador, Peru, and Venezuela). Chapter 9 by María Esperanza Dangond examines the content of this decision and its implications for trade in services in the Andean region. The author points out the ambitious nature of Decision 439, which foresees the complete elimination of all barriers to services trade among members of the Andean Community, along with the harmonization of national policies in those areas that are deemed to require this, such as regulatory issues for services or standards. Although it draws upon many of the concepts of GATS for definitions and concepts, the Andean Community agreement is different in several important ways. First, the most-favored-nation principle for trade in services among members of the Andean Community is an unconditional one. Moreover, national treatment is to extend to the area of government procurement of goods and services once a decision is established to this effect, or no later than the year 2002. Third, a specific timetable for complete liberalization of services trade is established.

The modality chosen for services liberalization by members of the Andean Community is similar to that chosen by MERCOSUR members—that is, a series of annual negotiations. These negotiations are to be based upon a consolidated inventory established by all five states containing national measures affecting either market access or national treatment for service providers from other members. Negotiations are to result in a complete removal of all barriers to services trade for Andean service suppliers within five years of the initiation of such negotiations. The Andean Decision is also unique in including a provision to bind the status quo with respect to treatment of service providers as of June 1998 and to move toward the harmonization of all relevant regulatory measures for services. Like MERCOSUR, the Andean Community also has established separate, services-related decisions, including decisions on competition policy and investment. The challenges faced by the Andean Community will be not only to ensure that these separate decisions are compatible with that on services, but also to establish the required inventories for the five members in order to fulfill the strict timetable for liberalization set out in the decision.

Central America has one of the oldest regional integration agreements in the Western Hemisphere (the Central American Common Market, or CACM, dating from 1960), but has not yet expanded this agreement to cover trade in services. Only construction services were included within the national-treatment obligation of the original agreement. A few stand-alone sectoral agreements have been concluded in order to facilitate road and maritime transport and the movement of personnel between the five Common Market members. In chapter 8, Alvaro Sarmiento describes the renovation of the CACM agreement through the signature of the Protocol of Guatemala in 1995. The latter foresees the extension of the agreement to services and underlines the importance for members of harmonizing national legislation in key service sectors such as banking, insurance, and capital markets. Following this mandate, CACM members have been exploring various approaches for designing a regional instrument for the liberalization of traded services and have made considerable progress in the outline of a Central American Treaty on Services and Investment.

Although no agreement has been finalized at the subregional level, the author points out that nonetheless various Central American countries have negotiated bilateral free trade agreements with Mexico covering the liberalization of trade in services (Costa Rica in 1995 and Nicaragua in 1998). Even more striking is the fact that Central America as a regional grouping has negotiated and concluded one NAFTA-inspired free trade agreement (with the Dominican Republic in 1998) and concluded negotiations with Chile in late 1999 on a similar free trade agreement. Thus the five members of the region have jointly taken on disciplines and obligations with respect to services trade and investment under the first agreement, and with respect to services trade only under the second agreement, though they have not yet been able to finalize an agreement among themselves in either of these two areas. The author points out the dichotomy and legal uncertainty created by such a situation and stresses the necessity for CACM members to rapidly conclude agreement on a legal instrument for services and investment that will promote liberalization and bring stability to service providers in the region. Such an agreement should also improve the efficiency of services in the domestic markets, particularly important for the development of "industrial clusters" within the region in sectors such as tourism and agribusiness, which need efficient support from service infrastructure in telecommunications, distribution, and transport.

In the Caribbean, members of the Caribbean Common Market (CARICOM) have also recognized the vast opportunities to expand services trade in their region and finalized an agreement in July 1998 for the liberalization of such trade. Like the Andean Community and the CACM, governments in the Caribbean region collectively decided in the late 1980s to reinvigorate their integration process and move to a deeper level of economic integration that would result in the creation of a single market (Declaration of Grand Anse, 1989). A series of nine protocols have since been drafted in an attempt to meet this objective. The chapter by Pamela Coke Hamilton analyzes the protocol addressed to services, formerly known as Protocol II: Establishment, Services, Capital.

The main provisions of Protocol II, which is not yet in force, consist of the right of any CARICOM national to provide cross-border services, to move capital throughout the region, and to establish new enterprises; the free movement of labor; and an effective standstill clause carrying the obligation not to impose any new restrictions once the protocol enters into force. One of the main innovations of Protocol II is contained in its provisions for the free movement of persons, in particular university graduates, professionals, and other skilled occupations. The qualifications of graduates of CARICOM institutions are to be recognized throughout the region, as well as those of other skilled workers, and work permits and passports are to be eliminated for all CARICOM nationals. If successfully implemented, these provisions will approximate the Caribbean region to that of a customs union with respect to the free movement of factors of production. The author outlines the current status of legislation to bring about the implementation of these provisions in the various member nations. The author also points out, however, that Protocol II is missing two key elements, most notably an MFN clause, and a clearly defined approach to the services liberalization process. She recommends that CARICOM members act as soon as possible to include specific language on MFN within the protocol and to outline the modality for regional liberalization in the services sector. Without these two critical components, the effective implementation of Protocol II may remain in doubt.

Part Three: Challenges and Conclusions

Part Three of the volume covers the challenges that the liberalization of services trade faces at the multilateral level and in the Western Hemisphere and also summarizes the discussion that took place at the conference on this issue held in Costa Rica in July 1999. The contributors in this section draw out considerations relevant to the negotiations of trade in services, particularly from the point of view of developing countries in the region. They evaluate the progress achieved so far by the subregional agreements on services in the Western Hemisphere and provide a synthesis of the discussion that took place at the conference.

The first chapter in Part Three, by Eduardo Lizano, makes the point that developing countries are in urgent need of achieving greater integration within the international economy, because the generally small size of their domestic markets does not provide the best conditions for achieving an optimum division of labor, scale economies, capital accumulation, or the adoption of new technologies. This point is particularly valid for services trade, where the quality, cost, and efficiency of key service sectors heavily influence the international competitive position of developing countries. The author examines the factors that might explain why developing countries are advancing so slowly toward the liberalization of their services markets. He stresses the importance for developing countries of participating actively in both multilateral and regional negotiations on services and of using those negotiations to provide leverage against the pressure of internal interest groups in various service industries that may be opposed to liberalization. The political economy argument for participating in services negotiations makes these a more viable means of market opening than that of unilateral liberalization. The broader the regional agreement, the more advantages it provides to developing participants for several reasons, including less trade diversion and lower administrative costs, greater ease of negotiation, and a wider market-broadening effect.

The chapter by Francisco Javier Prieto evaluates the degree of liberalization in services trade posited by GATS and the various subregional agreements discussed in Part Two, along with the strengths and weaknesses of the various agreements. In particular, the author discusses the two main approaches that have been developed for the liberalization of services trade—namely, the bottom-up approach of GATS and the top-down approach of NAFTA, to which the majority of countries in the hemisphere have subscribed. The strengths and weaknesses of both approaches are discussed.

The author points out the lack of provisions under NAFTA to ensure the ongoing dynamic of liberalization as well as the possibility to make reservations to the MFN principles and the lack of a built-in mechanism to negotiate the elimination of outstanding restrictions or nonconforming measures. Certain of these weaknesses have since been addressed in the NAFTA-type agreements on services negotiated by Mexico with various Latin American countries in the hemisphere. The WTO GATS approach to liberalization of services trade is also examined critically by the author who, similar to the other authors in the volume, finds many of the GATS provisions currently inadequate and in need of greater definition or elaboration. This is particularly true of the need to substantially reduce discriminatory treatment among member countries and to improve general disciplines so as to avoid the impairment or nullification of specific commitments. Improvement of GATS techniques on the scheduling of commitments is also cited as important, as well as the need to review and refine the GATS classification systems and to improve the provisions on transparency.

The author argues that liberalization initiatives at the subregional or broad regional level such as that offered by the Free Trade Area of the Americas (FTAA) process offer a *second-best* option for improving upon the insufficiencies of the multilateral institutional framework.

In terms of progress achieved to date, however, Prieto argues that the majority of existing subregional agreements have not yet generated an effective liberalization of services trade and that the commitments under such agreements have been limited on the whole to providing better transparency or greater judicial certainty. Existing agreements are critiqued as not having yet fulfilled an important task, namely the concerted and ongoing liberalization of services in a binding fashion.

However, the potential for wide-ranging liberalization contained in the subregional agreements of the hemisphere is great. Prieto reviews, in particular, the disciplines of the MERCOSUR and Andean Community agreements on services in order to draw some lessons for their possible application to the future hemispheric agreement on services currently being negotiated within the FTAA process. He argues that elements from nearly all of the subregional agreements could be used as building blocks for constructing an FTAA services agreement that would prove satisfactory to the concerns of all countries in the region and that would ensure mutually advantageous outcomes. The obligations of such an agreement could be implemented at different speeds by less-developed or smaller economies.

A hemisphere-wide FTAA agreement should allow for greater depth of reform and more substantive commercial opening in the services area than that which has been and could be achieved at the multilateral level, given the higher level of rapprochement between adjacent economies in the region. The breadth and depth of the disciplines to be included in a hemispheric services agreement, drawing upon the subregional models, should allow an FTAA agreement to converge with, underpin, and surpass services liberalization at the multilateral level.

The last chapter in the volume, by Maryse Robert, provides an overview and summary of the key issues debated at the San José conference and sets forth the main points made by speakers and participants during those two days of discussion. Conference participants emphasized the growth in services trade being made possible by rapid technological innovations, the importance of adequate regulatory changes and rule-making on the part of government authorities in response to such developments, the necessity of improving GATS for the purpose of the WTO multilateral services negotiations, including addressing existing MFN exemptions, reviewing the operation of GATS Article V, revising the GATS articles on market access and national treatment, and addressing and reconciling trade and regulatory objectives.

In particular, the author notes that conference participants focused on how to ensure greater liberalization of services trade in the future, because the current level of policy commitments on services at the multilateral level does not exceed the status quo for the most part. One of the main objectives of the current round of multilateral GATS negotiations is to reduce the imbalances in service commitments across members, sectors, and modes. The positive role that regional negotiations on services could play as a complement, and also as a means of stimulating the multilateral process, was frequently emphasized. For service providers, transparency in rules and in the provision of information is of the greatest importance. In this context, the adoption of a "negative list" approach in several of the regional integration agreements in the Western Hemisphere was cited as offering more transparency than the "positive list" approach of GATS because all sectors and measures are covered in the liberalization process except those that are specifically exempted and must be listed in annexes. It was emphasized that countries in the Western Hemisphere had much to gain by participating in multilateral and regional trade negotiations because they could take advantage of such opportunities as a way to lock in policies of reform and liberalization, and as a signaling device to international investors. This signaling function is always more powerful when bound in international agreements. Trade negotiations and liberalization of services trade, while not ends unto themselves, provide the means to promote efficiency and to generate growth and development. It is for this reason that all countries in the Western Hemisphere have an important stake in this process.

PART ONE

Crosscutting Services Issues

Improving the Architecture of the General Agreement on Trade in Services

GEZA FEKETEKUTY

ONE OF THE MAJOR ACHIEVEMENTS of the Uruguay Round of Multilateral Trade Negotiations was the negotiation of the General Agreement on Trade in Services (GATS), the first comprehensive framework for the global liberalization of trade in services. In addition to the legal framework, countries negotiated national commitments on access to their markets in individual sectors and subsectors, and on the treatment of foreign services and service suppliers within their national markets. The major thrust of this first round of negotiations on market access and national treatment was to commit governments to preserve the degree of access provided by current regulations. The difficult part of reducing the barriers built into existing government regulations was left largely to future rounds of negotiations.

The negotiators were aware of the need for further negotiations and agreed to resume them in the year 2000.[1] The agreement calls for successive rounds of negotiations for the liberalization of trade barriers, beginning with the round in 2000. It also calls for the resumption of negotiations on GATS rules, particularly with respect to subsidies, safeguards, government procurement, and regu-

An earlier version of this chapter appears in Sauvé and Stern (2000).

1. See Article XIX(1) of the General Agreement on Trade in Services, which says, "In pursuance of the objectives of this Agreement, Members shall enter into successive rounds of negotiations, beginning not later than five years from the date of entry into force of the WTO agreement and periodically thereafter, with a view to achieving a progressively higher level of liberalization."

lations "relating to qualification requirements and procedures, technical standards, and licensing requirements."[2] It tasks the Council for Trade in Services with the development of negotiating guidelines and procedures for each round of negotiations.[3] This chapter assesses the existing GATS provisions and their application, and makes suggestions for improving them.

An Initial Assessment of the Agreement

An assessment of the overall effectiveness of an international trade agreement such as GATS should be based on at least four criteria: the effectiveness of the negotiating procedures in achieving a reduction of trade barriers; the effectiveness of the disciplines built into the agreement in restraining the introduction of new trade barriers; the effectiveness of the legal framework and the dispute-settlement procedures in facilitating the settlement of disputes that arise over the interpretation of the commitments; and the effectiveness of the agreement in establishing a transparent and stable environment for enterprises engaged in international trade in services.

GATS was adopted in 1995. At this writing in 2000, it is too soon to form any conclusive judgments. The first round of negotiations on national commitments with respect to market access and national treatment was designed primarily to establish an initial set of national commitments that would preserve the existing degree of market access, rather than to achieve a substantial reduction in barriers to trade. Because demand for services continues to grow rapidly, the ability of the agreement to withstand political and economic pressures for protection has not been tested. Empirical evidence from other trade agreements such as the General Agreement on Tariffs and Trade (GATT) and the European Economic Community (EEC) suggests that such agreements often have to mature for a decade or two before either enterprises or governments actively use the agreement in managing their affairs.

Although the data required to evaluate the operational effectiveness of GATS are scarce, they do permit a preliminary assessment. Since the adoption of the agreement, there have been two multilateral negotiations under the GATS umbrella on market-access and national-treatment commitments—one on telecommunications services and the other on financial services.

The negotiations on basic telecommunication services led to the General Agreement on Basic Telecommunication Services (GABT) in February 1997,

---

2. See Articles VX(1), X(1), XIII(2), and VI(4) of the General Agreement on Trade in Services, respectively.
3. See Article XIX(3) of the General Agreement on Trade in Services.

which will, over time, open the provision of basic telecommunication services to international competition. Another result was the adoption of the Reference Paper that sets out a common framework for the regulation of competition in this area. In their submissions to the WTO on the preparation of the next round of multilateral trade negotiations, many governments have asked for a consideration of the wider application of the pro-competitive principles contained in the Reference Paper on telecommunications.[4]

The negotiations on financial services concluded in December 1997 were a more modest success. Though they resulted in few reductions in existing barriers to trade in financial services and in very few commitments with respect to cross-border sales of financial services, many governments agreed not to tighten existing barriers imposed on foreign financial institutions

Beyond the concrete results of the sectoral negotiations carried out to date, it is worth observing that the negotiation of GATS itself triggered a national debate in many countries on the somewhat encrusted national regulatory systems in services. This debate in many cases led to the substantial liberalization of both internal and external trade through autonomous domestic regulatory reforms. Although national experiences with autonomous adoption of domestic reforms vary considerably, as witnessed by the different experiences of East Asian economies, they provide an important lesson for future liberalization efforts. An essential requirement for successful liberalization may well be the development of national consensus among consumers, providers, regulators, economic officials, and trade officials that regulatory reform and trade liberalization in a particular sector will spur economic growth and are therefore in a country's own interest, whatever happens in the broader global context.[5]

The GATS Negotiating Procedures

Negotiations aimed at the liberalization of barriers to trade in services under the GATS umbrella have followed two approaches to date: a bilateral exchange of requests and offers, followed by the bilateral negotiation of market-access and national-treatment commitments on an item-by-item basis, across all services sectors; and plurilateral or multilateral negotiations focused on individual

4. See, for example, para. 5(b) of WTO document WT/GC/W/189, "EC Approach to Services," the paper submitted by the European Communities in preparation for the 1999 Ministerial Conference, and para. B.7 of WTO document WT/GC/W/116, "Communication from Australia," the paper submitted by Australia in preparation for the 1999 Ministerial Conference.

5. For an elegant and thorough discussion of the importance of approaching the liberalization of trade in services from the perspective of domestic regulatory reform, see Hoekman and Messerlin (2000).

sectors such as telecommunications, which covered not only market-access and national-treatment issues but also related regulatory issues.

As already noted, the relative success of these alternative approaches is difficult to evaluate. The initial round of across-the-board negotiations was more focused on covering as many sectors as possible with an initial set of commitments that reflected the current level of market openness than it was on achieving a substantial liberalization of barriers. The sectoral negotiations on telecommunications and financial services that were successfully concluded after the end of the Uruguay Round benefited from special factors such as the wish by many countries to remove most-favored-nation (MFN) exemptions and, in the case of telecommunications, the economic pressure generated by changes in technology.

The results require careful analysis because they go against the historical experience and firm belief of the trade policy community that crosscutting negotiations are more successful in achieving liberalization than negotiations focused on individual sectors. Crosscutting negotiations are usually considered more successful because interests in other sectors that stand to gain from liberalization offset the opposition of vested interests in any one sector. The underlying assumption is that in any given sector some countries are competitive and other countries are uncompetitive, and current providers in uncompetitive protected markets stand to lose as a result of negotiations. They will therefore pressure the governments involved not to reduce the protective barriers. Broad negotiations allow sectoral trade-offs between those who lose and those who gain in every country. The resistance of providers in uncompetitive services is compounded in many services sectors by the potential resistance of sectoral regulators who have a vested interest in preserving their existing regulations and protecting their bureaucratic turf.

The accumulated wisdom of trade negotiators has to be tempered, however, by recognition that liberalization in many services sectors cannot be achieved without substantial domestic regulatory reforms, and that such reforms cannot be achieved piecemeal and over the determined opposition of the regulators involved. As the less-successful efforts in areas such as maritime and air transport show, without the cooperation of regulatory officials and the opportunity to make the case that regulatory reform in a particular sector is to everyone's advantage, little progress can be made. The more recent experience of negotiations in the accounting sector reinforces this point. Although negotiations were successfully concluded, they fell short of the desired results because of the determined opposition of some regulators.

Another possible lesson from past trade negotiations is that negotiations organized around targets such as tariff-cutting formulas are likely to be more successful than negotiations based on item-by-item negotiations without some overall target or goal. Targets provide benchmarks against which results based on highly detailed bilateral negotiations can be measured. They also help improve the efficiency of negotiation, improve public comprehension, and enhance the consistency, clarity, and user-friendliness of the final schedules.[6] Both of the successful sectoral negotiations benefited from targets that provided a benchmark against which progress in the negotiations could be measured.

The remainder of this chapter addresses some of the weaknesses in GATS and recommends practical steps for strengthening the agreement.

The Conceptual Structure of GATS

The key difficulty in designing GATS was addressing the fact that barriers to trade in services are generally embedded in domestic regulations.[7] Unlike barriers to trade in goods, barriers to trade in services are not transparent barriers imposed at the border against foreign services. Cross-border flows of services are largely invisible. Governments that have tried to protect their local service suppliers from foreign competition have embedded the protective measures in domestic regulations focused on the local consumption or provision of services. For example, regulations may stipulate that only car insurance provided by a local firm satisfies the insurance requirement for car registration, or that only locally owned and established firms may sell car insurance to consumers.

Another challenge was that domestic regulations frequently limit trade even if they do not explicitly discriminate against foreign providers. This was a crucial point because historically the regulatory involvement of governments in the provision of services has been much more intensive in services than in manufacturing. Regulations often limit the number of firms, the number of employees, the number of distribution outlets, the services that can be sold, prices, marketing practices, and distribution channels. These types of regulations, which are nondiscriminatory in nature, protect existing firms from competition by new entrants, whether domestic or foreign. The rationale often provided for such intervention is that consumers need to be protected from the shady practices associated with excessive competition, or that consumers need to be assured of a stable supply of a reliable product at reasonable prices. Another rationale is that the market can support only a limited number of providers, or that all economic

---

6. Thompson (1999).

7. For an extensive treatment of the challenges facing the negotiation of a comprehensive agreement on trade in services, see Feketekuty (1988).

activities related to the provision of services that contain a monopoly component have to be regulated to protect the consumer interest.

A third challenge for the designers of GATS was that trade, investment, labor mobility, and foreign consumption are far more interwoven in services than in goods. The major argument for the negotiation of trade rules in services was that services were becoming tradable as a result of innovations in information technology, but it did not seem to make much sense to limit a trade regime to cross-border trade. After all, the bulk of services sold by foreign service providers to consumers are still being sold through locally established firms. Interestingly, when confronted by a choice between cross-border sales and local establishment of foreign providers, many regulators decided they would prefer the latter.

The GATS negotiators thus faced a threefold challenge: to remove discrimination in domestic regulations against services produced by foreign providers; to deal with nondiscriminatory regulations that had the effect of restricting trade; and to deal with four different ways in which services could be traded. Although the negotiators realized that the structure of the GATT rules would have to be changed to meet these challenges, the GATS rules were nevertheless a product of the GATT system. They innovated where they had to, but otherwise they adapted legal concepts and principles from the GATT system.

This grafting led to some of the major design flaws in the GATS regime. A review of the underlying structure of GATT is therefore useful in order to understand the GATS framework.

GATT Rules for Trade in Goods

The GATT rules for trade in goods are based on a few key notions: barriers should be imposed at the border; they should take the form of tariffs; the tariffs should be subject to negotiation; the tariffs resulting from such negotiations should be bound in national schedules; tariffs should be applied equally to goods imported from all member countries; and domestic regulations should not discriminate against foreign goods once they have crossed the border and their importers have paid the tariff. The GATT rules allow for exceptions to these basic rules, and they spell out how these rules are to be applied with respect to various government measures, but the core rules are those that implement the central notions just mentioned.[8]

Under GATT, the negotiation of tariffs (and quotas where permitted) is initiated through the bilateral exchange of requests and offers. Experience gained

8. For an elegant discussion of the underlying design of GATT, see Wilcox (1949).

from successive rounds of negotiations suggested that more liberalization could be achieved if bilateral negotiations were preceded by multilateral negotiations of agreed-upon targets or formulas.

The closest analog in goods to the central challenge in services of curbing the trade-restrictive impact of domestic regulations was the need to curb the trade-distorting impact of domestic standards. The GATT rules on standards give governments the right to pursue domestic social objectives through the establishment of compulsory standards for the goods sold in domestic markets, but they require that the resulting standards achieve the desired social objective in the least trade-distorting manner possible.

The Basic Structure of GATS

GATS addresses the trade-restrictive impact of regulations at three levels— through general provisions on domestic regulation, through sectoral annexes on the regulation of particular sectors, and through the negotiation of national commitments on regulations that affect trade. The GATS rules are based on the following key principles: regulations that restrict trade should be subject to negotiation;[9] the results of such negotiations should be bound in national schedules;[10] the resulting commitments should apply equally to services and service providers from all other member countries;[11] and regulations should not restrict foreign services or service providers, or discriminate against them, in a manner that is inconsistent with the binding commitments.[12] Moreover, the rules define trade not only as the cross-border delivery of services, but also as the foreign consumption of services, the delivery of services by foreign-owned but locally established enterprises, and the temporary entry of natural persons for the explicit purpose of providing a service locally.[13] The commitment to market access in services is less precise because barriers in services take the form of discriminatory regulatory requirements rather than tariffs, as is the case in goods.

This conceptual framework appears clear enough. The major problems of GATS are not the result of deficiencies in this basic framework. Rather, they are the result of the manner in which this underlying framework was implemented through the drafting of the legal provisions in GATS and the negotiation of the associated national schedules. After correctly analyzing the unique

9. Article XIX (Negotiation of Specific Commitments).
10. Article XX (Schedules of Specific Commitments).
11. Article II (Most Favored Nation Treatment).
12. Article XVI (Market Access) and Article XVII (National Treatment), respectively.
13. Article I (Scope and Definition).

requirements of an effective GATS regime for services, the negotiators frequently relied on GATT terminology and legal drafting, even where it did not provide the best fit. The ambitious nature of the undertaking and the continuing rapid pace of technological change in many services also led to inevitable shortcomings that will need to be addressed in future negotiations.

A more detailed assessment of the key shortcomings of the current GATS architecture and some recommendations for possible approaches to overcoming the weaknesses are set forth in the following sections.

The Hierarchy of Commitments in GATS

GATS provides for the negotiation of commitments at three levels—general provisions that are part of the GATS text, annexes that set out rules for particular sectors (such as telecommunications) or policy instruments (such as visas for temporary service providers), and national schedules of commitments on market access and national treatment. This architecture reflects the practical realities associated with the negotiation of increased disciplines. National schedules reflect the reality that the liberalization of trade barriers cannot be achieved overnight and that not every country can move at the same pace. Sectoral agreements reflect the fact that liberalization of trade in some sectors cannot be divorced from the establishment of compatible regulatory regimes, and in some cases from the modification of the current international regulatory regime. Sectoral agreements also may provide the best channel for achieving significant liberalization where the conditions are right, but the ability of any one country to liberalize its own regulations is facilitated in either economic or political terms by simultaneous reforms in other countries. The drafting of general GATS provisions for all services is, of course, the most efficient approach for advancing the liberalization of trade in services where such principles can be applied to all services.

The three-tiered structure is analytically sound, though it does not address whether more progress can be achieved toward particular objectives by concentrating negotiating resources at one level or another. The negotiation of the provisional agreement on accounting, for example, has raised the question whether more progress could be made by focusing on another professional service, by developing a crosscutting agreement for all professional services, or by improving the provisions of Article VI dealing with domestic regulation overall. No a priori answers can be provided on this question, and the real answer probably is that it depends on a political judgment of what can be achieved in different contexts, given current political and economic realities.

The three-tiered structure does raise questions about the relationship among the commitments at the three levels. For example, to what extent can reservations in national schedules override general provisions of GATS, or of sectoral annexes? Some provisions of GATS and of sectoral annexes obviously refer to the right of members to enter reservations in the national schedules, but what about the other provisions? If member countries agree to adopt new definitions in GATS or in an annex, would that alter the definitions employed in the national schedules where the country did not specify that it was using a national terminology? It may well be desirable to spell out the hierarchy of commitments that would apply under different circumstances.

Market Access and National Treatment

GATS recognizes that trade in services can be hampered either by discriminatory regulatory requirements imposed only on foreign services or by restrictive regulations imposed on both domestic and foreign services. However, the application of GATT concepts and terminology in GATS confuses the issue because they are used in ways that neither correspond clearly to their application in GATT nor clarify the intent of the commitments in the services context.

All quantitative limits on services or service providers are dealt with under the rubric of market access, regardless of whether such limits are being imposed on foreign services on a discriminatory basis or on both domestic and foreign services on a nondiscriminatory basis. National treatment is defined in the traditional GATT way as the nondiscriminatory application of domestic regulations to foreign services or service providers. This means that quantitative limits placed on foreign services or service providers fall under both the market-access and national-treatment provisions.[14]

The drafters of the agreement realized that this overlap could raise the question whether national commitments regarding the discriminatory application of quantitative regulatory controls should be entered as market-access

14. For an in-depth discussion see Mattoo (1997, pp. 112–29). Also see Low and Mattoo (2000, pp. 2–4). Unlike the authors of those works, I take the view that national-treatment commitments are to be viewed as independent of market-access commitments, except insofar as a discriminatory restraint listed under the market-access column ipso facto also constitutes a limitation on national treatment under the scheduling convention of Article XX. The difference in the two interpretations is likely due to a difference in the interpretation of the phrase "conditions and qualifications" in the following text of GATS Article XVII: "In the sectors inscribed in its Schedule, and subject to any conditions and qualifications set out therein, each Member shall accord to services and service suppliers. . . ." I interpret this language as requiring the explicit enumeration of an exception to national treatment in either the market-access or national-treatment column. I do not believe the entry of "unbound" in the market-access column satisfies this requirement.

or as national-treatment commitments in the schedules. To avoid duplication and confusion, Article XX(2) of GATS on the scheduling of commitments indicates that "measures inconsistent with both Articles XVI and XVII shall be inscribed in the column relating to Article XVI." Although this fix removes potential confusion with respect to the scheduling of discriminatory quantitative restrictions, it introduces a discrepancy between the text of the provisions on market access and national treatment and the content of the market-access and national-treatment columns in the national schedules. This difference between the articles and the schedules has introduced a conceptual confusion into the relationship between market-access and national-treatment commitments. Some countries have wrongly assumed that national-treatment commitments become operative only after they have made a commitment on market access.

The intermingling of commitments on discriminatory and nondiscriminatory barriers has the further effect of intermingling two laudatory but separate goals—trade liberalization and domestic regulatory reform. Removing discriminatory regulation, whether in quantitative or qualitative form, is all about trade liberalization. Removing nondiscriminatory restraints on services is frequently an exercise in domestic regulatory reform. The use of nondiscriminatory quantitative restraints more often than not reflects a country's approach to the regulation of activity in a services sector, and telling a country to eliminate such restraints is tantamount to saying it must reform its approach to the regulation of that sector.

The intermingling of commitments on discriminatory and nondiscriminatory quantitative restraints raises the hurdle for countries that are willing to tackle the liberalization of trade barriers or the reform of domestic regulation in a services sector, but not both simultaneously. Although nothing in the agreement requires them to do both simultaneously, the organization of the schedule does not easily allow countries to highlight progress on either trade liberalization or domestic reform.

It is easy to see how a GATT mind-set about traditional notions of market access and national treatment could lead to the current structure and terminology in GATS. However, the net effect has been to create confusion among businesses, trade officials, and other trade experts who are not thoroughly familiar with the details of the agreement. They naturally equate market access in services with the tariff bindings in GATT, and national treatment in services with its counterpart in GATT. They fail to grasp that market access in services is potentially a more far-reaching commitment, since it covers both discriminatory and nondiscriminatory restraints on the production and sale of services; in addition, the deviations from national treatment in services are not as damning as they would be in a GATT context, since national treatment in many services equates to the complete absence of barriers to trade and grants nondiscriminatory treatment both to services and to service providers.

To solve the problems with respect to market access and national treatment, the rule in Article XX should be reversed, and measures that impose quantitative limits on a discriminatory basis should be listed under national-treatment rather than market-access. This would allow countries to highlight progress on trade liberalization through the scheduling of commitments under the national-treatment column, and to highlight progress on domestic regulatory reform though the scheduling of commitments under the market-access column. Ideally, the market-access column would be relabeled "nondiscriminatory quantitative restrictions on services," and the sequencing of the two columns would be reversed, with the national-treatment column preceding the column on nondiscriminatory quantitative restraints. In an ideal world, the two relevant provisions of GATS would also be retitled and reversed. Making all these changes may prove too difficult, but at a minimum the scheduling convention in Article XX needs to be reversed.

Top-Down (Negative List) versus Bottom-Up (Positive List) Approaches

One of the hotly debated issues during the negotiations was whether the national schedules should list only deviations from an ideal state of national treatment and market access or whether they should list only positive commitments to provide national treatment and market access for a particular service and mode of supply.[15] The first approach was referred to as the top-down or negative list approach, and the second was referred to as the bottom-up or positive list approach. Those who favored a maximum degree of liberalization generally argued for the top-down, negative list approach; those who were more reluctant to see much liberalization argued for the bottom-up, positive list approach.

A top-down approach is more liberalizing because it automatically provides national treatment and market access to new services and services that no one really cares about. Moreover, a top-down approach provides more information for potential exporters, since importing countries must indicate in their schedules any deviation from national treatment or the use of any quantitative re-

15. Commitments in the national schedules are broken down by sector and services products within each sector, by mode of supply (cross-border trade, foreign consumption, establishment of foreign services firms, and temporary entry of natural persons who are service providers), and by market-access and national-treatment commitments.

straints with respect to any tradable service. Under a bottom-up or positive list approach, new services, services no one cares about, and services on which the importing country does not wish to make a commitment are not covered in a country's national schedule. Foreign exporters therefore have no information about the treatment they might expect on such services.

Aside from differences over the desired degree of liberalization in services, the negotiators ran into a practical problem. Some countries were simply not equipped to identify all national and local laws that might conflict with the national-treatment and market-access provisions. In some cases they did not have the personnel to do it. In other cases their regulatory systems were not sufficiently evolved to identify potential inconsistencies, and they did not want to constrain their future ability to develop their own regulatory approach or put themselves in the uncomfortable position of having to renegotiate their commitments.

In the end, the negotiators adopted a hybrid approach. In sectors where countries are prepared to make commitments, they must list their reservations to market access and national treatment. However, they assume no commitments with respect to sectors not inscribed in their schedules.

In sectors inscribed in their schedules, countries can list limitations on market access and national treatment by spelling out in some detail the specific services on which they are not making a market-access or national-treatment commitment, and/or the precise manner in which market-access or national-treatment commitments are circumscribed with respect to such services. Alternatively, a country may list the specific provisions in its laws for which it takes a reservation with respect to either market access or national treatment. In some cases a country may state that the commitment applies only to certain services or subsectors within a sector, and that it is making no commitments for other specific services or subsectors.

An examination of the schedules reveals that the issue is not primarily whether a top-down or bottom-up approach should be taken, but the degree of precision with which a country describes its limitations on market access and national treatment. There is not a huge difference between declaring a whole subsector unbound under a positive list approach and declaring it unbound under a top-down approach. In both cases little or no information is offered to service providers. Alternatively, a country could spell out in some detail the specific ways in which a particular law violates national treatment or imposes quantitative restraints.

Precision in the drafting of the reservations on national treatment and market access is desirable both because it provides greater assurance against arbitrary protectionist measures and because it gives potential exporters more information on the provisions they must satisfy. In other words, precision is desirable for the achievement of transparency, maximum liberalization, and greater certainty. The scheduling guidelines issued by the WTO Secretariat as guidance for the development of schedules specifically indicates that countries should not merely list a law or measure that contains inconsistent provisions, but should spell out the specific provisions that are inconsistent.[16] Many of the existing GATS schedules do not meet this standard, and one of the objectives of the coming negotiations should be to improve this aspect of the schedules.

It is not worth revisiting the debate over top-down versus bottom-up approaches. Not only would the outcome likely be the same, but it would also miss the more important issue regarding the care and precision with which a country spells out its limitations on national treatment and market access and the precise provisions of its laws that lead to these limitations. This cannot be accomplished through broad conceptual arguments. These issues should be addressed through a detailed and labor-intensive peer review of national schedules and the negotiation of a commitment by countries to bind a substantial portion of their schedules. Ironically, the schedules of new entrants have received a great deal more scrutiny than the schedules of existing members and therefore come closer to providing the kind of information that is desirable.

The Use of Negotiating Targets or Formulas

As noted earlier, one challenge for negotiators is to find an efficient approach to the negotiation of commitments on market access and national treatment. Each approach that has been used—bilateral negotiations based on an exchange of requests and offers, and sectoral negotiations based on sectoral targets—has its advantages and disadvantages. The strength of the bilateral negotiating approach is that it provides a broad basis for establishing a negotiating outcome that meets the interests of members, but its weakness is that it is very labor intensive and it is easy for negotiators to lose sight of the forest as they argue over each tree, The strength of the sectoral approach is that it sets a common target against which progress can be measured, and it allows countries to address common regulatory issues that might block progress in liberalizing restrictive regulatory measures. Its weakness is that it limits the possibility of satisfying the varied economic interests of members.

The question is whether the strength of the sectoral approach in setting a target could be applied on a more horizontal, cross-sectoral basis. In tariff negotiations under the GATT umbrella, tariff-cutting formulas, which were ap-

16. GATT Secretariat (1993).

plied across the board, served this purpose. Since barriers in services take the form of a wide variety of regulatory measures, the use of targets is likely to involve the establishment of a more varied set of objective criteria against which progress in the negotiations could be measured. Some of these criteria could be quantitative targets, and others could be qualitative targets for the treatment of certain types of common regulatory issues.

One type of quantitative target could be based on the number of sectors in which countries have made binding commitments and the degree to which such commitments cover both market access and national treatment and the four modes of services delivery. Negotiators might agree that developed countries cover, for example, 95 percent of all sectors and subsectors, and that developing countries cover, for example, 40 to 60 percent of their sectors and subsectors, based on their level of development. Similar percentages might be developed for the four modes.[17]

Another approach to the establishment of quantitative targets might be to negotiate targets for the elimination of quantitative restrictions listed in Article XVI; these are the restrictions that countries may not impose without listing them as exceptions in their national schedules in sectors where they have made any commitments. The restrictions covered in Article XVI include :

—limitations on the number of service suppliers, whether in the form of numerical quotas, monopolies, exclusive service suppliers; or the requirement of an economic needs test;

—limitations on the total value of service transactions or assets in the form of numerical quotas; or the requirement of an economic needs test;

—limitations on the total number of service operations or the total quantity of service output expressed in terms of designated numerical units in the form of quotas; or the requirement of an economic needs test;

—limitations on the total number of natural persons who may be employed in a particular service sector or that a service supplier may employ and who are necessary for, and directly related to, the supply of a specific service in the form of numerical quotas; or the requirement of an economic needs test;

—measures that restrict or require specific types of legal entity or joint venture through which a service supplier may supply a service; and

—limitations on the participation of foreign capital in terms of maximum percentage limit on foreign share-holding or the total value of individual or aggregate foreign investment.

17. For a thorough discussion of possible formulas, see Thompson (1999). Also see Low and Mattoo (2000, p. 18).

Some targets or formulas might suggest an approach to a common regulatory issue or problem. Such qualitative targets would serve as negotiating guidelines against which national measures could be compared. Negotiating guidelines do not become a binding part of the agreement.[18] If enough countries found a qualitative negotiating guideline useful, however, it could be given the status of a rule by being incorporated in a sectoral annex to GATS. The Reference Paper that forms part of the General Agreement on Basic Telecommunication Services is an example of such a guideline. The proposed rule could be open to any member for signature and apply only to members that signed, or it could be made a universal obligation, which would bind all members who did not specifically enter a reservation in their national schedule.

Improving the Rules on Domestic Regulation

Given the importance of the regulatory dimension in the liberalization process, Article VI (Domestic Regulation) plays a key role in the liberalization of trade in services. Article VI is the essential third leg of a three-legged stool, along with Article XVI (Market Access) and Article XVII (National Treatment). While Article XVI disciplines the use of quantitative restrictions and Article XVII disciplines discriminatory treatment of foreign services and service providers, Article VI disciplines more hidden forms of protection buried in domestic regulations and their administration.[19] Article VI(1) requires that "in sectors where specific commitments are undertaken, each Member shall ensure that all measures of general application are administered in a reasonable, objective, and impartial manner."

Article VI calls for the negotiation of more detailed disciplines that would help ensure that all measures are reasonable, objective, and impartial. Article VI even spells out the objectives of such disciplines by indicating that they shall aim to ensure that regulatory requirements are, among other things:

—based on objective and transparent criteria, such as competence and the ability to supply a service;

—not more burdensome than necessary to ensure the quality of the service;

—in the case of licensing procedures, not in themselves a restriction on the supply of the service.

Pending the negotiation of these detailed disciplines, Article VI(5) applies these objectives to any new measures that may nullify or impair commitments made in the schedules.[20]

The negotiation of the disciplines called for in Article VI above should clearly receive a high priority in the new round of negotiations in services, and the negotiators would do well to start by converting the objectives listed above into disciplines that would apply to all domestic regulatory measures with an impact on trade in services. Beyond these disciplines, they might consider the addition of several related principles to Article VI, including:

—*Transparency of regulatory objectives*. The social objective served by a particular law or regulation should be transparent; that is, it should be clearly stated at the time the regulation is adopted. A clear statement of the desired social objective helps to remove confusion over the purpose of the regulation. It also makes it a great deal easier to judge whether a regulation is the least burdensome necessary to accomplish the desired social objective. This principle is contained in the WTO agreement on accountancy services, which has been adopted on an ad ref basis.

—*Appropriate use of market mechanisms*. Governments should use market mechanisms to promote desired social objectives, whenever that is feasible. The use of across-the-board economic incentives and disincentives allows market forces to determine the most economically efficient manner of accomplishing the desired social goal. A corollary of this principle is that scarce resources should be auctioned whenever possible rather than allocated to incumbent firms on the basis of historic shares. An auction process is more likely to enable the most efficient firms to gain access to such resources and is more likely to ensure that the opportunity cost of using the scarce resource is properly reflected in the cost of supplying the service and the prices charged to consumers. Regulations that give existing producers or sellers preferential treatment in the allocation of scarce resources not only create domestic economic inefficiencies by discriminating against potentially more economically efficient new suppliers; they also distort international trade and competition. Moreover, such regulations create a significant risk that economic inefficiencies and trade distortions will be magnified by political and interest-group pressures and corruption.

—*Minimizing the scope of regulations*. Governments should seek to minimize the regulatory burden by limiting the scope of any regulation to what is necessary to accomplish the desired social objective. This principle could complement and reinforce the objective that government regulatory measures

20. For a thorough treatment of the shortcomings of the GATS disciplines on domestic regulation, see Nicolaïdis and Trachtman (2000).

should not be more burdensome than necessary to ensure the quality of the service. This corollary principle would require governments to limit the scope of regulations to what was necessary to achieve the regulatory objective. Minimizing the scope of regulations also helps to minimize their economic cost. The application of this principle is particularly relevant to the regulation of infrastructure services such as water, gas, electricity, telecommunications, and rail transportation. The tendency in the past has been for governments to regulate all aspects of economic activity in these sectors because the network for distributing these services often constituted a natural monopoly. In more recent years many governments have recognized that they can more efficiently protect consumers by separating the construction and operation of the distribution network from the provision of services over the network. The government can thus regulate access to and use of the network monopoly, while leaving the supply of the services over the network open to market competition. Efforts to restrict the scope of regulations to the minimum necessary to achieve the desired social objective help to limit the economic cost of such regulations and the potential distortion of international trade and competition.

—*Use of international regulatory standards.* Governments should use any international standards that would satisfy the desired social objectives. This principle is already included in Article VII(5), which deals with the negotiation of agreements recognizing the authorization, licensing, or certification of services suppliers by other governments. It requires that, "wherever appropriate, recognition should be based on multilaterally agreed criteria." This principle is also a core principle embedded in the GATT Agreement on Technical Barriers to Trade, otherwise referred to as the Standards Code.

Domestic Regulation and Electronic Commerce

As previously described, trade in services encompasses four modes of trade—foreign consumption, cross-border trade, the sale of services through a foreign-owned local establishment, and the provision of a service by the resident of another country who has gained temporary entry. Each mode is treated as a separate commitment in the national schedules. Countries thus have to specify the market-access and national-treatment commitments that apply to each mode of service delivery in a particular sector. (If a country is prepared to commit to a particular mode across all sectors, or if a reservation applies across all sectors, the schedule may contain a horizontal entry that applies to all sectors.) By addressing itself to the four modes, the services framework covers much more ground than GATT.

The advent of electronic commerce has created the need for a more precise definition of the four modes. Before the Internet and the burgeoning of electronic commerce, the definition of the four modes was fairly straightforward. Foreign consumption of a service occurred when a traveler to another country purchased and consumed a service abroad. Cross-border trade occurred by phone or by mail when the purchaser of a service was in one country and the seller in another country. The sale of a service through local establishment took place when a foreign-owned enterprise established a facility or a legal entity to produce or sell services in the local market. Finally, the sale of services through the temporary entry of a natural person took place when a provider physically traveled to the importing country to produce the service.

Today these distinctions have become blurred, and it is not clear which set of market-access and national-treatment commitments apply under different circumstances or whose regulatory jurisdiction applies under those circumstances. Take the issue of foreign consumption. If a consumer buys a service from a provider in another country over the Internet, under what circumstances should that transaction be treated as foreign consumption, as cross-border trade, or as a purchase from a locally established enterprise?

Some have argued that direct marketing to consumers in a particular country should be considered local establishment, subjecting the production of the service to the local regulatory jurisdiction of the country of the consumer. Likewise, if the purchaser acquires a service from a foreign producer who does not engage in targeted marketing, the sale might be considered cross-border trade, subjecting the sale of the service to the regulatory jurisdiction of the consuming country. But what if the consumer in question intends to consume the service abroad? Should the buyer's physical location at the time the order is placed or at the time of consumption determine regulatory jurisdiction and the applicable mode of delivery?

To make things even more complicated, how does the physical location of the Internet service provider (ISP) used by the consumer affect all of the above distinctions? Let us assume that a consumer in country A, using a local address in country B, acquires access to the Internet from an ISP in country B. For all practical purposes the purchaser will appear to the service provider to be a local resident. To what extent can the government of country A hold the seller responsible for meeting its regulatory requirements?

One answer to such questions would be to follow strictly the treatment of analog transactions involving more traditional methods of acquiring services and goods abroad. But it is not always clear where a service was produced and where the service provider is located. This is particularly true for the sale of information or another form of intellectual property by multinational firms established in many different countries.

An alternative approach would be to let the market sort out regulatory issues by allowing sellers and buyers to choose the regulatory jurisdiction that would apply to a particular transaction. Such an approach might be complemented by the development of private codes, which might receive some kind of recognition by individual governments, and would be enforced by all governments that subscribed to a particular code.

The Application of the MFN Principle

Another hotly debated issue in the negotiation of GATS was the application of the MFN principle, which for many countries is the cornerstone of the multilateral system. From an economic perspective, it avoids a distortion of the relative prices applicable to goods and services imported from or exported to different foreign countries. From a political-economic perspective, it puts all members of a multilateral system on a more equal footing. Small countries in particular feel that the MFN principle gives them more equal standing with large countries and protects them from excessive bilateral pressure. The MFN principle also helps prevent adverse political fallout from competitive bilateral negotiations, which historically contributed to a breakdown of global trade and exacerbated political tensions among countries between the two world wars.

On the other hand, some negotiators argued that differences in regulatory philosophy could lead to incompatible market structures. Also, differences in the quality of the regulations applied to service suppliers in different countries can affect the degree to which imported services meet the domestic regulatory objectives of the importing country in such areas as consumer protection and prudential supervision. Moreover, it was pointed out that international trade in certain services, such as international air passenger service, was currently governed by bilateral agreements, and that the application of the MFN principle in these sectors would require a new international regime.

The debate concluded with another compromise. The MFN principle was incorporated as a generic principle of GATS. However, countries were permitted to enter reservations on the application of the MFN provision in particular sectors. A number of countries availed themselves of this opportunity in heavily regulated sectors. After the subsequent negotiation of sectoral agreements on telecommunication and financial services, however, most countries withdrew their MFN reservations in these sectors.

Another part of the compromise was the introduction of two provisions that allow the negotiation of bilateral or plurilateral agreements on the mutual recognition of regulatory standards. Countries are allowed to negotiate such agreements without automatically extending the benefits to third countries, provided third countries are given the opportunity to negotiate accession to such agreements on equivalent terms. The first such provision is included in Article VII of GATS, which deals with the recognition of experience or education obtained, requirements met, or licenses or certifications granted in connection with the authorization, licensing, or certification of services suppliers. The second such provision is included in the Annex on Financial Services, which allows countries to recognize prudential measures of any other country for the purpose of determining whether a financial institution from that country meets requisite prudential standards.

Like GATT, GATS provides for an MFN exception for free trade agreements, which it calls economic integration agreements. However, the conditions set out in Article V of GATS for economic integration agreements are poorly drafted. Again, one suspects that the drafters borrowed heavily from the equivalent GATT provision without thinking through how the provision would be applied to services. It is difficult to see how the conditions set out in the article can be effectively monitored with the data that are normally available on trade in services. Moreover, it is unclear what kinds of barriers an economic integration agreement should be expected to eliminate and how much integration should be expected in areas such as labor mobility and the recognition of professional qualifications.

Here, too, there is little point in holding another conceptual debate over the application of the MFN principle. With respect to national MFN exceptions, countries should establish the conditions under which they are prepared to eliminate their MFN reservations in individual sectors and negotiate to satisfy those conditions.

With respect to mutual-recognition agreements, the negotiations should focus on the development of model instruments for accomplishing the regulatory objectives of member governments. Few bilateral mutual-recognition agreements have been negotiated under the terms of either GATS Article VII or the Annex on Financial Services to date, and there is no precedent for the accession of third parties. The negotiation of mutual-recognition agreements in services between the United States and the European Union under the umbrella of the Transatlantic Dialogue is one such effort. The Basle Accord among the countries that participate with the Bank for International Settlements could be seen as a prototype agreement on prudential supervision. How the accession of third parties under the terms of either Article VII or the Annex on Financial Services should be approached is not clear. It would be desirable to encourage experimentation in this area. Countries should explore a range of alternative approaches, including the development of voluntary codes and regulatory models.

Finally, the drafting of Article V should be improved. Negotiators should clarify the conditions that economic integration agreements should be expected to meet. Negotiators should also examine the kinds of data submitted by countries participating in such agreements as well as the data that might be readily available, and develop more meaningful guidelines for the examination of such agreements.

A Plan for the Progressive Future Integration of GATT and GATS

Because services are different from goods, GATS has evolved as a separate instrument for liberalizing trade in services and disciplining government regulations that affect trade in services. Earlier in this chapter it was suggested that some of the GATS provisions are confusing because the negotiators did not go far enough in recognizing the differences between goods and services. Thus it may be surprising that this chapter should end with a discussion of reasons to progressively integrate GATT and GATS in future negotiations. Yet there are several reasons to start thinking about the development of a common future framework for trade in goods and trade in services. This is not to suggest that the development of common disciplines should take up significant negotiating resources in the next round of negotiations. However, the fact that the current negotiations on transparency in government procurement apply to both goods and services is an indication that it is not too early to think about the accommodation of crosscutting agreements within the WTO structure.

It is likely that the current distinction between goods and services will be less important in the future. Much of GATT is built around the negotiation of tariffs and the maintenance of the benefits that accrue from tariff bindings. As tariffs on goods are eliminated, many of the provisions of GATT that apply uniquely to trade in goods will no longer matter. Moreover, much of the substance of trade negotiations in goods will shift to regulatory matters and industrial structure policy, issues at the core of GATS.

Although foreign investment and labor mobility are particularly important for trade in services, they are also increasingly relevant for trade in manufactured goods. It is somewhat of an anomaly that a firm that produces services can secure WTO commitments on the right to invest and establish, or on the entry of foreign professional personnel, but it cannot do so if it produces goods. What about firms that produce both goods and services on an integrated basis? Can they really separate management staff that supervises or advises manufacturing units from those who supervise or advise units producing services?

Moreover, many goods come bundled with a package of services. For many purposes such services are treated as goods when they are bundled together with the goods, and they are treated as services when they become separated. Where the unbundled goods and services are subject to different regulatory requirements, the difference in treatment can distort the most efficient way of packaging the components.

For all these reasons, it does not make much sense to negotiate commitments on establishment and labor mobility for service providers but not for goods providers. It is not clear at this stage how ministers will wish to address issues related to investment if or when they decide to launch another round of multilateral trade negotiations. At a minimum, they should decide to pursue investment commitments on a sector-by-sector basis, much along the lines currently possible under GATS.

Should WTO ministers decide to launch comprehensive negotiations on investment, they would need to decide whether the negotiations should cover both goods and services within a single framework or be divided between goods and services. Although any common agreement on investment would have to be reconciled with existing commitments in GATS under mode 3 dealing with establishment, it is difficult to imagine the negotiation of a comprehensive agreement on investment that did not apply to both goods and services.

Moreover, as the WTO regime for trade in goods is extended to investment, many of the GATS provisions will become highly relevant for trade in goods. For example, GATT deals with standards but not with regulations that affect the production process. Once investment in manufacturing is covered, the provisions of GATS Article VI on domestic regulation and the provisions of Article VII on recognition of certificates and licenses could apply equally to manufacturing enterprises. Conversely, many of the provisions of the GATT Standards Code could be applied to trade in services.

Similar considerations apply with respect to trade and competition policy. GATS has pioneered the integration of competition provisions into trade disciplines in the telecommunications area. If and when the WTO embarks on a broader consideration of competition issues, it will likely want to do so on an integrated basis and ultimately integrate the existing provisions under GATS into the new joint framework.

The globalization of production, which results in the unbundling and distribution of different steps in the production process to different countries, gives manufacturing many of the same characteristics as the production of services. Unbundled manufacturing contains many steps that may have been classified as manufacturing activities in the past but now fall into the category of business services. It can also be argued that partial processing of manufactured goods is more effectively treated as the production of a value-added service than as the manufacturing of a good. Traditionally, the concept of trade in goods has centered on the proposition that goods have an identifiable country of origin. It might be better to view partially manufactured goods that are shuttled from country to country as involving trade in services, rather than as goods that originated in the last port of call.

Hence there is a strong argument for integrating GATT and GATS rules on a step-by-step basis. One could imagine the development, over time, of new instruments that would establish common provisions for trade in both goods and services. Specific provisions of GATT and GATS could be replaced by new common provisions as negotiators succeeded in reconciling differences between the two agreements that do not arise from fundamental differences between goods and services. Ultimately provisions that are specific to either goods or services could be treated as special provisions contained in separate subsidiary chapters of the new common framework of disciplines.

These are long-term ideas that are unlikely to affect the near-term negotiations in either goods or services. However, the advent of negotiations on common issues such as transparency in government procurement argues for the establishment of an institutional structure that applies to both goods and services. Joint jurisdiction by both the Council for Trade in Goods and the Council for Trade in Services may be a good interim solution, but ultimately it may be more advisable to establish a Council for Common WTO Disciplines, just as the Dispute Settlement System falls under a joint body, the Dispute Settlement Body of the WTO.

Conclusion

The negotiation of the General Agreement on Trade in Services during the Uruguay Round was a major achievement. The negotiators made creative adjustments in the tool kit of GATT concepts and terms to fashion a set of disciplines suited for trade in services. In the end they proved too conservative in adapting the GATT tool kit. They did not make enough changes, and they did not think through the impact of the changes they did make on the legal structure of the new agreement. As a result, GATS suffers from ambiguities in key provisions, which undermine the value of negotiated commitments and the effectiveness of the agreement. The modest fixes to the agreement and the negotiating methodology described here would help strengthen the agreement and the associated schedules of national commitments.

References

Feketekuty, Geza. 1988. *International Trade in Services: An Overview and Blueprint for Negotiations*. Cambridge, Mass.: Ballinger.

General Agreement on Tariffs and Trade (GATT) Secretariat. 1993. "Scheduling of
    Initial Commitments in Trade in Services: Explanatory Note." MTN.GNS/W/164.
    Geneva (September).
Hoekman, Bernard, and Patrick Messerlin. 2000. "Liberalizing Trade in Services: From
    Reciprocal Negotiations to Domestic Regulatory Reform." In Pierre Sauvé and Rob-
    ert M. Stern, eds., *GATS 2000: New Directions in Services Trade Liberalization.*
    Brookings.
Howse, Robert. 1999. "Comments on Feketekuty, Nicolaïdis/Trachtman, and Zampetti
    Papers." Paper presented at a conference on services sponsored by the Brookings
    Institution, the American Enterprise Institute, and CSI. Washington, D.C., June.
Low, Patrick, and Aaditya Mattoo. 2000. "Is There a Better Way? Alternative Approaches
    under the GATS." Pierre Sauvé and Robert Stern, eds. *GATS 2000: New Directions
    in Services Trade Liberalization.* Brookings.
Mattoo, Aaditya. 1997. "National Treatment in the GATS: Corner-Stone or Pandora's
    Box?" *Journal of World Trade Law* 31 (February): 107–35.
Nicolaïdis, Kalypso, and Joel P. Trachtman. 1999. "From Policed Regulation to Man-
    aged Recognition: Mapping the Boundary in GATS." Paper presented at the confer-
    ence "Global Services Trade and the Americas." San Jose, Costa Rica, July 8–9.
Sauvé, Pierre, and Robert M. Stern, eds. 2000. *GATS 2000: New Directions in Services
    Trade Liberalization.* Brookings.
Thompson, Rachel. 1999. "Formula Approaches to Improving GATS Commitments:
    Some Options for Negotiations." Paris: Organization for Economic Cooperation and
    Development (OECD) Trade Directorate.
Wilcox, Clair. 1949. *A Charter for World Trade.* New York: Macmillan.
World Trade Organization (WTO). 1995. *The Results of the Uruguay Round of Trade
    Negotiations: The Legal Texts.* Geneva.
———. 1999. "Preparation for the 1999 Ministerial Conference: EC Approach to Ser-
    vices." WT/GC/W/189. Geneva (June 2).
———. 1998. "Preparation for the 1999 Ministerial Conference: Communication from
    Australia." WT/GC/W/116. Geneva (November 28).

CHAPTER TWO

Liberalization, Regulation, and Recognition for Services Trade

KALYPSO NICOLAÏDIS AND
JOEL P. TRACHTMAN

ONE OF THE CORE CHALLENGES for the negotiators in improving the WTO General Agreement on Trade in Services (GATS) and the other subregional agreements of the Western Hemisphere in services trade liberalization is to address the trade-restricting effects of national regulation. These are already addressed to a limited extent through transparency commitments, through the weak obligations contained in Article VI(5) (Domestic Regulation) of GATS, and more selectively, through national scheduling under market access and national treatment. Since 1995 the WTO GATS Working Party on Professional Services has sought to spell out more specific constraints on domestic regulation under the mandate of Article VI(4). The Council for Trade in Services issued recommendations for the accountancy sector in December 1998.

In this chapter we explore further options for policing domestic regulations under GATS and the subregional agreements, including criteria that should guide the fundamental trade-off between trade liberalization objectives and legitimate domestic constraints. Specifically, we suggest how developing more precise commitments under Article VI(4) of GATS, as well as implementing mutual recognition under Article VII (Recognition), may achieve this goal.

An earlier version of this paper appears in Sauvé and Stern (2000).

43

Mapping the boundaries between these modes of liberalization is one of the core challenges under GATS.[1]

The choice between (a) more general principles (such as national treatment, proportionality, or necessity) to be interpreted and applied as disciplines over time by panel rulings, and (b) more specific rules requiring recognition or harmonization achieved through political agreement—or the choice between methods of integration generally referred to as negative integration and positive integration—depends on the negotiators' evaluation of specific factors. In the more sensitive sectors, it could be premature to develop specific multilateral rules of recognition and harmonization in the short term.

GATS and the North American Free Trade Agreement (NAFTA) have thus far focused more heavily on *discriminatory* barriers to trade in services than on *nondiscriminatory* measures. However, nondiscriminatory regulatory diversity also poses a substantial barrier to international trade in services. Service providers must comply with multiple regulations: what is required, or permitted and normal, in one jurisdiction may be forbidden in another. In such circumstances, the benefits of free trade—economies of scale, consumer choice, and competitive disciplines—are lost. Because the types and level of the barriers vary in different circumstances, so do the trade costs. However, the regulatory benefits from diversity, assuming that they exist, vary also. An initial response to the problem of balancing the trade costs occasioned by regulatory autonomy and the regulatory benefits assumed to arise from autonomy is to engage in cost-benefit analysis case by case. However, cost-benefit analysis may be inefficient or otherwise unsatisfactory as a method of dealing with these problems. Moreover, even when the benefits of liberalization are deemed to outweigh its costs, the question remains whether the preferred method for achieving those benefits should be the application of general principles enforceable through panels or specific rules spelled out in political agreements.

This chapter examines different techniques currently available under GATS and NAFTA for allocating regulatory jurisdiction over services, in order to begin to evaluate the options for addressing the "trade and services regulation" problem.

Regulatory Jurisdiction in Services Trade

Under GATS, rules of national treatment alone simply permit host state regulation to be applied to foreign nationals operating in the host state. Similarly, rules of mutual recognition (or simply rules of recognition, as in the title of

---

1. The NAFTA (North American Free Trade Agreement) standards provisions contain a similar capability under Article 906(2), calling on parties to make their standards compatible, and under Article 913(2), establishing the role of the Committee on Standards-Related Measures.

Article VII) can be understood as rules that allocate regulatory jurisdiction to the home state even if that state offers services in, or to, residents of a host state. Rules of harmonization establish a kind of limited transnational regulatory jurisdiction insofar as they set a transnational substantive rule for application by national authorities, or in some cases by transnational authorities.

In addition, there are multiple types and phases of regulation. If there is harmonization of law, there are still regulatory barriers posed by the continuing fact of varying enforcers of the law engaged in licensing and supervision activities.[2] The key distinction here is between the prescriptive and enforcement aspects of jurisdiction. "Enforcement" jurisdiction refers to *regulatory control,* which encompasses the accreditation, supervision, and enforcement responsibilities of regulatory authorities. "Prescriptive" jurisdiction refers to the underlying substantive *rules*—that is, the *content* of the regulations that are enforced. Thus, regulation is a complex process, with varying "moments," each of which should be evaluated separately.

Prevailing allocations of regulatory jurisdiction are also increasingly challenged by more dispersed methods of providing services and more transnationally dispersed service providers. Cross-border provision of services, often by means of electronic technology, plays a leading role, while more service providers in financial services, telecommunications services, professional services, and other sectors engage in cross-border acquisitions or other means of establishment in multiple states. Regulation of service providers must be distinguished from regulation of service transactions, and appropriate measures designed for each.

Efforts to Date in the WTO, NAFTA, and Functional Organizations

Together, the trends described above may create pressures to move away from the traditional national treatment paradigm toward home country and transnational jurisdiction—or combinations thereof.

THE WORLD TRADE ORGANIZATION. The World Trade Organization (WTO) and GATS have only recently begun to address regulatory barriers to trade in

---

2. When we navigate between goods and services or among services, semantics matter. In the realm of goods, mutual recognition refers both to mutual recognition of standards and to mutual recognition of testing and certification procedures. In the realm of professional qualifications, mutual recognition is also used to refer both to the recognition of equivalence of the content of training and to the recognition of the home country's authority to certify such training through the granting of diplomas or other evidence of qualification. For financial services or more generally services provided by firms and requiring supervision of these firms, mutual recognition along the second dimension is usually referred to as home country control.

services. The original Uruguay Round GATS negotiations led to an open-ended framework agreement and centered on denials of national-treatment and market-access issues (Articles XVI and XVII). Although it addressed blatantly protectionist regulation, it generally declined to take on regulation with substantial regulatory justification.[3]

GATS imposes, therefore, few specific constraints on national regulatory autonomy. In fact, in the leading sector of financial services, the Annex on Financial Services specifically provides that nothing in GATS shall prevent a state from taking measures for prudential reasons.[4] In addition, Article XIV spells out some general conditions under which domestic regulations that may impose a burden on outsiders ought to be considered legitimate. At the same time, GATS Articles VI and VII provide several facilities for the development of further restrictions.

Article VI(4) of GATS calls on the Council for Trade in Services to develop any disciplines necessary to ensure "that measures relating to qualification requirements and procedures, technical standards and licensing requirements do not constitute unnecessary barriers to trade in services." Article VI(5) applies where a state has undertaken specific commitments, pending the entry into force of disciplines developed under Article VI(4). It prohibits the application of licensing and qualification requirements and technical standards that nullify or impair such specific commitments in a way that could not have been reasonably expected when the commitments were made and in a manner that is not based on objective and transparent criteria, is more burdensome than necessary to ensure the quality of the service, or, in the case of licensing procedures, is itself a restriction on the supply of the service. As we discuss later in the chapter, there are severe limitations on the possible application of this prohibition. Finally, Article VII encourages signatories to enter recognition agreements. It states: "For the purpose of the fulfillment, in whole or in part, of its standards or criteria for the authorization, licensing or certification of service suppliers . . . a member may recognize the education or experience obtained, requirements met, or licenses or

3. The preamble of the GATS recognizes "the right of Members to regulate, and introduce new regulations, on the supply of services within their territories in order to meet national policy objectives and, given asymmetries existing with respect to the degree of development of services regulations in different countries, the particular need of developing countries to exercise this right."

4. Similarly, the Annex on Telecommunications allows for limitations of access to include "measures necessary to ensure the security and confidentiality of messages," restrictions on resale or shared use, requirements to use specified technical interfaces for interconnection, requirements for the interoperability of telecommunication services, approval by type of terminals attached to the network, restrictions on interconnection of private leased or owned circuits, and last but not least, notification, registration, and licensing of foreign service providers.

certification obtained in a particular country." Presumably, domestic measures that escape the scrutiny of national treatment and Article VI(5) provisions will need to be dealt with (if at all) through Article VI(4) or Article VII.

THE NORTH AMERICAN FREE TRADE AGREEMENT. The North American Free Trade Agreement (NAFTA) contains limited constraints on domestic regulation. Article 904(4) generally prohibits standards-related measures that create unnecessary obstacles to trade. Contrary to GATT/WTO jurisprudence, it specifies that "an unnecessary obstacle to trade shall not be deemed to be created where: (a) the demonstrable purpose of the measure is to achieve a legitimate objective; and (b) the measure does not operate to exclude goods of another Party that meet that objective." This requirement can be described as combining minimum rationality with the principle of equivalence.

Article 905(1) of NAFTA requires use of international standards, except where such standards would fail to fulfill the regulating state's legitimate objectives. This requirement is substantially stronger than that of GATS. Article 906 requires recognition of exporting state standards where the exporting state demonstrates that its standards adequately fulfill the importing state's legitimate objectives. This requirement of recognition is substantially stronger than the facilitating approach of GATS Article VII. Article 906 also contains a general obligation of parties to make their standards "compatible." This is more mandatory in character than Article VI(4) of GATS but leaves open questions about how such a requirement may be enforced.

Article 1410(1) of NAFTA, relating to financial services, specifies that nothing in that part (which does not include Chapter 9) shall be construed to prevent the adoption or maintenance of reasonable measures for prudential reasons.

FUNCTIONAL ORGANIZATIONS AND COOPERATION WITH THE WTO. In connection with issues involving the overlap between trade competencies and other functional competencies, the WTO has expressed a willingness to defer to action by functional specialized organizations, such as the International Telecommunications Union and the International Organization for Standardization in telecommunications; the International Federation of Accountants, the International Accounting Standards Committee, and the International Organization of Securities Commissions in accounting; the Bank for International Settlements for banking, the International Civil Aviation Organization for aviation; Codex Alimentarius in food standards; and the International Labor Organization in labor standards.[5] Given the limitations on the applicability of non-WTO

---

5. Renato Ruggiero, the former director-general of the WTO, proposed the creation of a "World Environmental Organization" to serve as an environmental counterpart to the WTO.

law in the context of WTO dispute resolution, it seems odd that the WTO defers
to these other organizations. It may prove necessary to amend WTO law to
incorporate the results of these functional organizations' legislative efforts, or
to address these issues in WTO law initially. Furthermore, the WTO may prove
to be an attractive forum for these types of negotiations, insofar as the WTO
facilitates cross-sectoral exchanges of concessions.

What Is Left to Be Done?

It is difficult to determine how much more action needs to be taken to address regulatory barriers to trade in services. The determination cannot be made
in the abstract but must be made by reference to particular sectors in particular
states. The determination must be made on the basis of the benefits to those
particular states of reducing regulatory barriers, including compensation provided by other states in other sectors. Thus it will be important to evaluate the
costs and benefits of regulatory barriers and to place them on the table for
negotiations alongside concessions in services, goods, investment, intellectual
property, and the like in the next round of trade negotiations. States will no
doubt make sector-specific proposals and may find that there is enough congruence, or institutional spillover, among these proposals to adopt a more horizontal arrangement. In light of sectoral diversity, however, horizontal arrangements will probably be framed broadly, as standards for general application.

WHY DO MORE? THE VALUE OF REGULATORY AUTONOMY.   Regulatory autonomy is valuable for a number of reasons. States may simply have different
regulatory goals or methods, consumers different needs and habits. Regulatory
competition may provide benefits, first through regulatory autonomy, perhaps
enhanced by rules of recognition without harmonization. However, regulatory
competition may bring an unwelcome race to the bottom. Moreover, the value
of regulatory autonomy must also be weighed against three additional considerations. First, regulators are increasingly subject to the same pressures as commercial service providers: they need to regulate efficiently, at the least cost to
the taxpayer; waiving their regulatory prerogatives over foreign service providers helps in this regard. Second, regulatory cooperation can be good, by
spreading best practices in addition to facilitating trade. Third, given transnational
enterprise, regulators will need to cooperate in order to address the full jurisdictional scope of regulatory issues. Thus no single answer will apply across all
sectors and for all countries. Rather, it is necessary to devise an institutional

structure that will provide context-sensitive responses to particular regulatory circumstances.

DETERMINING APPROPRIATE INSTITUTIONAL OR REGULATORY STRUCTURES TO DO MORE. Several options are open to GATS negotiators, assuming they have a desire to impose greater disciplines on nondiscriminatory domestic regulation.

Laissez-regler. The first option is to do nothing legislatively (by "legislatively," we mean treaty-making or other international lawmaking). This approach might be suggested by considerations of subsidiarity: let the national government regulate as it sees fit (laissez-regler). This, of course, leaves open the question of whether some negative integration (or limited positive integration) should be effected adjudicatively. Laissez-regler is often accompanied by rules of national treatment, which, as discussed below, may shade into more intrusive standards.

Enhanced policed regulation. A second option would be to provide substantially stronger standards for domestic regulation in the resolution of disputes. They would go further toward disciplining nondiscriminatory national regulation on bases of disproportionality, necessity, or equivalence, or a more wide-ranging balancing test.

Harmonization and/or recognition. Third, the WTO could continue to expand its legislative program, with negotiations under Article VI(4) toward increased rule-based discipline, leaving less discretion to the dispute-resolution process than under the first and second options. Such a program might include rules of harmonization or rules of recognition, or both, negotiated and enforced multilaterally but is more likely in the short term to develop through the use of Article VII and restricted negotiations on recognition that might later be expanded. Within this program, case-by-case choices about how to combine harmonization and recognition would be appropriate.

FOUR SCENARIOS TO RECONCILE TRADE AND REGULATORY GOALS. As negotiators seek to "map boundaries" between these different modes and levels of constraints, they will need to decide where various regulatory measures and policies ought to fall along two separate dimensions: general standards versus specific rules, and a multilateral regime versus plurilateral arrangements.

Regulatory approach: general standards vs. specific rules. Following a distinction used in the legal lexicon, negotiators need to decide on the role of general standards usually applied through dispute resolution, on one hand and more specific rules usually established through treaty-making, on the other hand. In other words, to what extent should domestic regulations be policed through legal principles or political agreements?[6] Laissez-regler can apply to general standards or to specific rules, whereas enhanced policed regulation generally belongs to the former and recognition/harmonization to the latter. This choice ought to be based on criteria of feasibility and legitimacy, as will be discussed later. Clearly, these options can easily be combined on a case-by-case basis, such as for a given service sector and mode of delivery.

Institutional framework: multilateral regime vs. delegation to plurilateral arrangements. In addition, the WTO could rely on preexisting and new plurilateral arrangements that address domestic regulations outside the full-blown multilateral framework. Alternatively, or in combination, these can develop either more restrictive general standards among a subset of contracting parties or establish specific rules made through political deals, like mutual-recognition agreements (MRAs). Such plurilateral arrangements could be bilateral, regional, or functional. That regulatory measures might be addressed under this category would not mean, however, that they would fall outside the scope of the WTO, but simply that liberalization would be pursued under a bilateral or regional waiver or under a code-like approach. In this case, the authority to manage domestic regulatory measures is *delegated*, or at least relinquished, by the WTO.

There are thus four broad categories of approaches available under the WTO trade regime. Obviously, these approaches are not mutually exclusive and can be combined across as well as within sectors (see Table 2-1) .

This chapter maps the boundaries between these alternative approaches by spelling out what each would imply, the relative advantages of each, and the strategic relationships among them. We begin by discussing the characteristics, limits, and potential of the key GATS provisions relevant to option 1, namely national treatment under Article XVII, legitimate exceptions under Article XIV, and nullification and impairment under Article VI(5). We then discuss how these relate to the alternative options and propose a general framework for dealing with alternative regulations under GATS.

National Treatment under Article XVII

National treatment—which requires that foreigners be treated at least as well as locals—is a fundamental component of any structure for economic (and in-

---

6. We believe that the actual distinction used in the literature between "standards" and "rules" might be misleading in our context, in that here, "standards" is also used to refer to some of the domestic regulations per se, such as banking standards or professional standards. In this latter sense it conveys a notion of specificity rather than generality. To avoid confusion we use the terms "general standards" and "legal principles" interchangeably.

Table 2-1. *Mapping Boundaries in GATS*

Regulatory approach	Institutional framework	
	Multilateral (directly under WTO)	*Plurilateral (authority delegated by WTO)*
General standards (legal principles)	Article XVII national treatment Article VI(5) proportionality vs. Article XIV exceptions	EU/ECJ Equivalence/ proportionality
Specific rules (political agreements)	Article VI(4) agreements Possible further agreements	Bilateral or plurilateral MRAs under Article VII Possible further regulatory cooperation mechanisms

deed political) integration. In GATT, national-treatment obligations under Article III were initially intended to protect from defection the tariff concessions taken under Article II of GATT. However, Article III has grown in its use, in part because of the inherent difficulties in application of the standard of national treatment itself. The central problem (never solved in GATT) is how to determine when two products are similar enough—or when they are "like products"—to implicate the obligation to treat them alike. In order to find two products alike that are regulated differently, it is often necessary to disregard—to implicitly invalidate—the regulatory distinction applied under national regulation.

Under GATS, national treatment is not universal but is subject to the positive listing of the relevant service sector in the relevant member's schedule. In addition, it is subject within each listed sector to the negative listing of any exception to the national-treatment obligation in that schedule. Deciding that national treatment should not be a general principle as in GATT, but a concession to be bargained over, is one of the distinctive features of GATS, reflecting the fact that the starting point with services is a "zero-tariff situation." The core of a nondiscrimination obligation such as national treatment is the comparison between the favored good, service, or service supplier and the disfavored one. Article XVII sets up the comparison as being one between "like" services or service suppliers, referring on its face to the "like products" concept articulated pursuant to Article III of GATT.

Like Services and Service Suppliers

What makes two services "like"? For example, is the underwriting of a bond issue "like" a bank lending transaction? If so, why are different reserve requirements and capital requirements applicable? Does it matter for regulatory purposes that one transaction is effected by a bank that accepts insured deposits? Similarly, is Internet telephony "like" standard telephone service? More fundamentally, is it permissible to make distinctions between services on the basis of the identity and structure of the service supplier as well as the way the service appears to the consumer?

PRODUCT AND PROCESS DISTINCTIONS AND INSTITUTIONAL REGULATION VERSUS TRANSACTIONAL REGULATION. Under some GATT Article III jurisprudence, regulation of production processes is not "subject to" Article III and is therefore an illegal quantitative restriction under Article XI, unless an exception applies under Article XX. The distinction between product and process serves as a kind of territorially based allocation of jurisdiction, in which the product, which travels to the importing state, is permitted to be regulated by the importing state. On the other hand, the production process, which is assumed to take place in the exporting state, is not "subject to" Article III and is therefore unprotected from the strict scrutiny of Article XI (and regulation by the host state is only permitted if justified under Article XX).

The situation is quite different in GATS, where regulation of service providers is expressly validated and subject to the national-treatment criterion. Because the service provider—a person or a firm—may itself be a part of the continuing nature of the service, a different arrangement seems appropriate.

Furthermore, we must distinguish between the two main vehicles for trade in services: cross-border provision (including consumption abroad) and commercial presence.[7] In cases of commercial presence, the foreign service provider would, at least to some extent, be present in the territory of the service "importing" state and thus would be more naturally subject to the full territorial jurisdiction of that state.[8] The need for commercial presence indeed reflects the fact that a service is often "produced" and "consumed" simultaneously and in the same place. We have a much less "natural"—and more difficult—regulatory jurisdiction problem in connection with cross-border provision of services, whereby production and consumption need not happen in the same place. However, as seems to be recognized in Article XVII, the "importing" state should

7. GATS distinguishes among four modes of delivery, allowing states to list different exceptions to liberalization under each mode. The advent of electronic commerce is increasingly blurring the distinction between modes 1 and 2, and mode 4 can be seen as a variant on 3 for our purposes. The four modes are: (1) from the territory of one nation into the territory of another; (2) in the territory of one nation to a consumer in another nation; (3) by a service supplier of one nation through commercial presence in the territory of another nation; (4) by a service supplier of one nation through presence of natural persons of a nation in the territory of another nation.

8. Of course, it may be difficult to regulate a multinational corporation such as a bank, especially one that operates through branches, without regulating extraterritorially.

not, prima facie, be prevented from regulating the service provider in these cases.

On its face, the structure of Article XVII seems to indicate that a national service regulation imposed on a foreign service provider must meet two tests: it must provide treatment no less favorable than that accorded domestic like services, and the treatment must be no less favorable than that accorded domestic like service providers. Therefore, even if the service providers are not "like" and there is thus no possible basis for finding illegal discrimination between them, it is still possible that the services they provide may be "like," giving rise to a claim of violation of the requirement of national treatment. This might seem an absurd result and might invalidate, for example, a regulation that requires a bank to maintain reserves different from those maintained by an insurance company before making a loan, because although the service providers might not be "like," the services are.

Thus it would be better to read the two requirements above in the disjunctive—that is, to separate the evaluation of treatment of services from the evaluation of treatment of service providers. As a first step, this approach would simply evaluate regulation of services as services, by determining whether the regulation treats "like" services alike. If this were the case, regulation of service providers would be evaluated to determine only whether like service providers, as service providers, are treated alike. Using this interpretation, there would be no violation of national treatment if like services were treated differently where the reason for the difference in treatment is the regulation of the service provider *as* service provider. This is likely to be the interpretation that a WTO panel or the Appellate Body would apply. *In effect, such an approach would replicate the product/process distinction as a service/service provider distinction.* But unlike for products, host state regulation of the "process" or the service provider—often geographically located in the host state—would be validated (subject only to a strict national-treatment constraint). Laws regulating the service, as such, would only be evaluated to determine whether like services were treated alike, while regulations regulating the service provider, as such, would only be evaluated to determine whether like service providers were treated alike.

WHO SHOULD DETERMINE THE VALIDITY OF REGULATORY DISTINCTIONS? As noted at the beginning of this section, GATT/WTO dispute resolution has been unable to provide a predictable, consistent approach to determining when products are "like." We cannot expect GATS dispute resolution to do better. Thus, for example, we might ask whether two accountants, each with advanced university degrees from universities in different states, are "like service providers." Are two banks, each from different states where they are required to establish different levels of reserves, "like service providers"? Similarly, are the loans provided by these two banks "like services"? Under GATT jurisprudence, these questions cannot be answered predictably, or in the abstract, but must be determined on a case-by-case basis. Although this jurisprudence results in a degree of unpredictability, the Appellate Body has now addressed several cases, providing experience in how these multiple factors are likely to be viewed and applied (see Chapter 5 in this volume). The question posed here is whether case-by-case analysis by the dispute-settlement mechanism is superior to a more discrete, ex ante specification that could be provided by treaty-making or other quasi-legislative process.

PRUDENTIAL EXCEPTIONS.   Article 2.1 of the GATS Annex on Financial Services provides that nothing in GATS prevents members from taking any measures for "prudential reasons," including for "the protection of investors, depositors, policy holders or persons to whom a fiduciary duty is owed by a financial service supplier, or to ensure the integrity and stability of the financial system." The scope of this "prudential carveout" is unclear, especially because Article 2.1 continues, "Where such measures do not conform with the provisions of [GATS], they shall not be used as a means of avoiding the Member's commitments or obligations under the Agreement." This language seems to deny the exception where there is an intent to evade other GATS commitments. The exceptions included in the Telecommunications Annex do not include such a caveat. In addition, one might expect a measure to be attacked because it is not properly considered "for prudential reasons." It is difficult to predict how a WTO panel or the Appellate Body would approach this requirement. However, one possibility would be that it might be treated analogously to the treatment of Article XX(g) of GATT, which provides an exception from other GATT disciplines for measures "relating to the conservation of exhaustible natural resources." WTO dispute-resolution jurisprudence has required that measures sought to be justified under this provision be "primarily aimed" at such conservation. By analogy, in order for a measure to benefit from the "prudential carveout" of Article 2.1 of the GATS Annex, it would need to be "primarily aimed" at prudential regulation. This is just one of several possible ways that a WTO panel might approach the prudential carveout.

Relationship with General Exceptions, Article XIV

Importantly, even if a state is otherwise found to violate the national-treatment obligation of Article XVII (or other provisions of GATS), its regulation might still be permitted under the provisions of Article XIV (exceptions). Of course, Article XIV would only apply where there was an original violation of another provision of GATS. Article XIV parallels Article XX of GATT, providing certain domestic policy exceptions from the otherwise applicable GATT obligations. The most relevant bases for exceptions under Article XIV are for measures:

(b) necessary to protect human, animal or plant life or health;
(c) necessary to secure compliance with laws or regulations which are not inconsistent with the provisions of this Agreement including those relating to:
(i) the prevention of deceptive and fraudulent practices or to deal with the effects of a default on services contracts; (ii) safety. . . .

Both of these clauses incorporate a "necessity" test, which has been interpreted in the GATT context to require that the national measure be the least trade-restrictive alternative reasonably available to achieve the regulatory goal.

The exceptions under Article XIV would be available only if the national measures also met the requirements of the chapeau of Article XIV, which requires that such measures "are not applied in a manner which would constitute a means of arbitrary or unjustifiable discrimination between countries where like conditions prevail, or a disguised restriction on trade in services." The recent *Gasoline* and *Shrimp/Turtle* decisions of the WTO Appellate Body have interpreted the same language in the context of Article XX of GATT in a fairly restrictive manner. Given that the chapeau of Article XIV is identical to that of Article XX, one would expect the same type of scrutiny to be applied in services cases.

Nullification or Impairment and the Necessity Test under Article VI(5)

GATS Article VI (Domestic Regulation) spells out general obligations for service sectors that have been included by WTO members in their national schedules, except for measures that are the subject of reservations in these schedules under Articles XVII (National Treatment) and XVI (Market Access). In very vague terms, it provides that domestic regulations applied in a sector that a member has agreed to include under specific liberalization commitments must be administered in a "reasonable, objective, and impartial manner." Article VI also includes procedural guidelines requiring that decisions in cases where the supply of a service requires authorization in the host country must be issued "within a reasonable period of time," and that signatories establish tribunals and procedures to process potential complaints by foreign service suppliers.

Article VI(4) of GATS calls on the Council for Trade in Services to develop any necessary disciplines to ensure that measures relating to qualification requirements and procedures, technical standards, and licensing requirements do not constitute unnecessary barriers to trade in services.[9] Before the agreement and entry into force of more specific rules under Article VI(4), disciplines on national measures are contained in Article VI(5) for those sectors in which the importing member has undertaken specific commitments. In order for these disciplines to apply, two sets of criteria must be satisfied:

—The licensing or qualification requirements or technical standards must nullify or impair specific commitments in a manner that could not reasonably have been expected at the time the specific commitments were made.

—The measure must not be based on objective and transparent criteria, must be more burdensome than necessary to ensure the quality of the service, or in the case of licensing procedures, must in itself be a restriction on the supply of the service.

Nullification or Impairment

Nullification or impairment (N/I) has served as a central feature in GATT and WTO dispute resolution. Under Article XXIII of GATT, redress pursuant to the dispute-resolution system of GATT is only available in the event of N/I. In fact, it is possible, although infrequent, for N/I to serve as the basis for a successful complaint in the absence of an actual violation of GATT: so-called nonviolation nullification or impairment. Article VI(5) of GATS incorporates this concept of nonviolation nullification or impairment.

In a recent nonviolation nullification and impairment case, *Film*, the panel reviewed in detail the basis for certain U.S. expectations, in order to decide whether the United States had "legitimate expectations" of benefits after successive tariff-negotiation rounds.[10] As the complaining party, the burden of proof was on the United States to demonstrate its legitimate expectations. In order to meet this burden, the United States was required to show that the Japanese measures at issue were not reasonably anticipated at the time the concessions were granted.[11] Where the measure at issue was adopted after the relevant

9. It is worth asking what is left out of this list of types of measures. Was this provision intended to exclude any particular type or method of regulation?

10. "Japan—Measures Affecting Consumer Photographic Film and Paper," Panel Report WT/DS44/R (98-0886), adopted by Dispute Settlement Body (April 22, 1998).

11. Ibid., para. 10.7.

tariff concession, the panel established a presumption, rebuttable by Japan, that the United States could not have reasonably anticipated the measure.

The import of this approach in the services context is clear. The complaining party must show that the measures attacked were not reasonably anticipated. Thus long-standing regulatory practices or circumstances are protected. This means that domestic circumstances form a background for all concessions; as a matter of negotiation strategy, members of GATS must recognize this and bear the burden of negotiating an end to existing measures that reduce the benefits for which they negotiate.

It is worthwhile to compare this structure with that applicable to goods under GATT and under the two WTO agreements pertaining to regulatory standards: the Agreement on Technical Barriers to Trade and the Agreement on the Application of Sanitary and Phytosanitary Measures. Neither GATT nor these agreements include the N/I requirement in the prohibition itself. Therefore, in connection with trade in goods, determination of a violation of a provision of a covered agreement results in prima facie N/I under Article 3(8) of the DSU, placing the burden of rebutting the existence of N/I on the respondent. In the context of Article VI(5) of GATS, without N/I, there is no violation. Without a violation, there is no prima facie N/I. Consequently, it will be for the complaining party to show nullification or impairment. This will make it more difficult for national services regulation to be addressed under Article VI(5).

We may speculate as to why GATS relies on the N/I concept so heavily in this context. N/I is an extremely vague standard, but one that by itself has been difficult to meet. Thus, without the means to negotiate more specific disciplines on national regulation, N/I provides a modicum of more general discipline. It might be viewed as a "least common denominator," insofar as the parties could agree not to nullify or impair concessions earnestly made but could not agree on more pervasive, blanket restrictions on their national regulatory sovereignty. Thus Article VI(5) is first and foremost merely a standstill obligation.

The Necessity Test

Under this additional component of the Article VI(5) test, this chapter focuses on the requirement (incorporated from Article VI(4)(b)) that the national measure not be more burdensome than necessary to ensure the quality of the service. Even if it is possible to show that a national measure nullifies or impairs service commitments, a complainant would still be required to show that the national measure does not comply with the criteria listed in Article VI(4), the most likely of which is the necessity test examined here.

GATT dispute-resolution panels have taken a narrow view of what is "necessary" under Article XX of GATT, which contains language upon which Article VI(5) is modeled.[12] In order to be deemed necessary, the measure must be the least trade-restrictive measure reasonably available to achieve the regulatory goal. In the context of Article VI(4)(b), the reference is to measures "not more burdensome than necessary to ensure the quality of the service." The last clause could be very interventionist, since it sharply limits the permissible goals of regulation.

Furthermore, in a placement comparable to the inclusion of the N/I criterion in the substantive prohibition, here the necessity criterion is included as a parameter of the substantive prohibition, in addition to being included in the provisions of Article XIV(c) on exceptions. Therefore, in order to make out a violation of Article VI(5) under this clause, the national measure must be shown to be unnecessary in the sense described above.

Recognition and Necessity

Necessity has a complex relationship with recognition. That is, a necessity test, interpreted as a requirement that the national measure be the least trade-restrictive alternative reasonably available to address the regulatory concern, can be either an absolute requirement or a relative requirement. Thus a less restrictive option might make sense irrespective of the home regime, or conversely, it might only be justified in reference to the home country regulatory regime, as a *complementary* measure. In the latter case, where the home country regulatory regime satisfies the host country concerns, necessity may require recognition. This would be an extreme interpretation of necessity, stating in effect that *no* regulatory intervention on the part of the importing country is necessary at all.

New Disciplines under Article VI(4)

It is useful to begin developing an inventory of possible disciplines under Article VI(4), and to compare the operation of these potential disciplines with those already in place. These fall into two broad categories. On one hand, more stringent generalized legal standards are most likely in the short run. On the other hand, Article VI can serve as the legal basis for the inclusion of specific rules of recognition and harmonization in the longer run.

---

12. "Thailand—Restrictions on Importation of and Internal Taxes on Cigarettes," DS10/R, GATT Basic Instruments and Selected Documents 200 (37th Supp., 1990).

Enhanced Policed Regulation

In December 1998, the Council for Trade in Services adopted the "Disciplines on Domestic Regulation in the Accountancy Sector," which were developed by the WTO Working Party on Professional Services.[13] These disciplines apply to all member states that have made specific commitments in accountancy (positive list) but do not apply to national measures listed as exceptions under Articles XVI and XVII (negative list). For the most part, they further articulate and tighten the principle of necessity: that measures should be the least trade-restrictive method available to effect a legitimate objective. They have the following key features:

Necessity. WTO member states are required to ensure that measures relating to licensing requirements and procedures, technical standards, and qualification requirements and procedures are not prepared, adopted, or applied with a view to, or with the effect of, creating unnecessary barriers to trade in accountancy services. Such measures may not be more trade restrictive than necessary to fulfill a legitimate objective, including protection of consumers, quality of service, professional competence, and integrity of the profession. This necessity requirement is substantially stronger than that contained in Article VI(5) of GATS.

Transparency. WTO member states are required to make information regarding relevant regulation public; upon request, they must provide the rationale behind domestic regulatory measures in the accountancy sector.

Licensing requirements. With respect to residency requirements that are not subject to scheduling under Article XVII of GATS, WTO member states must consider whether less trade-restrictive means could be employed to achieve the relevant purposes, taking into account costs and local conditions. Where membership in a professional organization is required, member states must ensure that the terms of membership do not include conditions unrelated to the fulfillment of a legitimate objective.

Qualification requirements. WTO member states must take account of qualifications acquired in the territory of another member state, on the basis of equivalency of education, experience, or examination requirements. Examinations or other qualification requirements must be limited to subjects relevant to the activities for which authorization is sought. This last clause—expanding on the term "take account"—is obviously the most susceptible to different interpretations and will need to be spelled out through more specific rules.

Technical standards. Technical standards must be prepared, adopted, and applied only to fulfill legitimate objectives. In determining conformity, states

13. *WTO Focus*, December 1998, pp. 10–11.

must take account of internationally recognized standards of international organizations of which they are members.

From Policed Regulation to (Partial) Recognition and Harmonization under Article VI(4)

All the above options constitute alternative or complementary legal standards that can be enforced by dispute-resolution bodies. Article VI(4), however, could also be used eventually as a basis for more specific rules of harmonization or recognition that would apply to all the GATS contracting parties. This is what is suggested by the development of a framework mutual-recognition agreement for accountants, even if in a first stage this agreement is to be adopted by members on a bilateral or plurilateral basis under Article VII.

Specific rules with regard to licensing and qualification could be developed in two ways. GATS contracting parties could progressively establish a database—from the bottom up—clarifying what the relevant host country residual requirements should be for different professions in different countries.

Finally, harmonization, or at least the development of common "essential requirements" (as in the context of the European Union) could be envisaged under Article VI(4). Up to now, members have been reluctant to use the WTO to develop substantive international standards or regulations, preferring to delegate the task to regional or functional bodies. But if the disciplines outlined above were to create a certain amount of regulatory convergence among parties, perhaps the WTO could afford to become more proactive. For example, WTO disciplines could do more than simply urge contracting parties to "take into account" international standards (as stated in the technical standards clause) and could officially endorse specified international standards as the mandatory basis for recognizing foreign enforcement of those standards. Furthermore, WTO committees could themselves work on the wording of "multilateral essential requirements" even if those requirements were to be spelled out by more specialized bodies.

Additional Options: Delegation, Recognition, and Harmonization

Whereas Article VI(5) and the Article VI(4) work program contemplate policed regulation and perhaps legislation of multilateral rules of harmonization and recognition, Article VII of GATS provides for unilateral, bilateral, and plurilateral recognition regimes. In the longer run, it could even be the basis for a multilateral mutual-recognition regime.

Delegated Authority under Article VII

As already mentioned, Article VII does not mandate recognition but authorizes it. Through this provision the WTO gives its stamp of approval to nonmultilateral deals, such as regional agreements. Thus Article VII provides an exception from the most-favored-nation (MFN) obligations of Article II of GATS but makes up for it on the procedural front by outlining disciplines on recognition arrangements designed to prevent them being used to dilute entirely the MFN obligation.

Harmonization and the Limits of Recognition

A degree of harmonization is often a prerequisite for recognition. This is so because recognition requires acceptance of foreign regulation. Earnestly maintained national regulation cannot simply be replaced by foreign regulation through a rule of recognition without a determination that the foreign regulation satisfies enough of the host state's regulatory goals to serve as a satisfactory replacement. This can occur through regulatory convergence over time, facilitated by informal regulatory cooperation, exchange of data, and regulatory analysis. But if liberalization becomes a short-term political imperative, it is more likely to occur through formal harmonization. In the European Union, as well as in certain North American contexts (for example, the Multijurisdictional Disclosure System between the United States and Canada), essential harmonization has often been a predicate for mutual-recognition regimes. This experience indicates the need for a stronger link between Article VI(4) of GATS and Article VII.

Of course, laissez-faire adherents would argue for recognition without harmonization in order to promote regulatory competition. The issue here is, first, whether regulatory competition will result in a race to the bottom or a race to the top; second, whether the goal is to reach the bottom, the top, or somewhere in between, and third, how one defines the top and the bottom. In practice, this choice is made in the EU whenever a harmonizing directive is legislated. The directive will contain a particular degree of recognition and harmonization, anticipating and establishing the conditions for a particular level of regulatory competition.

This being said, it is important to note that although for underlying standards and criteria, harmonization is an alternative for use in eliminating barriers to access, on the enforcement side, mutual recognition is the *only* mechanism for liberalization short of supranational control. Unless we envisage the creation of supranational agencies responsible for controlling services firms, training professionals, and the like, mutual recognition of home country jurisdiction is the only alternative to host country control and traditional national treatment. Even if two countries adopt the same rules or both rely on international rules, mutual recognition of enforcement prerogatives is generally not extended as a matter of course.[14] In other words, "harmonization" as an alternative to either home or host country jurisdiction is not available along this second dimension. As a result, when we say that harmonization of the standards themselves provides a single rule from the economic actors' viewpoint, it does not necessarily follow that it provides a single point of control. In this light, mutual recognition of regulatory authority is thus the only path to market access.

Complementarity and Boundary between Articles VI and VII

What is missing in the WTO context is an entity like the European Commission, with real authority to initiate a legislative process toward "managed" recognition, including minimal harmonization, and with the ability to bring cases before a dispute-resolution tribunal to discipline national regulation. Also missing is broad agreement on the utility of the project. With an integrated program of rules, standards, and prospective rule-making, involving both dispute-resolution institutions and legislative institutions, sector-based solutions could be established to address the problem of regulatory barriers to trade in services. In short, there would be an institutional setting conducive to establishing a productive complementarity between general legal standards and specific treaty-based rules.

Nevertheless, the GATS framework provides an embryo for such conditions in the twin pillars of Articles VI and VII. We discussed earlier the relationship between the necessity test and recognition. In effect, and in certain cases, a strict reading of Article VI could eventually preempt the need for treaty-based recognition. But this is highly theoretical. Our diagnosis of widespread "managed mutual recognition" in practice would support the view that even politicians do not dare embark on a pure form of recognition amounting to total regulatory disarmament. This is, however, the only form of recognition judges would have at their disposal on the basis of an expanded interpretation of the necessity test. Judges cannot readily create systems, networks, and procedures for "managed" recognition.

14. This point is often overlooked by those who present harmonization as a complete alternative to mutual recognition. See, for instance, Sykes (1995). On the other hand, agreements such as the "positive comity" agreement between the European Union and the United States regarding competition law enforcement might be interpreted as providing a degree of mutual recognition of enforcement jurisdiction.

Yet Article VII does not exist in isolation from Article VI. These provisions work together to provide a complex system for managed mutual recognition. That is, the weak disciplines of Article VI(5), combined with strengthened disciplines developed under Article VI(4), can provide incentives for recognition under Article VII, or under other circumstances can accomplish the same goals as those sought under Article VII. We now turn to a more general analysis of the rationale, potential, and limits for choosing between or linking these two paths to liberalization.

Designing a Coherent Approach to Regulatory Jurisdiction

At the outset of this chapter, we argued that negotiators for services will be facing two fundamental choices. In determining a regulatory approach the choice will be between specific rules and general standards; and in designing an institutional framework, it will be between multilateral and plurilateral approaches. We now suggest some possible guidelines for making these choices.

The Regulatory Approach

The primary considerations in determining the regulatory approach are degree of specificity and locus of decision.

GENERAL STANDARDS VERSUS SPECIFIC RULES. The first core question facing GATS negotiators in the next trade round will be one of specificity: how specific should any new amendments be in policing domestic regulations? Even if regulatory options lie on a spectrum between two extremes, the choice is between general standards of policed regulation (including national treatment, nullification or impairment, proportionality, and necessity) and specific rules of recognition or harmonization. Here we draw on a literature developed mostly for the U.S. domestic context, which we seek to transfer to the international trade context. We speak of an "agreement" when talking about international trade; we speak of a "law" in the domestic context.

In general terms, a law is a "rule" to the extent that it is specified in advance of the conduct to which it is applied. Thus a law against littering is a rule in which "littering" is well-defined.[15] A law is a "standard" when it provides guidance to both the person governed and the person charged with applying the law

15. Even with the simple example of littering, there are issues that a law may not address. Must there be an intent not to pick up the discarded item? Are organic or readily biodegradable substances covered? Is littering on private property covered? Is the distribution of leaflets by air protected by rights of free speech?

but does not specify in detail the conduct required or proscribed.[16] Even with laws-as-rules there are always questions to ask, so that every law is incompletely specified in advance and therefore incompletely a rule. But with standards, the lack of specificity is more apparent and intentional.[17]

GATS itself provides examples of both approaches. Its General Obligations and Disciplines are obviously standards. The more specific "Disciplines on Domestic Regulation in the Accountancy Sector" still fall under this category. The model MRA in accountancy, on the other hand, constitutes a specific set of rules that are most likely to be adopted bilaterally or regionally.

Rules and standards should also be distinguished as a function of the locus of decision they privilege. Clearly, who makes the law affects its form and impact.[18] With rules, the legislature often "makes" the decision, whereas with standards, the adjudicator determines the application of the standard, thereby "making" the decision (this is contrary to the naive belief that the tribunal simply "finds" the law). Of course, courts can make rules pursuant to statutory or constitutional authority: the hallmark of a rule is that it is specified ex ante, not that it is specified by a legislature. However, at least in the international trade system, rules are largely made by treaty, and standards are largely applied by tribunals. Legislators in this case are national representatives negotiating on behalf of their member states, and adjudication is done through panels (or the WTO Appellate Body). The profound cost and benefit implications of the two approaches are explored below.

THE COSTS AND BENEFITS OF RULES AND STANDARDS. The choice of negotiating over rules or standards, and concurrently of whether national representatives or panels ought to make particular decisions, should be made using cost-benefit analysis, taking into account normative and strategic criteria.

First and most obviously, standards avoid *specification costs* associated with rule-making, including drafting costs, negotiation costs, and the use of general

16. Familiar constitutional standards in the U.S. legal system include requirements like "due process," prohibitions on uncompensated "takings," and prohibitions on barriers to interstate commerce. A well-known statutory standard is "restraint of trade" under the Sherman Antitrust Act.

17. The distinction between a rule and a standard is not necessarily grammatical or determined by the number of words used to express the norm or by who expresses the norm; rather, the critical distinction relates to how much work remains to be done to determine the applicability of the norm to a particular circumstance. Furthermore, and contrary to certain tenets of critical legal theory, this distinction assumes that language may be formulated to have core meanings, penumbral influence, and limits of application; see Hart (1994, chap. 7); Schauer (1991). If all language were equally indeterminate, there would be no distinction between a rule and a standard.

18. See Komesar (1994).

administrative resources. These savings can be significant in a multilateral context where more than 130 countries are negotiating together. Second, standards can be chosen on *efficiency grounds*. A public interest analysis may not give legislatures or trade negotiators enough information or predictive capacity to specify ex ante all of the details of treatment of particular cases. In the same vein, the rate of change of circumstances over time may favor the ability of courts to adjust, compared to what seem to be inflexible rules. This is especially true in the context of services, where technological change, particularly in relation to the Internet, sometimes overtakes attempts to lay out too-specific rules.

Efficiency may also result from differences in the strategic calculations made by the actors that make agreement possible:[19] "When the parties bargain over the entitlement when there is private information about value and harm, bargaining may be more efficient under a blurry balancing test than under a certain rule."[20] This is because under a more specific rule, the holder of the entitlement will have incentives to "hold out" and decline to provide information about the value to him of the entitlement. The cost of insecure contracts will generally not be equally shared. Under a standard, where presumably it cannot be known with certainty in advance who owns the entitlement, the person not possessing the entitlement may credibly threaten to take it, providing incentives for the other person to bargain.[21] Over time, rules may provide such benefits if tribunals develop exceptions to rules in a way that introduces uncertainty to their application.

Third, there are *strategic benefits* in avoiding ex-ante specification. The choice of standards may be a more explicitly political decision, either to agree to disagree for the moment, to avoid the political price that may arise from making a difficult decision too quickly, or to cloak the hard decisions in the false inevitability of judicial interpretation.[22] Standards may even help to mask or mystify a decision.[23] In the trade area, the strategic benefit is both external and internal. Externally, as with any ambiguous agreement, all sides may claim victory, at

19. A number of analysts have argued that the allocation of a legal entitlement may be more efficient if specified ex post by a judge rather than ex ante. For instance, Johnston analyzes rules and standards from a strategic perspective, finding that, under a standard, bargaining may yield immediate efficient agreement, whereas under a rule, this condition may not obtain. See Johnston (1995, p. 256). See also Rose (1988); and Trachtman (1998b).

20. Johnston (1995, p. 257).

21. Johnston points out that this result obtains only when the ex post balancing test is imperfect, because if the balancing were perfect the threat would not be credible. This provides a counterintuitive argument for inaccuracy of application of standards. Ibid., p. 272.

22. See Hadfield (1994, p. 550), citing Cohen and Noll (1991).

23. Abbott and Snidal (1998).

least initially. Internally, incompleteness is often used to avoid mobilization on the part of protectionist lobbies, and more generally, the intense domestic scrutiny associated with treaty-making. In the "Disciplines on Domestic Regulation in the Accountancy Sector," the negotiators avoided the political costs that would come with either recognition or harmonization. The costs may be borne later by the WTO dispute-resolution process if it determines that domestic regulation has violated the standards set, but these costs would be less general—felt in only one state at a time. (Interestingly, there is no formal rule of *stare decisis* or of general invalidation by virtue of the establishment of a legal principle.) The costs are incurred later, and are thus reduced in present-value terms.

Fourth, general standards help avoid *policy linkages* such as deciding how the policy expressed relates to other policies. This is critical in the trade area, where often the incompleteness of a trade agreement relates to its declining to address, or incorporate, nontrade policies. Thus, the "Disciplines on Domestic Regulation in the Accountancy Sector" allow some integration, without the need to constrain, in advance, the domestic regulation of accountants.

What are the arguments then for turning to more specific rules? First and foremost, rules are likely to provide a greater degree of *trade liberalization,* at least at first, than general standards. They are mechanisms to deepen and accelerate economic integration through political deals and reciprocal concessions. But this need not always be the case; in fact, agents can sometimes capture rule-making processes to carve out exceptions and safeguards that would not be specified under a standards-based approach.

Second, rules are generally thought to provide greater *predictability* both ex ante, as actors are able to plan and conform their conduct to the rule in question, and ex post, after the relevant conduct has taken place, when the parties can predict the outcome of dispute resolution. Both so-called primary and secondary predictability provided by rules can reduce costs for economic agents. Rules also provide compliance benefits: they are cheaper to obey because the cost of determining the required behavior is lower. They are also cheaper for a court to apply: the court must only determine the facts and compare them with the rule. To be sure, panels may construct exceptions in order to do what is, by their lights, substantial justice, thus reducing predictability. Moreover, predictability may not be a particularly important value, if, as with the "Disciplines on Domestic Regulation in the Accountancy Sector," the constraints imposed are not very intrusive and thus unlikely to affect many states or economic actors. In many cases, predictability is obtained at the cost of efficiency.

Third, the final outcome is likely to gain in *legitimacy*. At the core of the legitimacy issue is the degree of representativeness of constituents: which institution will most accurately reflect citizens' desires? There is no denying that in most liberal democracies the judicial branch has gained in legitimacy in relation to the legislative branch. At the international level, though, binding adjudication is still in its infancy and is not part of citizens' expectations of representative institutions.

RECOMMENDATIONS. Given the pros and cons of alternative approaches, we recommend the adoption of three guiding principles.

Choose a standard that maximizes the degree of liberalization within the limits of legitimacy in WTO. Of course, the choice between rules and standards depends, in part, on what standard is to be applied and who is to apply it. There are a number of available standards, which are applied in different circumstances. Merely naming them does not do justice to their diversity and subtlety in actual practice, or to the fact that they overlap in practice. Briefly, however, the various standards relate to national treatment, simple means-ends rationality, necessity/least-trade-restrictive-alternative tests, proportionality, balancing tests, and cost-benefit analysis.

In the recent Appellate Body report in the *Shrimp/Turtle* case, all of these standards were arguably applied together. They are all included to different extents either in current GATS provisions or in possible extensions of these provisions under the general principle of "enhanced policed regulation." In economic theory, the most efficient standard would be a cost-benefit analysis, which has the goal of maximizing the combination of trade benefits and regulatory benefits, net of trade costs and regulatory costs. However, there are good reasons, related to administrability and predictability, distributive concerns, commensurability, and interpersonal comparison of utility, why cost-benefit analysis is generally not used.

In order to use standards properly, GATS negotiators will need to consider these issues as they determine which standard or combination of standards should be applied to particular services issues or services sectors. Of course, an issue-by-issue or sector-by sector analysis might not mean that each issue or sector is treated differently. Rather there may be economies of scale or economies of scope that provide incentives for homogeneity of treatment.

Combine rules and standards when possible. When it is necessary to negotiate specific rules as a signal of political commitment to deeper liberalization but the complete fine-tuning of rules is too costly and inefficient, negotiators can seek to combine rules and standards in a single agreement. In particular, standards can be nested within rule-like agreements as safeguard mechanisms. Thus, for instance, most mutual-recognition clauses inside and outside the European Union include vaguely worded standards to the effect that host states are allowed to reassert regulatory jurisdiction in order to "protect the public good." It will be up to the courts to interpret such a vague standard with restraint, so as to respect prevailing notions of the "public good" in the countries concerned.

Adopt an evolutionary approach to rule-making. Negotiators may more consciously and explicitly adopt a staged approach to liberalization. Clearly, the strategic relationship between legislators and courts in this back-and-forth game cannot be mapped out in advance.[24] Nevertheless, standards may be used earlier in the development of a field of law, before sufficient experience is acquired to form a basis for more complete specification. In many areas of law, courts develop a jurisprudence that serves as a roadmap and forms the basis for codification—or even rejection—by legislatures. With this in mind, legislatures (or adjudicators) may set standards first and determine to establish rules later.[25] Thus the "Disciplines on Domestic Regulation in the Accountancy Sector" may form the basis for elaboration of a more detailed jurisprudence in the accountancy sector. As instances of the relevant behavior become more frequent, economies of scale will indicate that rules may be worth developing. For circumstances that arise only infrequently, it is more difficult to justify the promulgation of specific rules.

The Institutional Framework

Choices centered on the balance between general standards and specific rules will certainly depend on the institutional setting in which choice takes place. It is necessary to determine the level of aggregation among states at which to address particular issues or sectors. Different groupings of states will have varying common preferences and affinities. They may work together in regional groups, in bilateral pairs, or in other plurilateral groups, and they may overlap with one another and with the multilateral system in varying ways.

States will choose whether to engage in regional or multilateral integration on the basis of their own preferences and their own views about how to maximize their preferences. We do not address this substantive problem here but note that the choice of level of integration will depend, in part, on the degree of shared preferences in particular sectors, as well as on the institutional mecha-

24. Such strategic analysis is based on the tools of public choice or positive political theory. See, for example, Ferejohn and Weingast (1992). See also Sunstein (1995, p. 9613). ; and Cooter and Drexl (1994).

25. Kaplow (1998, p. 10); Kaplow (1992) See also, Sunstein (1995). It is clear that a rule of *stare decisis* is not necessary to the development of a body of jurisprudence by a court or dispute-resolution tribunal; see Palmeter and Mayroidis (1998). It is also worth noting that in a common-law setting, or any setting where tribunals refer to precedents, the tribunal may announce a standard in a particular case and then elaborate that standard in subsequent cases until it has built a rule for its own application.

nisms available at each level. Furthermore, economies of scope will arise from treating multiple issues together.

Conclusions

The choice between specific rules and general standards must be based on the particular service contexts in which it arises, and the choice may change over time. The choice of forum for these measures will depend on the degree of shared interests among states. GATS and NAFTA are wisely flexible in these respects, providing a facility for the development of rules and standards in multilateral, plurilateral, and regional contexts. But the default option in GATS today is a relatively weak set of general standards for application to domestic regulation—weaker than that applicable to technical standards relating to goods. We have sought to provide a roadmap to some of the boundaries that will need to be drawn in the upcoming round where the GATS agreement will be revisited.

These boundaries will have to be flexible and fluid and will need to adapt to prevailing economic, technological, and political circumstances. It is impossible to predict how these circumstances will change the constraint on regulatory jurisdictional allocation. But we can indicate possible alternatives.

On the technological front, advances in electronic-commerce technology might force states to contemplate transfers in regulatory jurisdiction that they had not envisaged before, simply because no recoverable assets would be located in the host territory. Alternatively, electronic identification technologies might develop to allow for the control of the territory of origin of potential clients or consumers and thus continued subjection of these consumers to their country's regulatory regime.

On the political and economic fronts, globalization combined with heightened emphasis on consumer needs, health, and protection might induce a citizens' revolt against further encroachment of regulatory sovereignty; a couple of highly publicized cases of flawed services subject to foreign regulations in key countries might suffice in turning the tide against deeper regulatory integration—especially if led by anonymous courts rather than elected politicians. Conversely, public opinion and politicians might be increasingly convinced that global governance is a necessary corollary to globalization and accelerate the pace toward trade-friendly global regulatory management.

References

Abbott, Kenneth W., and Duncan Snidal. 1998. "Why States Act through Formal International Organizations." *Journal of Conflict Resolution* 42 (Fall): 3–32.

Bhagwati, Jagdish. 1991. "Jumpstarting GATT." *Foreign Policy* 3 (Summer): 105–18.
Cohen, Linda R., and Roger G. Noll. 1991. "How to Vote, Where to Vote: Strategies for
    Voting and Abstaining on Congressional Roll Calls." *Political Behavior* 13(2):
    97–127.
Cooter, Robert, and Josef Drexl. 1994. "The Logic of Power in the Emerging European
    Constitution: Game Theory and the Division of Powers." *International Review of
    Law and Economics* 14(3): 307–26.
Drake, William, and Kalypso Nicolaïdis. 2000. "Services Trade in the Internet Age:
    Issues for the Millennium Round." In Pierre Sauvé and Robert Stern, eds., *GATS
    2000: New Directions in Services Trade Liberalization*. Brookings.
Ferejohn, John, and Barry Weingast. 1992. "A Positive Theory of Statutory Interpreta-
    tion." *International Review of Law and Economics* 12(2): 263–79.
Hadfield, Gillian K. 1994. "Weighing the Value of Vagueness: An Economic Perspec-
    tive on Precision in the Law." *California Law Review* 82(3): 541–54.
Hart, H. L. A. 1994. *The Concept of Law*. (2d ed.) Clarendon Law Series.
Howse, Robert. 1999. "Managing the Interface between International Trade Law and
    the Regulatory State: What Lessons Should (and Should Not) Be Drawn from the
    Jurisprudence of the United States Dormant Commerce Clause." In Thomas Cottier,
    Petros Mavroidis, and Patrick Blatter, eds., *Regulatory Barriers and the Principle of
    Non-Discrimination of World Trade Law: Past, Present and Future*. University of
    Michigan Press.
Johnston, Jason Scott. 1995. "Bargaining under Rules versus Standards." *Journal of
    Law, Economics, and Organization* 11(2): 256–81.
Kaplow, Louis. 1998. "General Characteristics of Rules." In B. Bouckaert and G. De
    Geest, eds., *Encyclopedia of Law and Economics*. Edward Elgar Publishers.
———. 1992. "Rules versus Standards: An Economic Analysis." *Duke Law Journal* 42
    (December): 557–629.
Komesar, Neil. 1994. *Imperfect Alternatives*. University of Chicago Press.
Mattoo, Aaditya. 1997. "National Treatment in the GATS: Corner-Stone or Pandora's
    Box?" *Journal of World Trade Law* 31 (February): 107–35.
———. 1999. "GATS and MFN." In Thomas Cottier, Petros Mavroidis, and Patrick
    Blatter, eds., *Regulatory Barriers and the Principle of Non-Discrimination of World
    Trade Law: Past, Present and Future*. University of Michigan Press.
Nicolaïdis, Kalypso. 1999. "Non-Discriminatory Mutual Recognition: An Oxymoron
    in the WTO Lexicon?" In Thomas Cottier, Petros Mavroidis, and Patrick Blatter,
    eds., *Regulatory Barriers and the Principle of Non-Discrimination of World Trade
    Law: Past, Present and Future*. University of Michigan Press.
———. 1997. "Promising Approaches and Principal Obstacles to Mutual Recognition."
    *International Trade in Professional Services: Advancing Liberalization through
    Regulatory Reform*. Paris: Organization for Economic Cooperation and Develop-
    ment.
———. 1996. "Mutual Recognition of Regulatory Regimes: Some Lessons and Pros-
    pects." *Regulatory Reform and International Market Openness*. Paris: Organization
    for Economic Cooperation and Development.
———. 1993. "Mutual Recognition among Nations: The European Community and
    Trade in Services." Ph.D. dissertation, Harvard University.

Palmeter, David, and Petros C. Mavroidis. 1998. "The WTO Legal System: Sources of Law." *American Journal of International Law* 92(3): 398–413.

Rose, Carol. 1988. "Crystals and Mud in Property Law." *Stanford Law Review* 40(3): 577–610.

Sauvé, Pierre, and Robert M. Stern, eds. 2000. *GATS 2000: New Directions in Services Trade Liberalization*. Brookings.

Schauer, Frederick. 1991. *Playing by the Rules*. Clarendon Law Series.

Sunstein, Cass R. 1995. "Problems with Rules." *California Law Review* 83(4): 953–1023.

Sykes, Alan O. 1999. "Regulatory Protectionism and the Law of International Trade." *University of Chicago Law Review* 66(1): 1–122.

———. 1995. *Product Standards for Internationally Integrated Goods Markets*. Brookings.

Trachtman, Joel P. 1999. "The Domain of WTO Dispute Resolution." *Harvard International Law Journal* 40(2): 333–77.

———. 1998a. "Cyberspace, Sovereignty, Jurisdiction and Modernism." *Indiana Journal of Global Legal Studies* 5(2): 561–81.

———. 1998b. "Externalities and Extraterritoriality." In Jagdeep Bhandari and Alan O. Sykes, *Economic Dimensions of International Law*. Cambridge University Press.

———. 1998c. "Trade and . . . Problems, Cost-Benefit Analysis and Subsidiarity." *European Journal of International Law* 9(1): 32–85.

———. 1996. "The Theory of the Firm and the Theory of the International Economic Organization: Toward Comparative Institutional Analysis." *Northwest Journal of International Law and Business* 17(2/3): 470–555.

———. 1995. "Trade in Financial Services under GATS, NAFTA and the EC: A Regulatory Jurisdiction Analysis." *Columbia Journal of Transnational Law* 34(1): 37–122.

Making Progress on Trade and Investment: Multilateral versus Regional Perspectives

PIERRE SAUVÉ

WHAT, IF ANYTHING, should governments do about the growing links between trade and investment? This topic has stirred much controversy and useful public debate worldwide in recent years and is likely to be of continued interest as long as investment remains a potential agenda item in a future WTO negotiating round, even as it is currently under discussion in the Free Trade Area of the Americas (FTAA) negotiations.

Multilateral Perspectives

The current investment policy landscape has much to impart about some of the forks in the road confronting governments involved in negotiations. Consider the following:

—Inflows and outflows of foreign direct investment (FDI) remain at unprecedented levels around the world in the absence of a multilateral set of disciplines. Worldwide foreign direct investment topped $800 billion in 1999, a rise of 25 percent since 1998. The United Nations Conference on Trade and Development (UNCTAD) estimates that the world's 60,000 transnational cor-

The views expressed in this paper are personal and should not be attributed to the Organization for Economic Cooperation and Development or its member countries. The author is grateful to Meriel V. M. Bradford, Edward M. Graham, Charles S. Levy, Maryse Robert, and Sherry M. Stephenson for helpful comments and discussions. The first section of this chapter draws on Sauvé and Wilkie (2000).

porations now produce about a quarter of world output. Their foreign affiliates notched up sales of $11,000 billion in 1998 compared with world exports of $7,000 billion, underlining the importance of international production rather than trade in reaching foreign markets. FDI has also become the single most important source of external finance for developing countries as a group, accounting for more than half of total capital inflows.

—The OECD-anchored Multilateral Agreement on Investment (MAI) failed to conclude negotiations satisfactorily. Its demise in 1998 was as swift and spectacular as its promise had once been.

—Internet-based policy advocacy by nongovernmental organizations (NGOs), particularly those concerned with environment, labor, and human rights issues (but also public interest groups concerned with consumer and development issues), has come of age. NGOs cut their teeth during the MAI negotiations and played some role in sidetracking the WTO's Seattle ministerial meeting of December 1999. It can be safely assumed that NGOs will be a mainstay of all future trade and investment policy discussions, regionally and multilaterally. This is a negotiating reality that governments need to better internalize and respond to.

—There is tepid support for an ambitious investment agenda among the Quad countries (Canada, the European Union, Japan, and the United States) and their respective private sectors, with Canada and the United States most obviously on the policy sidelines in the wake of strong domestic opposition to the MAI and to any WTO "cousin" in the investment field. It remains an open question whether such a cautious stance will have repercussions for the FTAA process.

—Slow-moving work on trade and investment at the WTO reflects the steep learning curve in this complex policy domain. This, in turn, has fueled the caution of many important developing-country members of the WTO, whose exclusion from the MAI talks provided them with a ready-made excuse to show continued reluctance on this policy front. Interestingly, the FTAA process has not to date encountered similar problems.

—A still compelling case is to be made on both economic and rule-making grounds for adapting the multilateral trading system to the realities of a globalizing world economy by doing for investment what has been done so successfully for trade since the inception of the General Agreement on Tariffs and Trade (GATT). In essence, this means allowing the benefits of open and contestable markets to be more easily and fairly reaped by developing legally binding disciplines with which to uphold the procompetitive values of transparency, predictability, and nondiscrimination in international commerce. Such logic, of course, also extends to negotiations conducted at the hemispheric level.

Scaling Back Multilateral Ambitions on the Trade and Investment Front

The policy landscape depicted in the previous section suggests that a multi-lateral journey on investment is likely to be very slow. Accordingly, and in light of the difficulties in Seattle, it may now be wise to scale back ambitions on trade and investment. This is so for several reasons.

To begin with, what market or policy failure would a body of multilateral rules for investment seek to redress? In other words, how crippling has the absence of a body of multilateral disciplines on investment protection and lib-eralization been for cross-border investment activity? As the investment fig-ures suggest, the answer can be given succinctly: not at all.

The increasing noise generated by the investment debate is taking place against a trend of continued unilateral liberalization in virtually all countries. There are, indeed, no compelling signals that these trends will change in the continued absence of a comprehensive, integrated set of multilateral rules. Unlike trade, whose cyclical forces of protectionist capture and policy reversals are always lurking on the near horizon, the broad direction of unilaterally decreed policy change on FDI has been, and remains, a one-way street—and a strongly liberalizing one at that.

Services, because of the infrastructural characteristics noted earlier, and for-eign direct investment, because of the intensity of the worldwide competition to attract it, share important "enabling" features that prompt countries by and large to do the right thing when it comes to regulating both areas. This is espe-cially true of investment (including investment in services, which absorbs close to 60 percent of global FDI flows these days), as is evidenced by the strongly unidirectional (and liberalizing) pattern depicted in UNCTAD's yearly compi-lation of the direction of change in national FDI regimes. Indeed, of the 895 policy changes made to host countries' (predominantly developing countries') investment regimes from 1991 to 1998, fully 843—or 94.2 percent—treated foreign direct investment more favorably than before.[1] The data suggest that the magic and invisible hand of the market takes care of many, if not most, problems on the investment (and services) front.

In addition, investment has already made its way into the WTO's body of rules, most notably in the Agreement on Trade-Related Investment Measures (TRIMs) and the General Agreement on Trade in Services (GATS). Admit-tedly, the Uruguay Round performed this feat in a largely incidental manner that today calls for greater coherence in rule-making. The main point, however, is that a solid foundation on investment has been laid.

---

1. See Sauvé (2000a, forthcoming).

Another reason to temper expectations is that the WTO Working Group on Trade and Investment amounts in all but name to a formal negotiating group. This reality undoubtedly explains part of the hardening of positions by many developing countries as the WTO Working Group wound up its initial mandate. That said, there remain subtle but important differences between a de facto and a de jure negotiating process to which WTO members need be sensitive. Letting the Working Group soldier on with its much-needed and excellent pedagogical work would better ensure that attention remains focused on the substantive elements of the trade-investment interface than a formal negotiation would allow.

Thus in the post-Seattle period, WTO members should strive to renew the Working Group's mandate until 2002, when the next ministerial meeting will be held, recognizing that countries are on a long and complex substantive and political journey. There is a need for time to pursue a pedagogical agenda, and for that agenda to take root and be accepted by the broader and more diverse WTO constituency. Ultimately that process should deliver its verdict on whether, all things considered, a consensus exists in favor of developing a WTO regime for investment.

There remains, finally, the all-important task of internalizing the many useful, if ultimately sobering, lessons from the decision to abandon the MAI. Many of these lessons are germane to how investment might be addressed in the future in the WTO and to the more immediate issue of whether changes to the architecture of existing rules are feasible. The following four questions would appear to warrant the more immediate scrutiny of policymakers:

—Should a multilateral regime address all forms of investment, including portfolio investment, or be more narrowly confined to flows of foreign direct investment?

—Just how big is the appetite for developing sweeping multilateral disciplines on investment protection, particularly in developed countries?

—Is a negative list approach to scheduling liberalization commitments, whereby all investment restrictions are eliminated unless explicitly reserved, politically and bureaucratically feasible?

—Is there a political market for introducing credible multilateral disciplines on investment incentives?

Where to Go in the Meantime

Two routes can be taken in attempting to answer these questions. Both, as it happens, lead in the same broad direction, emphasizing the incremental nature of the policy journey ahead.

A first way of looking at investment in the WTO 2000 agenda is to consider the three core components of any rule-making initiative on investment—protection, liberalization, and dispute settlement—and determine what is doable. The MAI talks revealed the limited political appetite for an intrusive policy agenda on investment protection matters in countries with highly developed regulatory systems. What may work well in the context of the highly asymmetrical power relations that characterize many bilateral investment treaties may not work among developed countries. So protection rules are perhaps best left in bilateral investment treaties, where some developing countries may derive important "signaling" benefits from them.

In turn, the lack of a compelling rationale for establishing a multilateral set of investment protection disciplines all but obviates the need for providing private investors with direct recourse to dispute-settlement procedures (so-called investor-state arbitration). A subject of considerable controversy in the North American Free Trade Agreement (NAFTA) and MAI contexts, direct private-party recourse is simply not on WTO radar screens. This leaves, therefore, one issue worth tackling: investment regime liberalization.

What is most feasible under *existing* WTO rules can be determined by taking a closer look at the WTO's existing investment-related provisions as they relate to the three core subjects covered by the multilateral trading system: goods, services (including people), and ideas (intellectual property). What bargains can likely be struck under each of these headings?

With respect to goods (chiefly manufacturing), two matters stand out: investment incentives, for which there is simply no political market, especially in countries with a federal system, for any substantive disciplines; and trade-distorting performance requirements (i.e., TRIMs), where the absence of a compensatory bargain on investment incentives and competition policy does not bode well for anchoring the future of investment talks in the WTO under either the TRIMs Agreement or the Agreement on Subsidies and Countervailing Measures. (Doing so would introduce some measure of countervailing discipline on the conduct of multinational investors in highly concentrated and imperfect markets.) The scope for significantly broadening the range of prohibited TRIMs may therefore be quite weak, despite the soundness of the economic rationale for doing so. One useful way of breaking the deadlock could be for the WTO and UNCTAD secretariats to team up in assessing the empirical effects of performance requirements on the development process. That task could form part of a renewed working group mandate.

Similar problems of political and developmental legitimacy arise for matters related to intellectual property. The welfare effects of the Agreement on Trade-Related Intellectual Property Rights (TRIPs) are being increasingly questioned on equity and developmental grounds. Reopening the TRIPs agreement in the coming round will be difficult in the best of circumstances. Even if one can argue that the agreement performs a useful investment-protecting function (which it does), the scope to alter it significantly or to address investment issues through it seems quite limited.

Services provide by far the largest potential for investment regime liberalization. Indeed, the great majority of discriminatory and presence-impeding measures maintained by governments in the investment area, including by developed countries, concern key service industries. These include the usual suspects of telecommunications, broadcasting and related audiovisual services, satellite services, energy services, distribution, financial services, civil aviation, and maritime transport. Simply put, the global investment liberalization game is very much services-centric, there being relatively few significant barriers to entry via FDI in manufacturing or in primary industries.

The Liberalizing Potential of Services

Future efforts on investment at the WTO are likely to focus on a liberalizing agenda for services. The first challenge will be to enhance the "investor-friendliness" of existing GATS rules and complete the unfinished framework of rules for services left over by the Uruguay Round by addressing issues that both investors and host countries care about. These could include: clarifying the scope of commercial presence, particularly as it concerns the operations of firms *before* establishment; beefing up multilateral disciplines on payments and transfers, which are arguably of greater importance to investors than concerns over expropriation-related matters; ensuring that the liberalization commitments of GATS members reflect the regulatory status quo; promoting greater regulatory transparency (including transparency on distortive and costly investment incentive programs); opening up government procurement markets, particularly for critical infrastructure services; encouraging greater activism on competition policy, as was usefully done in the WTO's landmark agreement on basic telecommunications in 1997; and providing for easier movement of key personnel and temporary entry of highly skilled workers.

Second, attention could be usefully devoted to devising "formula-based" approaches with which to achieve a progressively higher degree of investment regime liberalization. Formula-based liberalization could be either narrowly sectoral in design and scope, or horizontal in nature, focusing on restrictive barriers that cut across several key sectors and are common to many countries (such as quantitative thresholds on foreign ownership).

Summing up, a pragmatic approach to investment issues will be necessary for the next round of WTO negotiations. Although it is most unlikely that ambitious proposals for architectural reform will be up for consideration in the short to medium term, there remain other ways to clarify the status and scope of prevailing investment restrictions; make existing rules more investor-friendly; secure a higher overall level of liberalization commitments; and reach a more informed view on the appropriateness of embedding a comprehensive set of WTO investment disciplines in the medium term.

Regional Perspectives

Despite the sobering prospects for moving the multilateral agenda on trade and investment in the direction of an ambitious, comprehensive, and integrated set of rules and disciplines, the bar might be set higher at the hemispheric level. Indeed, quite apart from the fact that the desultory outcome of the WTO's Seattle ministerial may have given regionalism a new and strategic lease on life, prospects for moving forward on the trade-investment interface may be better in large parts of the Western Hemisphere than in most other regional or institutional settings.[2] An important challenge for FTAA negotiators will thus be to test this proposition and seek novel ways of addressing some of the political and legal sensitivities that the policy interface has raised in recent years.

Staying the Course on Unilateral Investment Regime Liberalization

An important test will be whether the countries in the region are willing to maintain the strongly liberalizing direction of policy change in FDI-related matters. Sustaining the process of liberalization through continuing unilateralism is without doubt the surest way of reaping the considerable, economywide, benefits that open services markets can deliver. Latin American governments have been, and remain, on the right path in opening up regulatory regimes governing services trade and investment. Maintaining openness and being prepared to go it alone must remain high on the domestic policy agenda.

Braving the chilly and fluctuating winds that greater market integration sometimes brings, governments in the hemisphere have overwhelmingly stuck to a liberalizing path in the field of services (including foreign investment in ser-

2. Another example of a favorable prospect for regionalism is that three Latin American countries—Argentina, Brazil, and Chile—were active observers of the MAI negotiating process (and might well have been founding members of the pact had it succeeded). Quite a few other countries in the region were also highly interested in the MAI negotiating process. In fact, had more Latin American countries been at the negotiating table from the outset (rather than just one OECD member, Mexico), there would have arguably been a stronger push to complete the agreement.

vices). They have done so out of a conviction, rooted in more than a decade of practice, that trade and investment in services are what make an economy tick. Services are key to all that an economy produces, brings to market, consumes, and exports.

The earlier recognition by Latin American governments that services are a key part of the economic infrastructure explains why services regimes in the region are more open than those of important trading partners in South and Southeast Asia. Early recognition of the economywide benefits of services liberalization also means that countries in the region have, with few exceptions, more readily embraced the need to promote privatization of key service industries, enforce competition policy more actively (or establish competition authorities where they did not previously exist), and develop procompetitive and market access–friendly regulatory regimes.

From a negotiating perspective, such developments have two broad implications. First, they imply that the FTAA process takes place in a highly propitious climate for ideas, a policy environment that is broadly supportive of further liberalization and open to experimentation and innovation in rule-design. That is rare nowadays, and it is a chance that should not go unnoticed or be squandered.

Second, the FTAA negotiations come at a time of considerable pent-up liberalization in the hemisphere. The impressive reservoir of mostly unilaterally decreed liberalization measures affecting trade and investment in services offers negotiators a wealth of options for moving the liberalization agenda forward in a concerted and balanced fashion.

Promoting Bound Liberalization

The reservoir of unilateral liberalization measures can be given much greater commercial value and political legitimacy if countries place a floor of juridical security and procedural transparency under it. The way to do that is for countries in the hemisphere to agree on the best means of progressively locking in the virtue for FDI that they have been prepared to practice domestically. That is the essence of sound international rule-making and must lie at the heart of what governments seek to achieve in the FTAA.

To be sure, the value of binding commitments can vary significantly from country to country, depending on factors as diverse as geography, market size, democratic legitimacy, credibility of property rights protection, and more. The point worth emphasizing is that many developing countries, and even a few developed ones, gain from the signaling effects that come from anchoring policy reforms in contractually binding agreements. For smaller, more peripheral countries, such signaling externalities may be of considerable importance, as the spectacular recent proliferation of bilateral investment protection agreements would appear to suggest. The sheer number of "modern" trade agreements signed in this hemisphere the past decade is a further indication of strong belief in the virtues of signaling.[3]

Addressing the Gap between Bound and Applied Levels of Market Openness

Recalling the analogy between *applied* and *bound* tariffs in relation to trade in goods, there exists today a particularly large gap between the level and quality of binding commitments on services trade that countries in the Western Hemisphere have lodged in various agreements (notably GATS) and the actual degree of openness that domestic regulations permit. Taking advantage of the FTAA process to narrow that gap by chipping away at the perverse, mercantilistic incentive to maintain it will do much to affirm the credibility of the hemisphere's integration journey. More important, it will also make the region more attractive to foreign investors and service suppliers.[4]

Countries in the region can take political solace from the fact that GATS Article V on economic integration leaves their negotiating coinage intact when it comes to investment in services affecting third countries (though the longer-term economic imperative should be to extend such benefits on the basis of most-favored-nation treatment in the WTO). That said, countries in the hemisphere should aim higher and adopt a NAFTA-like ratchet mechanism whereby unilateral liberalization measures (at least in liberalized sectors) governing trade and investment in services are automatically reflected in their FTAA commitments (albeit progressively, depending on countries' levels of development).

Acknowledging the Incremental Nature of Investment Regime Liberalization

Much as one can support the FTAA process and its demonstration-effect potential, and much as one can believe in the positive externalities embedded in the process of "getting there," it would be irresponsible not to strike a note of sobriety at this point. Liberalization of trade or investment in services is not something that happens quickly or on a linear trajectory. And it rarely, if ever,

---

3. See Sauvé (2000b, forthcoming).
4. UNCTAD (1999).

comes in large quantities. In the incremental world of liberalization it pays to know how to manage expectations and to temper the excessive demands or undue cynicism of key stakeholders.

Maintaining reasonable expectations is key to sustaining support for a liberalizing journey, the essence of which (when done properly) is its *longer-term, adjustment-promoting,* and *orderly* nature. Accordingly, one should never discount the considerable confidence-building value of locking in the regulatory status quo. That is indeed what most successful negotiations yield these days on "behind the border" (i.e., regulatory) issues.

Promoting Regulatory "Buy-In"

Securing the support and cooperation of regulators—so-called regulatory buy-in—is critical to forward movement on services and investment, both of which are areas of high regulatory activism. Doing so requires time and effort, and it is essential that regulatory agencies and their agents feel part of a rulemaking journey from the outset and encouraged to consider means of satisfying legitimate public policy objectives that do not unduly reduce market-access opportunities. Regulators must not come to feel like victims of a hostile takeover by bullying trade officials who are suspicious of the policy rationale that lies behind existing regulatory practices and institutions.

An open dialogue between trade and regulatory officials is the surest way of promoting procompetitive and market access–friendly regulatory reform. Further efforts should thus be undertaken to promote such a dialogue within the hemisphere, including through the establishment of ad hoc working groups linked to existing FTAA negotiating groups. Conferences should also be held more regularly to nurture such a dialogue. The ensuing liberalization dividends may well be reaped somewhat later as a consequence, but they are likely to be larger and rest on a sounder, more broadly convergent regulatory footing that promotes contestable markets.

Avoiding Undue Debates over the Architecture of Rules

FTAA negotiators are bound to engage in protracted debates on the pros and cons of differing approaches and architectures for securing the highest level of services and investment liberalization in the region. Though many trade policy officials are attracted by the geometry and intellectual niceties of such abstractions, negotiators should be encouraged to focus on outcomes more than means, and on content more than form. There is little doubt that a negative list approach to liberalization is better in theory, and for many reasons.[5] There is equally little doubt that the practice of negative listing causes many a bureaucratic and juridical headache. This is especially true for countries with scarce negotiating resources. It bears recalling, however, that the NAFTA architecture of top-down generic rules for investment, complemented by separate rules governing cross-border trade in services and the temporary entry of business people, has been widely exported within the Western Hemisphere. It is, indeed, a common feature of many of the more recent regional FTAs. Therefore, despite the reservations noted above, the FTAA negotiating groups on services and investment should certainly test the waters of negative listing. The key should be to emphasize its usefulness for assessing the efficacy of existing regulatory regimes.

A number of implications follow from this analysis, depending on which architectural fork in the road FTAA countries take. One implication is that regional consensus might be reached in a bottom-up, or GATS-like, manner. Past practice suggests that profoundly consequential differences in market access or liberalization are unlikely to arise from the choice of a negative- over a positive list approach. And there is little doubt that a hybrid, or GATS-like, approach is better suited to promoting progress in services trade and investment regime liberalization. That said, should a bottom-up approach be the chosen path, it would be preferable to avoid using the GATS approach of scheduling commitments by mode of supply, which has introduced an excessive degree of arbitrariness that countries can abuse by scheduling less commercially meaningful commitments. Anything that the FTAA negotiations can do to lessen the negotiating incentive for maintaining restrictions that condition national-treatment and market-access commitments is to be welcomed.

5. Conceptually speaking, a negative list approach is superior in areas of high regulatory density, such as investment and services. Such an approach locks in the regulatory status quo (that is, it ensures a standstill by allowing no wedge to be exploited between *binding* commitments and *applied* regulatory practices); it also guarantees the nondiscriminatory nature of all future regulatory undertakings; helps promote procompetitive regulatory reform; and forces governments to document in a highly transparent (and embracing) manner all discriminatory and restrictive practices they maintain. However, negative listing is also an approach fraught with difficulties and perverse incentives. Indeed the practice of negative listing, be it in NAFTA or the draft MAI, has been generally disappointing. It is taxing on bureaucracies (and would thus be problematic in a developing-country setting); sits uncomfortably with the political economy of federalism, particularly because subnational states tend to be regulatory activists in the areas of services and investment; and tends to prompt a knee-jerk resistance to change on the part of regulatory authorities while exacerbating the already formidable mercantilistic instincts of trade negotiators. The sobering result is the production of a messy phonebook of nonconforming measures (among which many are trivial) maintained at the federal level only; a need for open-ended unbound reservations in sensitive areas; and considerable caution over the legal and political consequences of buying into a permanent regulatory freeze. On the advantages of negative listing, see Sauvé (1996). See also Snape and Bosworth (1996).

Taking Regulatory Transparency Seriously

Even under a GATS-like model of liberalization, FTAA partners should be prepared to enhance transparency and promote regulatory reform by creating and exchanging nonbinding negative lists or inventories of nonconforming measures that affect trade and investment in services. Doing so would send a strong signal about the seriousness with which countries in the region take both of these important objectives. It would also help investors and service providers prepare to address the most significant barriers to achieving free trade and investment. Finally, it would create a most useful precedent from a WTO perspective, where the need for transparency is easily preached but less rigorously practiced.

A hybrid approach to liberalization is just as feasible for investment as it is for services, even if investment were treated in a generic, NAFTA-like manner in the FTAA. Indeed, as long as both investment (affecting goods and services in a generic manner) and trade in services are subject to the same scheduling treatment, *and* countries document the scope, nature, and sectoral incidence of access and presence-inhibiting measures (both discriminatory and nondiscriminatory), the debate over architectural issues need not take up too much time. But regardless of the outcome of this debate, FTAA countries should aim to bind autonomous measures of liberalization taken in scheduled sectors (the so-called ratchet effect).[6]

Adding Value through Regional Innovation in Rule-Making

Scarce negotiating energy should be targeted in the FTAA talks to making incremental, value-adding, and precedent-setting progress in areas where forward movement has proven difficult in other negotiating settings. These areas include taxation, where a constructive dialogue between tax and trade/investment officials is much in need (though the interface has yet to be taken up); investment incentives, where FTAA partners should at least agree on reporting requirements at the federal and subnational levels; and the movement of people, where a generic, NAFTA-like approach affirming the conceptual equivalence between the movement of skilled labor and the movement of capital would help internationally active firms deploy their skilled personnel and allow skilled workers from developing countries to share in the benefits of market openness.

Some of the useful lessons of the MAI's recent demise may be heeded concerning the scope of generic investment disciplines.[7] In particular, clearer dis-

6. Or, under a negative list approach, they should bind liberalization measures in sectors subject to MFN derogations or measures and sectors that are otherwise unbound.

7. For a fuller analysis of the reasons behind the MAI's failure, see Sauvé (1998).

tinctions may be needed between FDI and portfolio investment. FTAA partners could usefully explore allowing some degree of "variable geometry" between pre- and post-establishment obligations; between investment protection
and liberalization disciplines; and between investor-to-state and state-to-state
means of dispute resolution.

Despite the setback of the MAI negotiations and the lukewarm attitude of a
number of countries toward the trade-investment interface in the WTO setting,
FTAA countries should use their proliberalizing capital to tackle these issues in
an innovative, forward-looking manner.

Conclusions: Going Forward with Trade and Investment Liberalization

This chapter's closing proposition recalls in a somewhat circular way its
opening salvo, emphasizing once more that the FTAA process offers participating countries a rare opportunity to lock in the virtues at the hemispheric
level that they have shown in domestic policymaking. Few countries around
the world are in such a position. The highly propitious and proliberalizing climate of ideas that permeates the hemisphere is a precious resource. It should
not be wasted. Indeed, FTAA countries can do much to reenergize the sagging
spirit of trade and investment liberalization that has taken root in many quarters
of the world.

Taking some of the concrete steps outlined here would help pave the way,
through regional leadership, for a leap forward at the multilateral level. Much
has been said and written about the potential synergies and tensions between
regional and multilateral approaches to trade and investment liberalization.[8]
The FTAA process offers countries in the hemisphere a unique opportunity to
explore new avenues of liberalization and rule-making and to find novel solutions to familiar problems. If they are successful in doing so, FTAA partners
would be in a good position to lead by example in the WTO context.

The FTAA's window of opportunity is in all likelihood smaller in time and
scope today than it was at the time of the 1994 Miami summit. The time to be
bold and to chart an innovative path on investment and services is now. Now is
also the time to take concrete steps toward establishing the multilateral agenda
for the next negotiations. FTAA negotiators cannot afford to forget that there
will come a time when WTO members will be able to renew momentum at the
multilateral level.

8. See Stephenson (2000, pp. 509–29).

It is important that the FTAA process not be overtaken by the next WTO round. Staying ahead of the multilateral game and taking the best regional practices to the WTO negotiations in Geneva is, after all, what makes regional agreements synergistic with the WTO. Yet the risk of being overtaken by events and negotiating priorities is real if the FTAA partner countries do not soon begin to articulate a clearer sense of direction and purpose on the investment and services fronts.

References

Sauvé, Pierre. 2000a (forthcoming). "Canada, Free Trade and the Diminishing Returns from Regionalism." *UCLA Journal of International Law and Foreign Affairs* 5(1).

————. 2000b (forthcoming). "Developing Countries and the GATS 2000 Round." *Journal of World Trade* 34(2).

————. "Multilateral Attempts at Investment Rule-Making: Why So Difficult?" Paper presented at a Center for Business and Government seminar, John F. Kennedy School of Government, Harvard University (November 10). Available from the author at pierre_sauve@harvard.edu.

————. 1996. "Services and the International Contestability of Markets." *Transnational Corporations* 5 (April): 37–56.

Sauvé, Pierre, and Christopher Wilkie. 2000 "Investment Liberalization in GATS." In Pierre Sauvé and Robert M. Stern, eds., *GATS 2000: New Directions in Services Trade Liberalization*. Brookings.

Snape, Richard, and Malcolm Bosworth. 1996. "Advancing Services Negotiations." In Jeffrey J. Schott, ed., *The World Trading System: Challenges Ahead*. Washington: Institute for International Economics.

Stephenson, Sherry M. 2000. "GATS and Regional Integration." In Pierre Sauvé and Robert M. Stern, eds., *GATS 2000: New Directions in Services Trade Liberalization*. Brookings.

United Nations Conference on Trade and Development (UNCTAD). 1999. *World Investment Report 1999*. Geneva.

CHAPTER FOUR

Regional Agreements on Services in Multilateral Disciplines: Interpreting and Applying GATS Article V

SHERRY M. STEPHENSON

ARTICLE V OF THE WTO General Agreement on Trade in Services (GATS) provides for WTO members to participate in regional trade arrangements that discriminate against the services or service providers of other countries. Thus Article V grants coverage for preferential treatment extended to services trade in derogation of the MFN obligation of GATS Article II. The underlying rationale behind this derogation is that the preferential arrangement should contribute to the further liberalization of the multilateral trading system. The exemption from the MFN obligation, however, must be based on certain requirements set out in GATS Article V, some of which are similar to those of Article XXIV of the General Agreement on Tariffs and Trade (GATT) and some of which are different.

At the present time there is considerable confusion and lack of clarity surrounding the interpretation of these requirements, which is undermining the credibility of the multilateral trading system. Just as lack of respect for and the absence of a universal interpretation of the conditions set out in Article XXIV for goods were major weaknesses of GATT, similar problems are hindering the application of GATS Article V for services. Few regional agreements have been notified to the WTO. For those whose service provisions are being examined under the WTO Committee on Regional Trading Agreements, no pronouncement has yet been made about their compatibility with multilateral dis-

An earlier version of this chapter appears in Sauvé and Stern (2000).

ciplines. The majority of regional agreements containing provisions on services have not been notified to the WTO and are therefore without multilateral oversight.

The need for a strong and viable GATS Article V is more pressing than ever, given the large number of regional trading agreements that have been signed or extended to the services area since the conclusion of the Uruguay Round in December 1993, most of which contain provisions to liberalize trade in services. For countries that are members of more than one integration agreement, the consistency of these agreements is also important. A further complication is that several sectoral stand-alone agreements on services have been concluded that may have no legal cover under GATS if they have not been notified under the list of most-favored-nation (MFN) exemptions or folded into a broader integration arrangement.

For all of the above, it is imperative that guidelines be developed and agreed to for the interpretation and application of the conditions set forth in GATS Article V. This article is the nexus between multilateral disciplines and market-access commitments on services that countries agreed to in the Uruguay Round and the numerous, and growing, set of integration agreements that contain services provisions. Without a clarification of Article V for services (and Article XXIV for goods) the contribution of economic integration agreements to multilateral trade liberalization will remain controversial and the link between the two imprecise and undefined.

This chapter first considers the background to the drafting of GATS Article V. It then examines the main areas of ambiguity surrounding the interpretation of the article at this writing. Last, the paper reflects on the questions that are raised by the application of GATS Article V to a future agreement on services within the Western Hemisphere in the context of the Free Trade Area of the Americas (FTAA) process.

The Drafting of GATS Article V

During the Uruguay Round negotiations, a draft provision on preferential trade for services was introduced by the European Union and supported by Switzerland, Australia, and New Zealand. Economic integration agreements only became an issue in the negotiations at the end of 1988, when ministers agreed at the Montreal Mid-Term Review to include this discussion in the services negotiations. In December 1989 a text was circulated by the chairman of the negotiating group on services that included a provision for a derogation to the nondiscrimination principle, "under conditions to be negotiated [for example, regional integration arrangements, free trade areas, preferential trading arrangements among developing countries]. Such arrangements shall, *inter alia*, not create any new, or raise existing, barriers to trade in services in relation to other signatories and shall in this respect be subject to multilateral discipline and surveillance."[1]

During the negotiations on how to draft Article V, some participants felt it important to use Article XXIV of GATT as a basis and examine only regional agreements with services provisions that fall under Article XXIV of the GATT. Other participants felt that each economic integration agreement should be examined on its own merit with respect to services, independently of its content covering trade in goods. In the end a rather opaque compromise was reached. An economic integration agreement on services is to be examined under specific criteria with respect to services trade only. However, the agreement may also be considered in its "entire economic context." The meaning of the latter was not explained by the drafters of the article.

GATT Article XXIV provided the background for the inclusion of the concept "substantially all trade" in GATS Article V. The negotiators generally felt that certain criteria were needed to apply to the services area in order to allow agreements to deviate from the nondiscrimination principle. The "Dunkel text" of December 1991 contained a proposed draft of Article V.[2] At the end of 1991 a footnote to Article V:1(a) setting out the criteria for "substantially all trade" in the area of services was added to the draft text. The final version of Article V found in the WTO GATS is almost identical to that set out in the Dunkel draft.

Article V of GATS is different from its counterpart, Article XXIV of GATT, in two important ways. Whereas the GATT article is called "Customs Unions and Free Trade Areas," GATS Article V is called "Economic Integration." The GATS article contains no reference to formal integration structures, and its provisions do not distinguish between the two. Unlike GATT, GATS does not call for economic integration to be "regional." This fact corresponds to economic logic, since services trade under the four modes of supply is not linked to a regional dimension, nor does it necessarily gravitate toward regional markets.

Article V Disciplines and Multilateral Examination

The main provisions of GATS Article V pertinent to the discussion here are set out below for easy reference.

1. GATT Secretariat, WTO Committee on Regional Trade Agreements, "Systemic Issues Related to 'Substantially All Trade,'" Background Note WT/REG/W/21/Rev.1 (February 5, 1998), derestricted.
2. The "Dunkel text" of December 1991 was named for Arthur Dunkel, the director-general of GATT at that time.

Article V—Economic Integration:

1. This Agreement shall not prevent any of its Members from being a party to or entering into an agreement liberalizing trade in services between or among the parties to such an agreement, provided that such an agreement:

(a) has substantial sectoral coverage,[3] and

(b) provides for the absence or elimination of substantially all discrimination, in the sense of Article XVII, between or among the parties, through:

(i) elimination of existing discriminatory measures, and/or

(ii) prohibition of new or more discriminatory measures,

either at the entry into force of that agreement or on the basis of a reasonable time-frame except for measures permitted under Articles XI, XII, XIV and XIV bis.

2. In evaluating whether the conditions under paragraph 1(b) are met, consideration may be given to the relationship of the agreement to a wider process of economic integration or trade liberalization among the countries concerned.

4. Any agreement referred to in paragraph 1 shall be designed to facilitate trade between the parties to the agreement and shall not in respect of any Member outside the agreement raise the overall level of barriers to trade in services within the respective sectors or subsectors compared to the level applicable prior to such an agreement.

The three requirements set out in Article V that must be met by all economic integration agreements that provide for preferential, discriminatory treatment on trade in services are that such agreements must: cover "substantially all trade" (with respect to number of sectors, volume of trade, and modes of supply); result in the removal of "substantially all discrimination" between the parties to an agreement; and not raise the overall level of barriers to trade in services to services suppliers from countries outside the agreement. These requirements were loosely drafted and imprecise and thus are the source of some confusion. Many of the concepts have been borrowed from GATT Article XXIV but do not readily apply to trade in services with the aggregated data that are

---

3. Footnote in the text of Article V: "This condition is understood in terms of number of sectors, volume of trade affected and modes of supply. In order to meet this condition, agreements should not provide for the *a priori* exclusion of any mode of supply."

presently available. Interpretation of the above requirements has therefore proved to be very difficult.[4]

The Committee on Regional Trading Agreements (CRTA) was established in 1997 within the WTO and given the mandate to examine regional trade and economic integration agreements and to develop a consensus on the interpretation of both GATT Article XXIV and GATS Article V. Although both the earlier GATT Committee on Trade and Development and the present CRTA have discussed how to interpret the systemic issues raised by preferential agreements in the area of goods, very little discussion has taken place on this question with respect to services. A detailed consideration of the systemic issues raised by GATS Article V only began in late 1998.

At the end of 1998, WTO members reported that their progress in the adoption of reports on the compatibility of integration agreements with WTO requirements had been impeded by a lack of consensus on the interpretation of the rules relating to regional trading agreements (RTAs), such as those discussed in the following section.

More fundamentally, the rules governing services are unclear about the kinds of barriers that an economic integration agreement should be expected to eliminate. Barriers to trade in services are by their nature very different from barriers to trade in goods because they consist of measures set out in laws, decrees, and regulatory practices. Liberalization of trade in services as defined under GATS calls for the removal of discriminatory practices by sovereign governments in the treatment of foreign service providers. This rule would apply to any manner in which a service might be supplied (that is, through cross-border trade, commercial presence in the domestic market, or movement of personnel). Removal of discrimination can be effected through domestic legislation, through the conclusion of mutual-recognition agreements that recognize the qualifications of foreign service providers as equivalent to those of domestic service providers, or through the harmonization of national laws and regulatory practices. The removal of all discrimination would allow for almost a total merging or integration of a country's domestic market with a foreign market. If some discrimination remained, domestic suppliers would continue to be favored over foreign suppliers. Exactly what degree of integration WTO members should expect in areas such as foreign direct investment, labor mobility, and the recognition of professional qualifications is extremely unclear.

---

4. Geza Feketekuty has written that it is difficult to see how the conditions set out in Article V can be monitored effectively with the kind of data that are normally available at present on trade in services. See chapter 1 in this volume.

Clarifying the Interpretation of GATS Article V

The issues raised by the interpretation of GATS Article V are complex, and discussion of the systemic issues that will help determine the compatibility of regional agreements with multilateral obligations has barely begun. Thus the interpretation of the issues raised in this section is still not settled.

The Meaning and Measurement of "Substantial Sectoral Coverage"

A fundamental requirement of all economic integration agreements on services is that they provide liberalization in "substantially all sectors." However, it is not clear what GATS Article V means in this regard or whether "substantial sectoral coverage" should be determined on a sector-by-sector basis, on a subsector-by-subsector basis, or on a completely disaggregated basis. Would a liberal interpretation of this requirement allow for the exclusion of one or more subsectors? Would it allow for the exclusion of an entire sector (such as that of air transport services in various Western Hemisphere agreements)? Should members of an economic integration agreement be expected to meet a higher standard than that set by GATS (under which much of the transport sector, including air transport and maritime transport services, are effectively excluded at present)?

One wonders how much weight should be allotted to a sector that was excluded from the coverage of liberalization. This brings up the difficulty of measuring trade in services. It is almost impossible at present to measure the volume of trade covered by an integration agreement on services because of the limited availability of accurate data on services trade and the aggregate nature of the categories reported in statistical publications.[5] The only internationally comparable source that includes categories of services trade is the fifth edition of the *Balance of Payments Manual* (BOPM5), published by the International Monetary Fund in 1993. However, the BOPM5 includes fewer than thirty categories of services trade. The difficulty is compounded by the fact that what is needed for the relevant calculation is not the value of trade in services for the world market but the value of intraregional trade in services (among the members of a given integration agreement). When they exist, these data must be extracted from national accounts and national trade statistics and may not be comparable from country to country or from agreement to agreement.

Therefore a key question is how to calculate the affected volume of trade in a situation where an entire sector may be excluded from an agreement or where

5. See Stephenson (1999).

a given service sector may be less than fully liberalized. If a services sector is fully or partially excluded from the coverage of an integration agreement, it would be almost impossible to determine its economic importance because at present so few data exist for calculating the percentage represented by that sector in total intraregional trade in services. In the absence of such data, a more feasible alternative would be to calculate the importance of the excluded sector or subsector in the combined gross domestic product (GDP) of the members of a given agreement. A suggestion has been made to adopt a minimum percentage target for the volume of services trade to be covered by an integration agreement, as measured by the combined volume of domestic services activity of the included service sectors.[6] However, at this writing the WTO Committee has not discussed what this minimum percentage might be.

It is also unclear whether the GATS requirements in Article V would allow for the exclusion of a mode of supply for one service sector only (such as the cross-border supply of financial services in the case of the agreements signed by Chile). It is equally unclear whether the admonition to not exclude a priori any mode of supply extends to particular categories within one of the modes (such as the exclusion of the movement of labor other than professional service providers, as is the case for the majority of agreements in the hemisphere). Should all labor mobility related to trade in services be included?[7]

Equally important, does an integration agreement have to cover investment? Because GATS defines investment as the most important mode of supply for services trade, it would seem that no agreement that excluded investment would be consistent with multilateral rules. However, in some services sectors there are significant restrictions on investment conditions. Governments require foreign suppliers to establish themselves locally before they are allowed to sell their services to local consumers, a requirement that amounts to an a priori exclusion of cross-border trade in these services. Can this be considered a violation of Article V?

In the Western Hemisphere, all of the integration agreements on services either include a separate chapter containing comprehensive investment disciplines (those agreements modeled on the NAFTA approach) or define investment as a mode of supply within the agreement (the Southern Cone Common Market [MERCOSUR]; the Andean Community). In the case of the latter approach, in-

6. This suggestion was made in an informal paper presented by Hong Kong, China, to the members of the WTO Council for Trade in Services in May 1999.
7. Note that this is a requirement under all of those agreements with the stated aim of being or becoming customs unions. This is not the case for free trade agreements. GATS Article V requirements do not distinguish, however, between the two forms of integration agreements. This would seem to have strong implications for labor mobility.

vestment protocols have been developed separately or are being completed. It will be important to see how the link between the investment and services components of these two integration agreements is articulated and whether the approaches to liberalization are compatible between the two areas.[8] If not, service suppliers will be subjected to a confusing situation that would also be unclear from a legal standpoint.

The Meaning of "Substantially All Discrimination"

Another requirement set out in GATS Article V is for integration agreements to provide for the "absence or elimination of substantially all discrimination." This is understood in terms of GATS Article XVII on national treatment, which provides that treatment granted to service suppliers from other parties to an integration agreement be no less favorable than that accorded to domestic service suppliers. Granting unqualified national treatment among the members of an integration agreement would be the equivalent of providing free trade for services: no discriminatory barriers (except possibly those of a quantitative nondiscriminatory nature) would exist to the establishment of member firms or to cross-border sales of services by member firms. The main question is whether such a requirement can be measured quantitatively and to which sectors it should apply. Clearly all sectors included in an integration agreement should be covered; for those sectors, the question is how to measure the extent of liberalization achieved. What types of discriminatory measures, besides those that fall under the enumerated GATS articles, should be considered as legitimate exceptions from this requirement?

Article V lists specific other GATS articles in which measures are exempt from eliminating "substantially all discrimination." These articles are: Articles XI (IMF Provisions on Payments and Transfers), XII (Balance of Payments), XIV (General Exceptions related to health, safety, taxation, and public order), and XIV *bis* (National Security). Not included are Articles VII (Recognition), X (Emergency Safeguard Measures), XIII (Government Procurement), and XV (Subsidies). Article V also does not refer to the two annexes on air transport services and financial services. It is not clear whether such omissions make it impossible for members of an integration agreement to discriminate against

---

8. For example, it would be problematic for service suppliers to be faced with an agreement that provided for a positive list of services commitments on the one hand, including those on foreign direct investment, and with an agreement on investment on the other hand that adopted a negative list approach to investment decisions overall (for both goods and services). This would be the case for an investment agreement that contained a pre-establishment discipline for market access.

each other in important areas such as the licensing of professional service suppliers, the granting of domestic subsidies, and government procurement of services. Likewise, do these omissions mean that members of an integration agreement are not allowed to apply emergency safeguard measures to their services trade with each other?

The agreements on services in the Western Hemisphere do not yet eliminate or harmonize licensing requirements for professional service suppliers. One mutual-recognition agreement was concluded by the engineering profession in 1995. The agreement has been approved by all Canadian provinces and Mexican states, but in the United States only the state of Texas has ratified it. A text for recognizing the qualifications of legal consultants was also agreed to in 1995 but has not yet been adopted in any country. Recognition agreements are stalled, although they are being considered by the professions of architects, accountants, nurses, land surveyors, and actuaries. Thus NAFTA has not yet eliminated or harmonized the licensing requirements for professional service suppliers among its members.

All of the other NAFTA-type free trade agreements in the Western Hemisphere also contain chapters on professional services, whose aim is to promote recognition of the equivalency of these requirements. It is not clear that any progress has been made to date on this objective for the members of these agreements. Such provisions are also present in the two customs unions, the Andean Community and MERCOSUR. The Andean Community is drafting a decision that will elaborate a general framework containing the conditions for the recognition of titles and mandatory licenses, as well as other requirements for the exercise of professional service activities. In the case of MERCOSUR, professional bodies are to play the dominant role in proposing and drafting resolutions for the mutual recognition of professional qualifications. One such resolution has been adopted for the professions of architects, agronomists, geologists, and engineers. This resolution, however, covers only those professionals already in possession of a work contract and who intend to stay abroad no more than two years. Thus a long-term liberalization is not yet foreseen, even for those four professions. Clearly the stringent application of the requirement under Article V to harmonize or recognize the qualifications of professional service suppliers among the members of integration agreements in the Western Hemisphere would make it difficult for those agreements to be compatible with multilateral disciplines.

With respect to safeguards, many of the integration agreements in the hemisphere do not contain an article providing recourse to emergency safeguard action (the case of NAFTA; the Group of Three; the bilateral agreements between Chile and Mexico and between Chile and Canada; and the Andean Community Decision on Services). However, the other integration agreements do include a safeguard provision. It is difficult, however, to imagine how safeguard action among members to an integration agreement would be compatible with the requirement to both liberalize trade among members and not raise the level of barriers to outside members. Again, however, this question has not been discussed in the WTO.

Most agreements in the hemisphere do not include an explicit provision to eliminate subsidies between members. Therefore this area remains unclear, as does the interpretation of the disciplines expected on subsidies by GATS.

When discrimination in a given service sector is not completely eliminated among members to an integration agreement, how its economic impact should be evaluated is still open to debate. Does the existence of discrimination between the suppliers of professional services hold more weight than the maintenance of discrimination in the provision of educational services? Or health services? How to evaluate the economic significance of remaining discrimination has not yet been explored.

Last, GATS Article V requires the elimination of "substantially all discrimination" by members to economic integration agreements within a reasonable time frame. The question is then what may be considered reasonable. In the Understanding on the Interpretation of Article XXIV of GATT 1994 that resulted from the Uruguay Round, a "reasonable time frame" is taken to mean no longer than ten years for goods. A recent proposal to the Council for Trade in Services has suggested that this time frame be no longer than five years.[9] However, this issue has not yet been discussed for services.

The Meaning of Not Raising the Overall Level of Barriers to Services Trade

Once again Article V is unclear about how to interpret the meaning of the injunction not to raise the barriers to trade in services for parties outside an integration agreement in individual service sectors or subsectors. In practice, how can such a requirement be tested or evaluated?

First, the difficulty of calculating the overall level of barriers to services trade in effect before the formation of an integration agreement makes this requirement nearly impossible to translate into practice. Barriers to trade in services are present in laws, decrees, and regulatory practices, and their quali-

9. This proposal was made in a paper by Japan at an April 1999 meeting of the WTO Council for Trade in Services. The proposal suggests that the WTO requirement to eliminate discrimination in the sectors covered by an economic integration agreement be met within five years after the agreement is in place. Japan made a similar proposal in 1997.

tative nature makes it virtually impossible to attach to them a quantitative value. Calculating tariff or price equivalents for the trade-restrictive effect of most national laws and regulatory practices has proved impossible and most likely will continue to run into enormous data and methodological difficulties, greater for some sectors than for others. One proposed alternative is to require that an agreement on services not reduce the level of trade in any service sector or subsector after its entry into force, or that it not reduce the growth of trade in any sector or subsector for members of an integration agreement below a historical level.[10]

A related question again has to do with the nature of changes to barriers to trade in services. In the case of a customs union arrangement that calls for regulatory barriers to services trade to be gradually harmonized, is an agreement not to reduce the level or the growth of trade significantly different from an agreement that says its members may choose to lower or reduce barriers on the basis of equivalency or mutual recognition? Does the choice of an approach to eliminating discrimination have an effect on the treatment of third parties? Would it be easier for third-party service suppliers to join a mutual-recognition agreement than to comply with harmonized regulatory standards? Does this question also relate to the concept of the "wider process of economic integration" set out in Article V(2)?

Other Problems Surrounding GATS Article V

Besides the problems of interpretation and application, other problems render Article V unsatisfactory as well. These include: the lack of notifications of regional and economic integration agreements to the WTO for examination in the Committee on Regional Trading Arrangements and the hesitation of developing countries to participate in this process; the existing sectoral stand-alone agreements on services and their relationship to GATS Article V obligations; and the status of Article V in relation to the regional and economic integration agreements included in the list of Annex I measures or MFN exemptions.

Reluctance to Notify the WTO of Economic integration Agreements

There seems to be a general reluctance to notify both regional trading arrangements and economic integration agreements to the WTO for examination

---

10. This suggestion for an alternative means of evaluating this Article V requirement was proposed by Hong Kong, China, in its paper to the WTO Council for Trade in Services of March 1999.

by the WTO Committee on Regional Trade Agreements. A study done by the WTO Secretariat for the purpose of drawing a global picture of RTAs identified more than 130 such agreements (not a comprehensive count), of which only 60 had been notified to GATT/WTO. This leaves 74 nonnotified RTAs.[11] Several of these RTAs have incorporated provisions on trade in services. These parties to integration agreements on services are not in compliance with WTO disciplines and appear to be unwilling to participate in this important review process.

In the Western Hemisphere at the end of 1999, ten bilateral or subregional integration agreements covering services had been signed or had entered into force.[12] These agreements, along with the date of their signature (S) or entry into force (F), are the following:

North American Free Trade Agreement	January 1994 (F)
Group of Three Free Trade Agreement	January 1995 (F)
Mexico-Bolivia Free Trade Agreement	January 1995 (F)
Mexico–Costa Rica Free Trade Agreement	January 1995 (F)
Chile-Canada Free Trade Agreement	July 1997 (F)
MERCOSUR Protocol on Services	December 1997 (S)
Central America–Dominican Republic Free Trade Agreement	April 1998 (S)
Andean Community Decision 439 on Services	June 1998 (F)
Mexico-Nicaragua Free Trade Agreement	July 1998 (F)
Chile-Mexico Free Trade Agreement	August 1999 (F)

At this writing, only two of these ten agreements have been notified to the WTO for examination under GATS Article V. These agreements are NAFTA (notified in March 1995) and the free trade agreement between Canada and Chile (notified in November 1997). The lack of compliance with one of the basic requirements of GATS by the parties to the other eight integration agreements in the Western Hemisphere is clearly a matter of concern, particularly since all appear to be "GATS plus" agreements, in content or in their long-term liberalization objectives.

Two of the agreements foresee the complete removal of barriers to services trade among the members to the arrangements within a stated period of time, specifically a ten-year period for the members of MERCOSUR and a five-year period for the members of the Andean Community. The stated objective

11. Not all of these 74 agreements would need to be notified to the WTO, however; only those containing binding provisions for preferential treatment fall under multilateral obligations. This would still leave a considerable number of nonnotified agreements.

12. Organization of American States (1999).

of the former agreement is to carry out "successive rounds of negotiations in order to complete the MERCOSUR liberalization program for services within a ten-year period, counted from the date of entry into effect of the Services Protocol." The latter calls for "the progressive liberalization of subregional trade in services, in order to reach a Common Market in Services, through the elimination of restrictive measures within the Andean Community" (Decision 439 in date of June 1998). This ambitious liberalization goal is not present in any of the other integration agreements that contain provisions on services (with the exception of the European Union single-market agreement).[13]

Although they do not call for full liberalization of services, all of the agreements initiated and signed by Mexico (the Group of Three and the bilateral free trade agreements with Bolivia, Costa Rica, Chile, and Nicaragua) do contain a built-in dynamic for future liberalization. Each member is obligated to continue opening member services markets through future negotiations that aim to "eliminate the remaining restrictions set out in the list of non-conforming measures."[14]

The lack of willingness by MERCOSUR and the Andean Community to notify the WTO of the agreements that cover all or most service sectors and modes of supply and that seem to provide for the future removal of substantially all discrimination in services trade among members is puzzling. However, their reluctance may be linked to the fact that the liberalizing process for services is in its early stages. MERCOSUR members have not revealed the lists of commitments they have begun to exchange among themselves, and the Andean Community has not yet developed the inventories of national laws and regulations from which they are to begin negotiating removal of discriminatory measures. Few of the free trade agreements have published the lists of reservations or nonconforming measures to the scope of services liberalization that are to accompany the treaties. In the case of NAFTA and the agreement between Chile and Canada, such lists are an integral part of the text, thus making these agreements highly transparent (for measures at the federal level).[15] The Group of Three finalized the list of reservations after the conclusion of their agree-

13. All of the integration agreements that postulate the complete removal of restrictions to internal services trade are agreements that by their stated objective are customs unions, not free trade agreements.

14. This obligation for future liberalization appears in Article 10.09 of the Group of Three Treaty, Article 10.09 of the Mexico/Chile Free Trade Agreement, Article 9-08 of the Mexico/ Bolivia and Mexico/Costa Rica Free Trade Agreements, and Article 10.09 of the Mexico/Nicaragua Free Trade Agreement. Mexico is on the verge of concluding a new free trade agreement with the three countries of the northern triangle in Central America—namely, El Salvador, Guatemala, and Honduras.

15. See chapter 12 by Francisco Javier Prieto in this volume.

ment (in 1997), and each member country published these separately. Thus for the other agreements within the Western Hemisphere a critical element of transparency is missing from the process of services liberalization that certainly would constitute a stumbling block for a multilateral examination under the WTO.

However, in their reluctance to notify the WTO of recent economic integration agreements on services, countries in the Western Hemisphere may be overlooking paragraph 3(a) of Article V that allows for more lenient examination to be extended to such agreements among developing countries:

> 3. (a) Where developing countries are parties to an agreement of the type referred to in paragraph 1, flexibility shall be provided for regarding the conditions set out in paragraph 1, particularly with reference to subparagraph (b) thereof, in accordance with the level of development of the countries concerned, both overall and in individual sectors and subsectors.

Although the article allows for flexibility with respect to the elimination of "substantially all discrimination" in services trade, it does not precisely define the notion of "more favorable treatment." Eight of the ten integration agreements in the Western Hemisphere covering services have developing-country membership only, but not one of these has yet been notified to the WTO. This lack of compliance with the Article V notification requirement can only serve to weaken the one link that could ensure the compatibility and congruence of the parallel multilateral and regional liberalization processes.[16]

Overlapping Membership in Regional Trade Agreements

Another troubling phenomenon is the increasingly common tendency for WTO members to be party to more than one economic integration agreement simultaneously. According to a study prepared by the WTO Secretariat, twelve countries in the Western Hemisphere have signed more than four RTAs.[17] Mexico is a party to no fewer than six different agreements covering services, and several countries are party to two different agreements (Bolivia, Canada, Chile, Colombia, Costa Rica, Nicaragua, and Venezuela). Certain anomalies have arisen in this context. For example, the members of the Central American

---

16. Outside of the Western Hemisphere, this appears to be the case only for the members of the Association of Southeast Asian Nations (ASEAN), who signed a protocol on services in 1995.

17. The WTO Secretariat also noted that fourteen European countries were party to thirty-five different RTAs.

Common Market have signed a free trade agreement with the Dominican Republic covering services, although they do not yet have an agreement among themselves. Colombia and Venezuela have agreed to completely eliminate barriers to services trade between themselves in the context of the Andean Community but have not agreed to the same thing in the context of the Group of Three Treaty they signed with Mexico.

This overlapping membership in RTAs and economic integration agreements on services has resulted in a complex web of rules for administering and enforcing the provisions of the agreements. It has been remarked that such multiple rules may run counter to the primary objective of RTAs, which is to facilitate trade among members, resulting in overall trade creation but not to raising barriers to trade with third countries.

Stand-Alone Sectoral Agreements

It is a little-known fact that within the Western Hemisphere a great number of stand-alone agreements have been reached in the area of services. In a study carried out in 1997 for the FTAA Working Group on Services using information received from the participating countries, the OAS Secretariat classified no fewer than 167 sectoral agreements on services of various types (41 at the subregional level and 126 at the bilateral level).[18] The large majority are in the areas of professional services and transport services (with 67 agreements relating to air routing). It is striking that more than half of the sectoral agreements have been signed since 1990.

The legal status of these agreements is unclear at present. Agreements on cooperative and technical assistance that do not contain liberalizing provisions would not seem to conflict with GATS Article V requirements. However, agreements that provide for statutory preferential treatment better than that provided to other trading partners should have been notified to the WTO as part of Annex II of MFN Exemptions to the GATS, or they should have been the object of a waiver request, as discussed in the following paragraphs. Since there have been no requests made to the WTO for waivers on services measures, some of these sectoral agreements now presumably exist in a legal gray area.

In the area of telecommunications, a Draft Convention on the provision of value-added telecommunications services was negotiated in 1997 by members of the OAS under the aegis of the Inter-American Telecommunication Commission (CITEL). The Convention covers such matters as the standard of treatment, interconnection with the public network, terminal equipment, rights of

18. Organization of American States (1998).

end users, and others. It is not clear whether the Convention is meant to be applied on a nondiscriminatory basis or a preferential basis among countries in the Western Hemisphere only. If the intention is to give preferential treatment, then the Draft Convention would conflict with the basic MFN principle and would need to comply with GATS Article V provisions. In that case, it is unlikely that a single service sector could qualify under these provisions. Although it was possible for WTO members to list measures and agreements such as a sector-specific telecommunications agreement as MFN principle exemptions in their 1994 schedules, this possibility expired when GATS entered into force in January 1995. The only other channel open for making such a sector-specific agreement consistent with GATS would be to seek a waiver from the MFN obligation under Article IX(3). Such waivers must be justified by exceptional circumstances, should in principle be temporary, and are subject to annual review.

In light of the above, members of CITEL decided to transmit the Draft Convention to the FTAA Negotiating Group on Services in August 1998 for consideration and use in the FTAA process. The negotiating group has not yet discussed the Draft Convention.

Notification of Integration Agreements as MFN Exemptions

Also worrisome is the fact that many WTO members have claimed wide-ranging exemptions for preferential trade agreements through notifying these under Annex II or their list of MFN exemptions, rather than having their agreements examined by the WTO Committee on Regional Trade Agreements. Presumably their purpose is to avoid the examination process under GATS Article V because of uncertainty over whether such agreements would be deemed compatible with multilateral obligations.

This brings into question the purpose of the existing Annex II on MFN Exemptions and the MFN article itself. Article II(1) of GATS states that the MFN obligation is to be immediate and unconditional for services supplied by any other WTO member and that it is to apply to "any measure covered by this Agreement." Although the scope of application of such measures is wide, it would not include the provisions of economic integration agreements, which are subject to the provisions of Article V. Measures covered by preferential agreements that contain comprehensive disciplines on services are part and parcel of a larger package and should not be considered on an individual sectoral basis or listed in the GATS MFN Annex.

In the GATS lists of MFN exemptions, several sector-specific discriminatory measures are included that originate in preferential integration agreements;

most of these are in the audiovisual sector (37), road transport services (24), maritime transport services (14), telecommunications services (18), and financial services (10).[19] Additional analysis would be necessary to determine which of these measures stand alone and which fall under services agreements with comprehensive disciplines and sectoral coverage. Because it is not known what will happen to this annex in the next round of GATS 2000 negotiations, it also cannot be predicted what will happen to exemptions that have been inscribed in national schedules to cover integration agreements. This issue will likely be discussed in the negotiations.

Application of GATS Article V to a Future FTAA Agreement on Services

What will be the relationship of GATS Article V to a future FTAA Agreement on Services? To be deemed compatible with the rules and disciplines of the multilateral trading system, a future FTAA agreement on services must fulfill the requirements set out in Article V. Thus a future agreement must cover "substantially all sectors" and "remove substantially all discrimination" among participants in the Western Hemisphere. The interpretation of these obligations will depend on the outcome of the deliberations in the WTO Committee on Regional Trade Agreements and how these are defined by WTO members.

Political and economic reality will dictate, however, that a regional agreement encompassing countries in the Western Hemisphere that account for one-quarter of the world's GDP and one-fifth of world trade will come under close scrutiny in the WTO. Such an FTAA agreement would rival that of the European Union in economic and trade terms. Thus the conditions of GATS Article V would most likely be closely reviewed and strictly applied in this context because the FTAA agreement would have such a large weight in international trade.

At another level, what type of subregional preferential treatment could be envisaged, if any, between the parties to a future FTAA agreement? Although the MFN principle in its unconditional form has been the backbone of the vast majority of trading agreements in the world economy, in the FTAA context could the MFN principle be interpreted in a conditional manner within a future FTAA agreement covering services?

This concern arises because the FTAA process is taking place in a region where several integration agreements already exist and where it may be desir-

---

19. This information is contained in table 2 of Mattoo (1998). This paper contains a thorough and interesting discussion on the role of the MFN provision in the services area.

able for some agreements to achieve deeper levels of local integration than that at the broader regional level. For example, the San José Ministerial Declaration (March 1998) reads: "The FTAA can co-exist with bilateral and sub-regional agreements, to the extent that the rights and obligations under these agreements are not covered by or go beyond the rights and obligations of the FTAA (paragraph f. of the section on General Principles)." Thus the San José Declaration could be interpreted as allowing special preferences between smaller groups of countries in the hemisphere (which go beyond the obligations or liberalization of a future FTAA agreement) to be maintained alongside a regional trade agreement. If the declaration is read in this manner, then several questions arise:

—How would it be possible for a broader FTAA agreement on services containing a conditional MFN clause to be compatible with GATS Article V, which requires that an economic integration agreement achieve the "absence or elimination of substantially all discrimination, in the sense of Article XVII (National Treatment), between or among the parties"?

—How would such an agreement fulfill the mandate given by ministers and endorsed by heads of state to create a free trade agreement for the hemisphere?

—If varying degrees of MFN treatment were envisaged within an FTAA agreement, how could this be brought about?

—Can the MFN principle be thought of as open to gradual implementation within the region so that at some point all countries would reach the same level of liberalization and MFN treatment?

—Should exceptions to the MFN principle, if unconditional, be thought of as permanent exemptions or temporary, time-bound reservations, subject to future liberalization?

In addition, the question arises whether differential or conditional MFN treatment could be given to countries *outside* the Western Hemisphere. This might be desirable for members of different subregional agreements that are involved in simultaneous integration processes, both within and outside the FTAA, and who might wish to enter into a mutual economic integration agreement.

Conclusions

At this point in time, it is difficult to reach any definitive conclusions about either the interpretation or the application of GATS Article V, given the limited discussion that has taken place on this discipline within the WTO and the lack of clarity surrounding its provisions. However, it is certainly possible to conclude that Article V is being observed at present more in the breach than in practice, at least with respect to multilateral notification and examination. The result is a low degree of transparency in the provisions and disciplines of economic integration agreements, which are being negotiated in increasing numbers. The analysis in this chapter makes clear that rather than serving to underpin the basis of economic integration efforts, Article V is at present a weak and ineffective discipline. Its weaknesses may undermine the trading system in the future if it is not strengthened in the GATS 2000 negotiations. Article V is the only formal link in the world economy between multilateral and regional efforts at services liberalization.

References

Feketekuty, Geza. 2000. "Assessing the WTO General Agreement on Trade and Improving the GATS." In Pierre Sauvé and Robert M. Stern, eds., *GATS 2000: New Directions in Services Trade Liberalization*. Brookings.

———.1998. "Setting the Agenda for Services 2000: The Next Round of Negotiations on Trade in Services." Paper presented at "The Future of Services Trade Liberalization—Services 2000," a conference sponsored by the Coalitions of Service Industries. Ditchley Park, England (April).

Mattoo, Aaditya. 1998. "Most-Favoured Nation Treatment and the GATS." Draft paper presented at "Most-Favoured Nation: Past and Present," a World Trade Forum conference. Neuchatel, Switzerland (August).

Organization of American States. 1999. *Provisions on Trade in Services in the Trade and Integration Agreements of the Western Hemisphere*. Washington.

———. 1998. *Sectoral Agreements on Services in the Western Hemisphere*. Washington.

Sauvé, Pierre. 1997. *Preparing for Services 2000*. CSI Occasional Paper 4. Washington: Coalition of Services Industries.

Sauvé, Pierre, and Robert M. Stern, eds. 2000. *GATS 2000: New Directions in Services Trade Liberalization*. Brookings.

Stephenson, Sherry M. 1999. "Regional Agreements on Services within APEC and Disciplines of the Multilateral Trading System." Paper presented at the meeting of the APEC Group on Services. Wellington, New Zealand (February).

CHAPTER FIVE

Dispute Settlement in the Services Area under GATS

HECTOR A. MILLÁN SMITMANS

TWO IMPORTANT ISSUES relating to dispute settlement need to be considered in the context of the GATS negotiations aimed at liberalizing trade in services. One concern is whether the rules and procedures that were originally set up to deal with trade in goods and have been extended to trade in services and trade-related aspects of intellectual property rights are adequate and will be adequate for electronic commerce and the new technological innovations. The second is what consequences the overlapping dispute-settlement rules and procedures concerning services at the multilateral, regional, and subregional levels have and whether a single global architecture for dispute settlement for the services sector would be more effective.

This chapter considers these issues and the decisions that will have to be adopted at the political level in the context of future negotiations over services. The chapter reviews the implementation of the WTO Understanding on Rules and Procedures Governing the Settlement of Disputes (DSU) as it applies to the General Agreement on Trade in Services (GATS).

Dispute Settlement under the WTO Agreement

Pursuant to Article IX:2 of the WTO Agreement, the Ministerial Conference and the General Council have the exclusive authority to adopt interpretations of the agreement and of multilateral trade agreements such as GATS. In the case of GATS they are to exercise this authority on the basis of a recom-

mendation by the Council for Trade in Services. The decision to adopt an interpretation shall be made by a three-fourths majority of the members.

The WTO and GATT 1994, and GATT 1947 previously, contain rules aimed
at ensuring the enforcement of the rights and obligations set out in the respective agreements and to give redress in the case of nullification or impairment of
benefits or impediments to the attainment of the objectives of the agreements,
even when the circumstances do not involve violations of the obligations or
provisions of the agreements.[1] Article 3.2 of the DSU makes the dispute-settlement system of the WTO a central element in providing security and predictability to the multilateral trading system. The members recognize that it pre-
serves their rights and obligations under the covered agreements and clarifies
the existing provisions of those agreements in accordance with customary rules
of interpretation of public international law.

The WTO Agreement entered into force on January 1, 1995, and the DSU
has been in operation for over five years. The DSU is available exclusively to
the 137 WTO members (as of May 2000) for consultations and the resolution
of disputes pursuant to the covered WTO agreements, the WTO Agreement,
and the DSU itself.[2] The General Council of the WTO, which is composed of
the representatives of all the members, discharges the responsibilities of the
Dispute Settlement Body (DSB) provided for in the DSU.[3] If the complaining
party so requests, the DSB shall establish a panel composed of three or five
panelists, whose function is to assist the DSB in discharging its responsibilities
under the DSU and the covered agreements.[4]

During the period 1995–2000, members notified the WTO of some 193 complaints about 151 distinct matters. At this writing in early 2000, there were
some twenty-one active cases before the Dispute Settlement Body; in thirty-
four cases Appellate Body and panel reports had been adopted, and thirty-two
cases were settled or inactive.[5]

---

1. General Agreement on Tariffs and Trade (GATT 1947), of October 30, 1947, Articles XXII
and XXIII; General Agreement on Tariffs and Trade (GATT 1994), of April 15, 1994, Articles
XXII and XXIII; and Marrakesh Agreement Establishing the World Trade Organization (WTO
Agreement) of April 15, 1994, Article II:2 and Annex 2, "Understanding on Rules and Procedures Governing the Settlement of Disputes" (DSU); all in WTO, *The Results of the Uruguay
Round of Multilateral Trade Negotiations—The Legal Texts* (Geneva).
    2. DSU Article 1.1.
    3. WTO Agreement, Article IV:3.
    4. DSU Articles 4.7, 6.1, 8.5, and 11.
    5. WTO Secretariat, "Overview of the State-of-Play of WTO Disputes," May 5, 2000. The
references to the dispute-settlement cases are excerpted from the "Overview."

Article XXIII of GATS gives a member recourse to the DSU if that member believes that any other member has failed to carry out its obligations or specific commitments under GATS. The general obligations and disciplines are set out in Parts I, II, IV, V, and VI of GATS. The specific market-access commitments are subject to the provisions of Part III of GATS and to the terms, limitations, and conditions agreed and specified in the respective schedules. If the DSB considers the circumstances serious enough, it may authorize members to suspend the application to other members of obligations and specific commitments in accordance with Article 22 of the DSU.

This chapter focuses on WTO dispute-settlement cases involving services in which the provisions of GATS have been invoked. The following provisions of GATS have been invoked so far in the WTO for the purpose of dispute settlement: Articles I (Scope and Definition), II (Most-Favored-Nation Treatment), III (Transparency), V (Economic Integration), VI (Domestic Regulation), XVI (Market Access), XVII (National Treatment), XXI (Modification of Schedules), and XXVIII (Definitions). The next section provides a description in chronological order of the cases in which GATS provisions have been invoked. Some have been completed, and others are still under consideration by the DSB (as of May 2000).

The DSU establishes the rules and procedures governing the settlement of disputes, but it is up to the complainant to identify the cause of action. Pursuant to Article 6.2 of the DSU, the complainant must identify the specific measures at issue and provide a brief summary of the legal basis for the complaint. Pursuant to Article 12.7 of the DSU, the report of the panel must set out the findings of fact, the applicability of relevant provisions, and the rationale behind any findings and recommendations. Pursuant to Article 17.6, 17.12, and 17.13 of the DSU, an appeal shall be limited to issues of law covered in the panel report and legal interpretations developed by the panel; the Appellate Body shall address each of the issues raised during the appellate proceeding; and the Appellate Body may uphold, modify, or reverse the legal findings and conclusions of the panel. GATS provisions were not invoked in some WTO cases dealing with issues such as the conformity of laws, regulations, and administrative procedures with the obligations under Article XVI:4 of the WTO Agreement, and with provisions of the multilateral trade agreements (MTAs) concerning export income and specific taxation issues, distribution measures, the procedures applicable to business confidential information, the right to representation by private counsel, the issue of GATT practice, the issue of overlap of agreements, the rules of interpretation, and others. However, the DSB may in the future be asked to consider whether recommendations and findings concerning provisions of other MTAs may also be relevant in services cases.[6]

Overview of Cases

European Communities (EC)—Regime for the Importation, Sale, and Distribution of Bananas, complaint by Ecuador, Guatemala, Honduras, Mexico, and the United States (WT/DS27). The original complainants in this case (all except Ecuador) had requested consultations with the European Communities (EC) on this issue on September 28, 1995 (WT/DS16). After Ecuador's accession to the WTO, the current complainants again requested consultations with the EC, on February 5, 1996. The complainants alleged that the EC's regime for importation, sale, and distribution of bananas was inconsistent with GATT 1994 Articles I, II, III, X, XI, and XIII, as well as with provisions of the Agreement on Import Licensing Procedures, the Agreement on Agriculture, the Agreement on Trade-Related Investment Measures (TRIMs), and GATS. A panel was established at the DSB meeting on May 8, 1996. At the request of the EC under Article 9.2 of the DSU, the panel prepared four separate reports (including a joint report on Guatemala and Honduras) with identical factual aspects and different findings to the extent that the initial written submissions were different.[7] The panel found that the EC's banana import regime and its licensing procedures for the importation of bananas were inconsistent with GATT 1994. The panel further found that the Fourth Lomé Convention waiver of December 9, 1994, waives the inconsistency with GATT 1994 Article XIII, but not inconsistencies arising from the licensing system.[8] The reports of the panel were circulated to members on May 22, 1997. The European Communities, Ecuador, Guatemala, Honduras, Mexico, and the United States appealed certain issues of law and legal interpretations developed by the panel. The Appel-

---

6. United States, Tariff Increases on Products from the European Communities (WT/DS39), complaint by the European Communities. United States, sections 301–310 of the Trade Act of 1974 (WT/DS152), complaint by the European Communities. Belgium, Netherlands, Greece, Ireland, and France, Certain Income Tax Measures Constituting Subsidies (WT/DS127, 128, 129, 130 and 131), complaint by the United States. Korea, Taxes on Alcoholic Beverages (WT/DS 75 and 84), complaint by the European Communities and the United States. Chile, Taxes on Alcoholic Beverages (WT/DS 87 and 110), complaint by the European Communities. United States, Tax Treatment for Foreign Sales Corporation (WT/DS 108), complaint by the European Communities. Australia, Subsidies Provided to Producers and Exporters of Automotive Leather (WT/DS126), complaint by the United States.

7. WT/DS27/R/USA, 7.399.

8. BISD (Basic Instruments and Selected Documents) Supplement no. 40, Vol. 1, p. 26. (BISD is an annual WTO publication.)

late Body upheld most of the panel's findings but reversed the panel's findings that the inconsistency with GATT 1994 Article XIII was waived by the Fourth Lomé Convention waiver, and that certain aspects of the licensing regime violated Article X of GATT 1994 and the Agreement on Import Licensing Procedures. The report of the Appellate Body was circulated to members on September 9, 1997.[9]

At its meeting on September 25, 1997, the Appellate Body report and the panel reports, as modified by the Appellate Body, were adopted by the DSB. On November 17, 1997, the complainants requested that the "reasonable period of time" for implementing the recommendations and rulings of the DSB be determined by binding arbitration, pursuant to Article 21.3(c) of the DSU. The arbitrator found the reasonable period of time for implementation to be fifteen months and one week, specifically the period from September 25, 1997, to January 1, 1999. The report of the arbitrator was circulated to members on January 7, 1998. The period for implementation set by arbitration expired on January 1, 1999. The EC has subsequently revised the contested measures. On August 18, 1998, the complainants requested consultations with the EC (without prejudice to their rights under Article 21.5) for the resolution of the disagreement between them over the WTO-consistency of measures introduced by the EC in purported compliance with the recommendations and rulings of the panel and the Appellate Body. At the DSB meeting on November 25, 1998, the EC announced that it had adopted the second regulation to implement the recommendations of the DSB and that the new system would be fully operational from January 1, 1999. On December 15, 1998, the EC requested the establishment of a panel under Article 21.5 to determine that the implementing measures of the EC must be presumed to conform to WTO rules unless challenged in accordance with DSU procedures.

On December 18, 1998, Ecuador requested the reestablishment of the original panel to examine whether the EC measures to implement the recommendations of the DSB were WTO-consistent. At its meeting on January 12, 1999, the DSB agreed to reconvene the original panel, pursuant to Article 21.5 of the DSU, to examine both Ecuador's and the EC's requests. Jamaica, Nicaragua, Colombia, Costa Rica, Côte d'Ivoire, the Dominican Republic, Dominica, St. Lucia, Mauritius, and St. Vincent indicated their interest in joining as third parties in both requests, while Ecuador and India indicated their third-party interest only in the EC request. On January 14, 1999, the United States, pursuant to Article 22.2 of the DSU, requested authorization from the DSB to suspend concessions to the EC in the amount of U.S.$520 million. At the DSB

9. WT/DS27/AB/R.

meeting on January 29, 1999, the EC, pursuant to Article 22.6 of the DSU, requested arbitration about the level of concessions to be requested by the United States. The DSB referred the issue to the original panel for arbitration. Pursuant to Article 22.6 of the DSU, the request for the suspension of concessions by the United States was deferred by the DSB until the determination, through arbitration, of the appropriate level of concessions to be suspended.

In the panel requested by the EC, pursuant to Article 21.5 of the DSU, the panel found that, because Ecuador had challenged the WTO-consistency of the EC measures taken in implementation of the DSB recommendations, it was unable to agree with the EC that the EC must be presumed to be in compliance with the recommendations of the DSB.[10] Pursuant to Article 21.5 of the DSU, the panel requested by Ecuador found that the implementation measures taken by the EC in compliance with the recommendations of the DSB were not fully compatible with the EC's WTO obligations.[11] In the arbitration, under Article 22.6 of the DSU, necessitated by the EC's challenge to the level of suspension sought by the United States (U.S.$520 million), the arbitrators found that the level of suspension sought by the United States exceeded the level of nullification and impairment suffered as a result of the EC's new banana regime not being fully compatible with the WTO. The arbitrators accordingly determined the level of nullification suffered by the United States to be U.S.$191.4 million.[12] At its meeting on April 19, 1999, the DSB took note of the statements made by the members and, pursuant to the U.S. request under Article 22.7 of the DSU, agreed to grant authorization to suspend the application to the European Communities and its member states of tariff concessions and related obligations under GATT 1994, consistent with the decision of the arbitrators contained in document WT/DS27/ARB.[13]

Trade in Goods Issues

A long list of issues was raised by the complainants and the respondent. The parties reiterated many of these issues as appellants and appellees. A brief description of some of them follows.

A preliminary issue was the right of the United States to bring claims under GATT 1994. The Appellate Body stated that a member had broad discretion in deciding whether to bring a case against another member under the DSU and that the United States was justified in bringing its claims under GATT 1994 in

10. WT/DS27/RW/EEC.
11. WT/DS27/RW/ECU.
12. WT/DS27/ARB, 8.1.
13. WT/DSB/M/59, p. 11.

this case. Because the United States was a producer of bananas, a potential export interest could not be excluded. The internal market of the United States for bananas could be affected by the EC banana regime, in particular by the effects of that regime on world supplies and prices of bananas.[14] The Appellate Body considered that the request for the establishment of the panel was sufficiently specific to comply with the minimum standards established by Article 6.2 DSU. It was sufficient for the complaining parties to list the provisions of the specific agreements alleged to have been violated.[15]

The Appellate Body concluded that the Agreement on Agriculture did not permit the European Communities to act inconsistently with the requirements of Article XIII of GATT 1994.[16] The Appellate Body also addressed in detail the scope of the waiver granted under GATT 1947, which waived the provisions of Article I:1 of the General Agreement until February 29, 2000, to the extent necessary to permit the European Communities to provide preferential treatment for products originating in the African, Caribbean, and Pacific (ACP) States as required by the relevant provision of the Fourth Lomé Convention,[17] without being required to extend the same preferential treatment to like products of any other contracting party.[18] The Appellate Body examined the provisions of the Fourth Lomé Convention insofar as necessary to interpret the Lomé waiver.[19]

The conclusions of the Appellate Body were as follows: the duty-free access afforded by the European Communities to all traditional ACP bananas was required;[20] the duty-free access for the 90,000 tonnes of nontraditional ACP bananas and the margin of tariff preference in the amount of 100 ECUs per tonne granted to all other nontraditional ACP bananas were required;[21] and the allocation of tariff quota shares to the traditional ACP States that supplied bananas to the European Communities before 1991 in the amount of their pre-

---

14. WT/DS27/AB/R, 136 and 138.
15. WT/DS27/AB/R, 141.
16. WT/DS27/AB/R, 158, 162, and 163.
17. In May 2000, the Fiji Convention among the European Communities and the African, Caribbean, and Pacific (ACP) States will replace the Fourth Lomé Convention with a series of regional free-trade agreements and include provisions on aid, development policies, good governance, and other issues. The Fiji Convention will last twenty years (*Financial Times*, February 11, 2000). On February 29, 2000, the European Communities and Tanzania on behalf of the ACP States requested a waiver for concluding negotiations on a new ACP-ECP Partnership Agreement (GC/W/IP7). The request is under consideration in the WTO Council for Trade in Goods.
18. WT/DS27/AB/R, 166.
19. WT/DS27/AB/R, 167, 171.
20. WT/DS27/AB/R, 172.
21. WT/DS27/AB/R, 173.

1991 best-ever export volumes was required.[22] However, the allocation of other tariff quota shares was not required.[23]

The Appellate Body also upheld the findings of the panel that the nondiscrimination provision of GATT 1994, specifically Articles I:1 and XIII, applied to the relevant EC regulations, irrespective of the number of separate regimes for the importation of bananas.[24] The Appellate Body agreed that import-licensing procedures for tariff quotas were within the scope of the Agreement on Import Licensing Procedures.[25] Article 1.3 of the Licensing Agreement and Article X:3(a) of GATT 1994 did not preclude the imposition of different import-licensing systems on like products when imported from different member countries.[26] The requirement to match import licenses with export certificates that provided an advantage to some members not given to other members was inconsistent with Article I:1 of GATT 1994.[27] The EC procedures and requirements for the distribution of licenses for importing bananas among eligible operators within the European Communities were within the scope of Article III:4 of GATT 1994.[28]

GATS Issues

The bananas case is the first WTO case in which members invoked the provisions of GATS. The panel reports (WT/DS27/R/ECU, WT/DS27/GTM, WT/DS27/HND, WT/DS27/R/MEX, WT/DS27/USA), as well as the reports of the Appellate Body (WT/DS27/AB/R) and the arbitrators (WT/DS27/ARB), have reviewed in detail the arguments concerning nullification or impairment of benefits under the provisions of GATS made by the complainants. The panel was able to rule on GATS aspects because the European Communities and their

22. WT/DS27/AB/R, 174.
23. WT/DS27/AB/R, 175, 176, 177.
24. WT/DS27/AB/R, 191.
25. WT/DS27/AB/R, 191.
26. WT/DS27/AB/R, 198, 201, 204. The general interpretative note to Annex 1A of the WTO Agreement provides that in the event of a conflict between a provision of GATT 1994 and a provision of another agreement in Annex 1A, the provision of the other agreement shall prevail to the extent of the conflict.
27. WT/DS27/AB/R, 206–07.
28. WT/DS27/AB/R, 211; WT/DS27/AB/R, 214. Hurricane licenses are granted, on an ad hoc basis, to operators who "include or directly represent" a producer adversely affected by a tropical storm and thus unable to supply the EC market. Hurricane import volumes enter in addition to the 2.553 million tonne tariff quota and are subject to the third-country (non-ACP) in-quota tariffs (ECU 75 per tonne). Hurricane licenses may be used to import bananas from any source (WT/DS27/R/USA, paras. III.15 and II.28). WT/DS27/AB/R, 216.

member states have made commitments on distribution in their GATS schedules (GATS/SC/31 and Suppl.). The main points raised are summarized hereunder.

The Appellate Body noted that the U.S. standing under GATS had not been challenged and that the claims under GATS and GATT 1994 relating to the EC regime were inextricably interwoven in this case.[29] The Appellate Body reversed the conclusions of the panel that all the GATS claims made by Guatemala and Honduras and certain claims under Article XVII of GATS made by Mexico were not included within the scope of the case because all five complaining parties jointly had made claims under GATS and requested the establishment of the panel. The terms of reference of the panel in this case were established in the request for the establishment of the panel.[30]

Articles II and XVII of GATS are the main provisions invoked in this case.

The first issue considered by the panel and the Appellate Body was whether GATS applied to the EC import-licensing procedures. The second was whether GATS overlapped with GATT 1994 or whether the two agreements were mutually exclusive. The Appellate Body upheld the panel's finding that there was no legal basis for an a priori exclusion of measures within the EC banana import-licensing regime from the scope of GATS. On the issue of whether GATS and GATT were mutually exclusive, the Appellate Body agreed with the panel that the EC banana import-licensing procedures were subject to both GATT 1994 and GATS, and that GATT 1994 and GATS may overlap in their application to a particular measure. The specific aspects of the measure examined under each agreement could be different. Under GATT 1994, the focus was on how the measure affects the goods involved. Under GATS, the focus was on how the measure affects the supply of the service or the service suppliers involved.[31]

With respect to the definition of wholesale trade services and the application of that definition, the Appellate Body noted that the European Communities had made a full commitment for wholesale trade services (CPC [Provisional Central Product Classification] 622), with no conditions or qualifications, in its Schedule of Specific Commitments under GATS (GATS/SC/31, April 15, 1994, p. 52). The Appellate Body agreed with the panel that the operators as defined in the relevant regulations of the European Communities were indeed suppliers of wholesale trade services within the definition set out in the headnote to sec-

29. WT/DS27/AB/R, 137.
30. WT/DS27/AB/R, 147.
31. WT/DS27/AB/R, 220, 221, and 222.

tion 6 of the CPC. The CPC characterized the principal services rendered by wholesalers as reselling merchandise.[32]

On the issue of integrated companies, the Appellate Body agreed that even if a company is vertically integrated, and even if it performs other functions related to the production, importation, distribution, and processing of a product, to the extent that it is also engaged in providing wholesale trade services that company is a service supplier within the scope of GATS.[33]

Another critical issue was whether Article II(1) of GATS applied only to de jure, or formal, discrimination or also to de facto discrimination. The Appellate Body disagreed with the panel's interpretation of Article II of GATS in light of the national-treatment obligation of Article III of GATT 1994 because Article II of GATS relates to MFN treatment. The panel should have compared the MFN obligation in Article II of GATS with the MFN and MFN-type obligations in GATT 1994. According to the Appellate Body, the obligation imposed by Article II of GATS was unqualified. The ordinary meaning of this provision did not exclude de facto discrimination. The Appellate Body concluded that "treatment no less favorable" in Article II(1) of GATS should be interpreted to include de facto as well as de jure discrimination.[34]

The Appellate Body declined to rule on arguments challenging the panel's factual conclusions that de facto discrimination had continued to exist after the entry into force of GATS and on the burden of proof concerning which companies were juridical persons of another member, the market shares of companies engaged in wholesale trade services in bananas within the European Communities, and the nationality of the majority of operators. Factual findings are beyond review by the Appellate Body.[35]

With respect to whether the EC licensing procedures were discriminatory under Articles II and XVII of GATS, the Appellate Body noted that there was no provision in GATS comparable to Article II:1 of GATT 1994 and that it had rejected the aims and effects theory with respect to Article III:2 of GATT 1994. The Appellate Body concurred with the panel's conclusion that the allocation to Category B operators of 30 percent of the licenses allowing for the importation of third-country and nontraditional ACP bananas at in-quota tariff rates created less-favorable conditions of competition for like service suppliers of complainants' origin and was therefore inconsistent with the requirements of

32. WT/DS27/AB/R, 225 and 226.
33. WT/DS27/AB/R, 227.
34. WT/DS27/AB/R, 231, 233, and 234.
35. WT/DS27/AB/R, 237 and 239.

Article XVII of GATS. (Most of the suppliers of EC [or ACP] origin were classified in Category B for the vast majority of their past marketing of bananas, and most of the suppliers of complainants' origin were classified in Category A for the vast majority of their past marketing of bananas.)[36] The Appellate Body also concurred with the panel that the allocation to Category B operators of 30 percent of the licenses for importing third-country and nontraditional ACP bananas at in-quota tariff rates was inconsistent with the requirements of Article II of GATS.[37]

The Appellate Body upheld the panel's legal conclusion that the activity function rules providing the allocation to ripeners of a certain proportion of the Category A and B licenses allowing the importation of third-country and nontraditional ACP bananas at in-quota tariff rates created less-favorable conditions of competition for like service suppliers of complainants' origin and were therefore inconsistent with the requirements of Article XVII of GATS. The Appellate Body also accepted the panel's conclusion of fact that the vast majority of operators who include or directly represent EC or ACP producers were service suppliers of EC (or ACP) origin.[38] With regard to hurricane licenses, the Appellate Body did not accept the argument that the aims and effects of a measure were relevant in determining its consistency with Articles II or XVII of GATS.

Concerning the nullification and impairment of benefits, the Appellate Body upheld the panel's finding that the European Communities had not succeeded in rebutting the presumption that its breaches of GATT, GATS, and Licensing Agreement rules had nullified or impaired benefits of the complainants, with the modification that this finding should be limited to the U.S. and EC obligations under GATT 1994. The panel had erred in extending the scope of the presumption of nullification or impairment of benefits in the meaning of Article 3.8 of the DSU to claims made under GATS as well as to claims made by the complaining parties other than the United States. The European Communities' attempted rebuttal applied to only one complainant, the United States, and to only one agreement, GATT 1994.[39]

36. Category A operators are those that have marketed third-country and/or nontraditional ACP bananas; they are allocated 66.5 percent of import licenses allowing the importation of bananas at in-quota rates. Category B operators are those that have marketed EC and/or traditional ACP bananas; they are allocated 30 percent of import licenses. Category C operators are those that started marketing bananas other than EC and/or traditional ACP bananas in 1992 or thereafter ("newcomer" category); they are allocated 3.5 percent of import licenses.

37. WT/DS27/AB/R, 241 and 244.

38. WT/DS27/AB/R, 246 and 248.

39. WT/DS27/AB/R, 250 and 254.

Decision by the Arbitrators

United States. The United States requested the DSB to authorize the suspension of the application to the EC and its member states of tariff concessions and related obligations under GATT 1994 covering trade in the amount of U.S.$520 million. The EC objected to the level of suspension proposed by the United States and requested arbitration on the level of nullification or impairment. The DSB decided to submit the matter to the arbitration of the original panel. The arbitrators determined that the level of nullification or impairment suffered by the United States was U.S.$191.4 million per year. Excerpts of the relevant sections of the decision by the arbitrators concerning GATS are reproduced hereunder.[40]

The United States had alleged that EC Regulations 1637/98 and 2362/98 perpetuate nullification and impairment caused by the previous EC regime, which was found to be inconsistent with the EC's obligations under Articles II and XVII of GATS. More specifically, the United States had alleged (1) that the revised licensing procedures perpetuated the violations of Articles II and XVII of GATS (the most-favored-nation treatment and national-treatment clauses) found by the original panel and the Appellate Body in the *Bananas III* case,[41] and (2) that the enlargement of the license quantity reserved for "newcomers" to 8 percent and the criteria for acquiring "newcomer" status under the revised licensing procedures were inconsistent with Article XVII of GATS.[42]

The arbitrators stated that the consideration of alleged inconsistencies under GATS's national treatment and MFN clauses usually presupposes a two-step examination. For purposes of Article XVII, it was necessary to examine whether the domestic and foreign services or service suppliers at issue were "like" and whether services or service suppliers of the complainant's origin were treated less favorably than those of domestic origin. For purposes of Article II, it was necessary to examine whether services or service suppliers originating in different foreign countries were "like" and whether services or service suppliers of the complainant's origin were subject to less-favorable treatment than those of other members' origin.[43]

The arbitrators recalled the findings with respect to particular aspects of the license allocation procedures that applied under the previous regime to third-

---

40. WT/DS27/ARB.

41. WT/DS27/R/ECU, WT/DS27/R/GTM, WT/DS27/R/HND, WT/DS27/R/MEX, WT/DS/27/R/USA. The earlier *Bananas I* and *II* disputes preceded WTO and were initiated by different GATT 1947 contracting parties in 1992 and 1993.

42. WT/DS27/ARB, 5.34.

43. WT/DS27/ARB, 5.37.

country and nontraditional ACP imports within the tariff quota, to the extent they were relevant here:

—"that the allocation to Category B operators of 30 percent of the licenses allowing the importation of third-country and nontraditional ACP bananas at in-quota tariff rates created less-favorable conditions of competition for like service suppliers of complainants' origin and was therefore inconsistent with the requirements of Articles II and XVII of GATS."[44]

—"that the allocation to ripeners of 28 percent of Category A and B licenses allowing the importation of third-country and nontraditional ACP bananas at in-quota tariff rates created less-favorable conditions of competition for like service suppliers of complainants' origin and was therefore inconsistent with the requirements of Article XVII of GATS."[45]

—"that the allocation of hurricane licenses exclusively to operators who included or directly represented EC (or ACP) producers created less-favorable conditions of competition for like service suppliers of complainants' origin and was therefore inconsistent with the requirements of Article XVII (or II) of GATS."[46]

These findings had been upheld by the Appellate Body.[47]

The arbitrators also examined the structure of the revised regime because the Appellate Body had noted in the past, in *Japan—Alcoholic Beverages*,[48] that a measure's "protective application can most often be discerned from the design, the architecture, and the revealing structure of a measure." Although the dispute on *Japan—Alcoholic Beverages* concerned claims under GATT 1994, they believed that the Appellate Body's description of de facto discrimination under GATT 1994 might also give some guidance in analyzing whether there is de facto discrimination under GATS.[49]

In light of all their considerations, the arbitrators were of the view that the United States had shown that the revised EU license allocation system for bananas prolonged, at least in part, less-favorable treatment in the meanings of Articles II and XVII GATS for wholesale service suppliers of U.S. origin. The United States had also shown that its service suppliers did not have access to import licenses on terms equal to those enjoyed by service suppliers of EC/ACP origin under the revised regime and carried on from the previous re-

44. Panel reports on *Bananas III*, paras. 7.341 and 7.353.

45. Panel reports on *Bananas III*, para. 7.368.

46. Panel reports on *Bananas III*, para. 7.393 (and para. 7.397).

47. WT/DS27/ARB, 5.39.

48. Appellate Body report on *Japan—Taxes on Alcoholic Beverages*, WT/DS8/AB/R, WT/DS10/AB/R, WT/11/AB/R, adopted on November 1, 1996, p. 31.

49. WT/DS27/ARB 5.71.

gime through measures constituting effective discriminatory barriers to distribution.[50]

Therefore, the arbitrators were of the view that the revised license allocation
system reflecting past performance and license usage during the 1994–1996
period displayed de facto discriminatory structure. It was also their view that
under the revised regime U.S. wholesale service suppliers were accorded less-
favorable treatment than EC/ACP suppliers of those services, in violation of
Articles II and XVII of GATS.[51]

The arbitrators stated that although any potential service supplier originating in a third country was not de jure precluded from acquiring "newcomer"
status, in their view the criteria for demonstrating the requisite expertise to
qualify as an importer of bananas as a "newcomer" created in their overall
impact less-favorable conditions of competition for service suppliers of the
United States or other members than for like service suppliers of EC origin. In
this respect, the arbitrators recalled the Appellate Body's statement in *Japan—
Alcoholic Beverages*[52] that a measure's "protective application can most often
be discerned from the design, the architecture, and the revealing structure of a
measure."[53]

In light of these considerations, the arbitrators concluded that the criteria for
acquiring "newcomer" status under the revised licensing procedures accorded
to U.S. service suppliers de facto less-favorable conditions of competition in
the meaning of Article XVII than to like EC service suppliers.[54]

With respect to GATS, the arbitrators stated that under the revised regime
U.S. suppliers of wholesale services were accorded de facto less-favorable treatment in the allocation of licenses for purposes of distribution than EC/ACP
suppliers of those services, in violation of Articles II and XVII of GATS; in
addition, they said that the criteria for acquiring "newcomer" status under the
revised licensing procedures accorded to U.S. service suppliers de facto less-
favorable conditions of competition than to like EC service suppliers, in violation of Article XVII of GATS.[55]

Thus, it was the view of the arbitrators that U.S. benefits under the revised
EC regime were nullified or impaired.[56]

50. WT/DS27/ARB, 5.79.
51. WT/DS27/ARB, 5.80.
52. Appellate Body report on *Japan—Taxes on Alcoholic Beverages*, WT/DS8/AB/R, WT/
DS10/AB/R, WT/DS11/AB/R, adopted on November 1, 1996, p. 31.
53. WT/DS27/ARB, 5.94.
54. WT/DS27/ARB, 5.95.
55. WT/DS27/ARB, 5.97.
56. WT/DS27/ARB, 5.98.

Services Issues in the Banana Dispute

The European Communities had raised one preliminary issue regarding the scope of service transactions that may be included in the determination of nullification or impairment in light of the reach of the specific commitments bound in the EC's GATS schedule. It had contended that the revision of the UN Central Product Classification (CPC) system affected the interpretation of the scope of its market-access and national-treatment commitments on "wholesale trade services" that the EC had bound in its GATS schedule under the distribution sector. The EC submitted that the Provisional CPC had been replaced in the meantime by the Central Product Classification —Version 1.0 (Revised CPC), and that the Revised CPC sought to create a system of service categories that were both exhaustive and mutually exclusive. Therefore, in the EC's view, any services related to wholesale trade transactions that also fall into another CPC category should be assessed on that basis—that is, they should not be considered to be covered by the EC's commitments on wholesale trade services.[57] The European Communities had added that the specific commitments bound in its GATS schedule were still valid.[58]

The United States had contended that the scope of the EC's specific commitments under GATS, which were bound in the EC GATS schedule, could not be affected by the subsequent modification of the Central Product Classification list. Consequently, it was still the Provisional CPC that mattered for purposes of interpreting the scope of the EC's commitments on wholesale trade services.[59]

The arbitrators noted that the specific commitments bound by the European Communities in its GATS schedule with respect to the service sectors or subsectors at issue in the original case were categorized according to the Services Sectoral Classification List, which refers to the more detailed Provisional CPC.[60] They also recalled that in *Bananas III* the parties disagreed whether the panel's terms of reference comprised the narrower subsector of "wholesale trade services" or encompassed the broader sector of "distributive trade services" as described in a headnote to section 6 of the provisional CPC. The relevant defi-

---

57. The European Communities noted that, according to the "Correspondence Tables between the CPC Version 1.0 and Provisional CPC," item 62221, "Wholesale trade services of fruit and vegetables," corresponds in the CPC Version 1.0 to 61121, "Wholesale trade services, except on a fee and contract basis, fruit and vegetables."

58. WT/DS27/ARB, 6.20.

59. WT/DS27/ARB, 6.21.

60. Article XXVIII (e) of GATS: "'sector' of a service means, (i) with reference to a specific commitment, one or more, or all, subsectors of that service, as specified in a Member's Schedule, (ii) otherwise, the whole of that service sector, including all of its subsectors."

nition of the Provisional CPC of "wholesale trade services" reads: "Specialized wholesale services of fresh, dried, frozen, or canned fruits and vegetables (Goods classified in CPC 012,013,213, 215)."

"Distributive trade services" are described as follows:

> Distributive trade services consist in selling merchandise to retailers, to industrial, commercial, institutional, or other professional business users, or to other wholesalers, or acting as agent or broker (*wholesaling services*) or selling merchandise for personal or household consumption including services incidental to the sale of the goods (*retailing services*). The principal services rendered by wholesalers and retailers may be characterized as reselling merchandise, accompanied by a variety of related, subordinated services, such as: maintaining inventories of goods, physically assembling, sorting, and grading goods in large lots; breaking bulk and redistribution in smaller lots; delivery services; refrigeration services; sales promotion services rendered by wholesalers.[61]

The arbitrators recalled that with respect to both wholesale and distributive trade services, the EC had included bound specific commitments on liberalization of market access and national treatment in its GATS schedule without specific conditions or limitations, and without scheduling any MFN exemptions. The original panel had limited its findings to the narrower subsector of "wholesale trade services."[62]

It was not entirely clear to the arbitrators how, in the EC's view, the new categorization of service sectors according to the Revised CPC should affect the classification of service sectors on the basis of which the European Communities had bound its specific commitments on market access and national treatment in its GATS schedule. Therefore, it was not clear how the principle of the mutually exclusive categorization of service sectors could affect the reach of the EC's "wholesale trade services" commitments to those service transactions that did not fall into any other category of the Revised CPC. In any event, the arbitrators did not see how the revision of the CPC could retroactively change the specific commitments listed and bound in the EC GATS schedule. Indeed, at the hearing, the EC had stated that such a change in the EC's specific commitments bound in its GATS schedule could only be made consistently with the requirements of Article XXI of GATS on the "Modification of Schedules."[63]

61. WT/DS27/ARB, 6.22.
62. WT/DS27/ARB, 6.23.
63. WT/DS27/ARB, 6.24.

In the view of the arbitrators, for purposes of the calculation of nullification or impairment under GATS, in light of the EC's commitments on "wholesale trade services," what mattered was that, according to the UN CPC descriptions quoted above, the *principal* services rendered by *wholesalers* relate to reselling merchandise, accompanied by a variety of related, *subordinated* services, such as maintaining inventories of goods; physically assembling, sorting, and grading goods in large lots; breaking bulk and redistribution in smaller lots; delivery services; refrigeration services; and sales promotion services. They considered that this rather broad variety of *principal* and *subordinated* services should constitute the benchmark against which the United States could possibly claim nullification or impairment for losses in its actual or potential trade with the European Communities.[64]

The arbitrators also emphasized that, according to Article XXVIII (b) of GATS, the "supply of a service" (such as wholesaling) includes "the production, distribution, marketing, sale, and delivery of a service." They also recalled that, pursuant to Article XXVIII (d, f, g, l, m, n) of GATS, the origin of a service supplier is defined on the basis of its ownership and control. Therefore, for the calculation of nullification or impairment by reference to losses of actual or potential service supply, it did not matter whether the lost services related to trade in bananas from the United States or from third countries to the EC, or to bananas wholesaled within the EC, provided that the suppliers of wholesale services harmed were commercially present in the EC and were U.S.-owned or U.S.-controlled. These considerations were subject to the conclusion above that WTO members that are the countries of origin of bananas have the right to claim nullification or impairment for actual or potential losses in the supply of service transactions that add value to bananas up to the f.o.b. stage, and that such claims cannot be made by the United States under Article 22.6 of the DSU.[65]

The arbitrator's report and the reports of the panels were issued to the parties on April 6, 1999, and circulated to members on April 9 and 12, 1999, respectively. On April 9, 1999, the United States, pursuant to Article 22.7 of the DSU, requested that the DSB authorize suspension of concessions to the EC equivalent to the level of nullification and impairment—that is, U.S.$191.4 million. On April 19, 1999, the DSB authorized the United States to suspend concessions to the EC as requested.

Ecuador. The report of the panel requested by Ecuador, under Article 21.5 of the DSU, was adopted by the DSB on May 6, 1999. On November 8, 1999,

---

64. WT/DS27/ARB, 6.25.
65. WT/DS27/ARB, 6.26.

Ecuador requested authorization from the DSB to suspend the application to the EC of concessions or other related obligations, pursuant to Article 22.2 of the DSU, in the amount of U.S. $450 million.[66] Considering that the economic cost of withdrawal of concessions in the goods sector alone would have a greater impact on Ecuador than on the EC, that the nullification or impairment of benefits amounts to over 50 percent of all exports of goods by the EC to Ecuador, and that these goods are essential for the Ecuadoran economy, exercising its rights under Article 22 of the DSU, Ecuador requested authorization to suspend concessions and other obligations under the GATS and TRIPS (Trade-Related Intellectual Property Rights) Agreements. Ecuador proposed to suspend concessions or obligations stemming from trade-related intellectual property rights in the following categories set out in Part II of the TRIPS Agreement: Section 1: Copyright and related rights; Article 14: Protection of performers, producers of phonograms (sound recordings), and broadcasting organizations; Section 3: Geographical indications; and Section 4: Industrial designs. Ecuador also proposes to suspend concessions and obligations in the following subsector in its schedule of specific commitments under GATS: 4. Distribution services, B. Wholesale trade services (CPC 622). In addition, Ecuador reserved the right to suspend tariff concessions or other tariff obligations granted in the framework of GATT 1994 in the event that these may be applied in a practicable and effective manner.

The suspension of concessions or other obligations would apply to the following EC member states: Austria, Belgium, Finland, France, Germany, Greece, Ireland, Italy, Luxembourg, Portugal, Spain, Sweden, and the United Kingdom.[67] At the DSB meeting on November 19, 1999, the EC, pursuant to Article 22.6 of the DSU, requested arbitration on the level of suspension of concessions requested by Ecuador.[68] The DSB referred the issue of the level of suspension to the original panel for arbitration. Pursuant to Article 22.6 of the DSU, the request for the suspension of concessions by Ecuador was deferred by the DSB until the determination, through arbitration, of the appropriate level for the suspension of concessions.[69] This case was decided by the arbitrators on March 24, 2000 (WT/DS27/ARB/ECU). This is the first time that a member has requested authorization to cross-retaliate under the DSU and where retaliation would include a specific commitment under GATS as well as certain sections of the TRIPS Agreement.

---

66. WT/DS27/52.
67. WT/DS27/52.
68. WT/DS27/53.
69. WT/DSB/M/71, p. 13.

The arbitrators noted that Ecuador had submitted statistics that displayed the inequality between Ecuador and the European Communities in support of its argument that circumstances were serious enough to justify suspension across agreements: Ecuador's population is 12 million, while the EC's population is 375 million. Ecuador's share of world merchandise trade is less than 0.1 percent, whereas the EC's world merchandise trade share is in the area of 20 percent. The EC's share of world trade in services is 25 percent; no data are available for Ecuador because its share is so small. The GDP at market prices in 1998 was U.S.$20 billion for Ecuador and U.S.$7,996 billion for the fifteen EC member states. In 1998 the EC's GDP per capita was U.S.$22,500, whereas Ecuador's per capita income was U.S.$1,600. Following the evaluation of the various counterfactual regimes, the arbitrators chose to use the same counterfactual as in the U.S./EC *Bananas III* to ensure that there was consistency and in particular no double counting with respect to the nullification and impairment borne by the United States. The arbitrators assumed that the volume of Ecuador's banana exports to the EC would increase (at the expense of other suppliers) to the level of its best-ever exports during the past decade (745,058 tonnes in 1992), that the share of those bananas distributed in the EC by Ecuadoran service suppliers would rise to 60 percent, and that the proportion of those distributed bananas for which Ecuadoran service suppliers are given import licenses would rise to 92 percent (assuming that the remaining 8 percent of the available import licenses are those reserved for newcomers, consistent with the assumption used in the U.S./EC *Bananas III* arbitration). The arbitrators determined that the level of Ecuador's nullification and impairment was U.S.$201.6 million per year. The arbitrators suggested that Ecuador submit another request to the DSB for authorization of suspensions of concessions or other obligations consistent with the decision of the arbitrators of a level not exceeding U.S.$201.6 million per year.

With regard to GATT, the arbitrators concluded that, in this case, it would be practicable and effective for Ecuador to suspend concessions or other obligations under GATT for the import of consumer goods destined for final consumption by end-users in Ecuador from the European Communities amounting at least to U.S.$60.8 million (WT/DS27/ARB/ECU, 99,125,166,169,170, 173 (a),(b)).

With regard to GATS, the arbitrators considered the EC's submission that in 1998 trade in services between the European Communities and Ecuador was estimated to be equivalent to U.S.$197.54 million. However, the parties had not provided information on which proportion of this trade in services was covered by Ecuador's commitments under GATS. Therefore they could not ascertain to what extent such trade concerned modes of supply that Ecuador had bound in service sectors covered in its GATS schedule. Accordingly, these statistics did not undermine the analysis of the effectiveness and practicability of suspending Ecuador's commitments on services with respect to different modes of supply. Therefore, the arbitrators concluded that Ecuador had followed the principles and procedures of Article 22.3 DSU in considering that it was not practicable or effective for it in this case to suspend commitments or other obligations under GATS with respect to principal sectors other than "distribution services." The arbitrators concluded that Ecuador could request and obtain authorization by the DSB to suspend commitments under GATS with respect to "wholesale trade services" (CPC 622) in the principal sector of distribution services (WT/DS27/ARB/ECU, 119,120, 173 (c)).

With regard to TRIPS, the arbitrators concluded that to the extent that suspension requested under GATT and GATS was insufficient to reach the level of nullification and impairment indicated, Ecuador could request and obtain authorization by the DSB to suspend its obligations under the TRIPS Agreement with respect to the following sectors of that agreement: Section 1: Copyright and related rights, Article 14 on "Protection of performers, producers of phonograms (sound recordings) and broadcasting organisations"; Section 3: Geographical indications; and Section 4: Industrial designs (WT/DS27/ARB/ECU, 139–165, 173 (d)). An authorization by the DSB to suspend the treatment provided for in the TRIPS provisions would concern the nationals of the thirteen EC member states listed in Ecuador's request for suspension. (Of the fifteen EC member states, Denmark and the Netherlands were excluded) (WT/DS27/ARB/ECU,141).

The arbitrators' decision emphasized that the suspension of concessions or other obligations was in principle a temporary action, pending the removal of the WTO-inconsistent measure at issue, a solution remedying the nullification or impairment of benefits, or a mutually satisfactory solution. It was obviously impossible to suspend concessions or other obligations for a particular amount of nullification or impairment under one sector or agreement and simultaneously for that same amount under another sector or a different agreement. However, once a certain level of nullification or impairment has been determined by the arbitrators, suspension may be practicable and effective only for part of that amount. In such a situation, suspension for the residual amount of nullification or impairment may be practicable or effective in another sector under the same agreement or possible only under another agreement, as was the case in this dispute. In the eventuality that Ecuador found itself in a situation where it was not realistic or possible for it to implement the suspension authorized by the DSB for the full amount of the level of nullification and impairment in all of the sectors and/or under all agreements mentioned above combined, the arbitrators expressed their trust that the parties to the dispute would find a mutually satis-factory solution (WT/DS27/ARB/ECU, 165, 176, 177).

The interpretation developed by the arbitrators and its application in this case strengthen significantly the capacity of the members with small econo-mies to seek the effective enforcement of panel conclusions and recommenda-tions through the cross-retaliation mechanism. This decision without question reinforces the credibility of the WTO dispute settlement system.

In pursuance of Article 22 of the DSU, Ecuador and the other parties to the case will now have to decide when and how to pursue this matter further.

On May 5, 2000, Ecuador requested authorization by the DSB to suspend with regard to the European Communities and its member states (with the ex-clusion of Denmark and the Netherlands) the application of tariff concessions and related obligations stemming from GATT 1994, GATS and the annexes thereto, and the TRIPS Agreement, for U.S.$201.6 million, the amount deter-mined in the decision of the arbitrators of March 24, 2000, as being equivalent within the meaning of Article 22.4 of the DSU to the level of nullification and impairment suffered by Ecuador as a result of the WTO-inconsistent aspects of the EC import regime for bananas. Ecuador requested authorization by the DSB to suspend concessions or other obligations under GATT 1994 concerning the categories of goods in respect of which, in the view of the arbitrators, the sus-pension of concessions was effective and practicable. Ecuador's request under GATT 1994 applies to the nondurable consumer products and durable con-sumer products included in the list attached to document WT/DS27/54 whose imports from the European Communities into Ecuador during 1999 were worth U.S. $62.1 million. In accordance with Article 22.3(a) of the DSU, Ecuador requested authorization by the DSB to suspend commitments under GATS with respect to wholesale trade services (CPC 622) in the principal sector of distri-bution services. In view of the fact that the requested suspension of conces-sions under GATT 1994 and GATS was insufficient to reach the level of nul-lification and impairment of U.S. $201.6 million indicated by the arbitrators, Ecuador requested authorization by the DSB, pursuant to Article 22.3(c), to suspend its obligations with regard to the EC under the TRIPS Agreement with respect to the following sectors: Section 1: Copyright and related rights, Article 14: "Protection of performers, products of phonograms (sound recordings) and broadcasting organizations"; Section 3: Geographical indications; and Section 4: Industrial designs (WT/DS27, p. 2). Article 22.7 of the DSU stipulates that the DSB shall, upon request, grant authorization to suspend concessions or other obligations where the request is consistent with the decision of the arbi-trators. At its meeting on May 18, 2000, the DSB considered Ecuador's request (WT/AIR/1298) and authorized Ecuador to suspend to the European Communities and its member states as requested, concessions, commitments, and related obligations under GATT 1993, GATS, and the TRIPS Agreement. Ecuador has stated that instead of these measures it would rather negotiate compensation from the EC for the amount of the trade losses determined by the arbitrators.

The May 5, 2000, status report on the implementation of the recommendations and rulings in the dispute regarding *European Communities—Regime for the Importation of Bananas* states that no agreed conclusions have been reached yet (WT/DSU27/51/Add.8) and reports that no new events that would substantially modify the situation have occurred since the report was presented in April. The EC has developed a proposal for the reform of the banana regime. The proposal envisages a two-stage process comprising a tariff rate quota system for several years that would be replaced by a tariff-only system no later than January 1, 2006. The proposal includes a possible license distribution system for the tariff rate quota regime. The EC has stated that if no feasible administrative system of license distribution in a tariff quota regime can be found, the EU would envisage negotiations under Article XXVIII of GATT 1994 to replace the current system with a tariff-only regime (WT/DS27/51). Pursuant to Articles 22.8 and 21.6 of the DSU, this matter is under continuous surveillance by the DSB.

The DSB has also considered the following case related to the bananas dispute.

European Communities (EC)—Regime for the Importation, Sale, and Distribution of Bananas, request for consultations by Guatemala, Honduras, Mexico, Panama, and the United States (WT/DS158). This request, dated January 20, 1999, was in respect of the implementation of the recommendations of the DSB in *European Communities—Regime for the Importation, Sale, and Distribution of Bananas*. The complaining parties noted that the fifteen-month period of time for the EC to implement the DSB's recommendations and rulings had ended on January 1, 1999. The complaining parties contended that the EC had modified its regime in a manner that would not permit the dispute to conclude at that time with a solution acceptable to their governments, and as a result, jointly and severally requested consultations with the EC concerning the EC banana regime established by EC Regulation 404/93, as amended and implemented by Council Regulation 1637/98 of July 20, 1998, and EC Commission Regulation 2362/98 of October 28, 1998. The complaining parties contended that their objective was to clarify and discuss in detail with the EC the various aspects of the EC's modified banana regime, including their effect on the market, the complainants' concerns about the regime's WTO-inconsistency, and ways that the EC might modify its regime in order to produce a satisfactory settlement of this dispute. The consultations are pending.

United States—The Cuban Liberty and Democratic Solidarity Act, complaint by the European Communities (WT/DS38). On May 3, 1996, the European Communities requested consultations with the United States concerning the Cuban Liberty and Democratic Solidarity (LIBERTAD) Act of 1996 and other legislation enacted by the U.S. Congress regarding trade sanctions against Cuba. The EC claimed that U.S. trade restrictions on goods of Cuban origin, as well as the possible refusal of visas and the exclusion of non-U.S. nationals from U.S. territory, were inconsistent with U.S. obligations under the WTO Agreement. Violations of GATT 1994 Articles I, III, V, XI, and XIII, GATS Articles I, II, III, VI, XI, XVI, and XVII, and the GATS Annex on Movement of Natural Persons Supplying Services were alleged. The EC also alleged that even if these measures by the United States were not in violation of specific provisions of GATT or GATS, they nevertheless nullified or impaired its expected benefits under GATT 1994 and GATS and impeded the attainment of the objectives of GATT 1994. The EC requested the establishment of a panel on October 3, 1996. The DSB established a panel at its meeting on November 20, 1996. At the request of the EC, dated April 21, 1997, the panel suspended its work. The panel's authority lapsed on April 22, 1998, pursuant to Article 12.12 of the DSU.

Japan—Measures Affecting Distribution Services, complaint by the United States (WT/DS45). This request, dated June 13, 1996, concerns Japan's measures affecting distribution services (not limited to the photographic film and paper sector) through the operation of the Large-Scale Retail Store Law and other laws, which regulate the floor space, business hours, and holidays of supermarkets and department stores. Violations of GATS Articles III (Transparency), VI (Domestic Regulation), XVI (Market Access), and XVII (National Treatment) were alleged. The United States also alleged that these measures nullified or impaired benefits accruing to the United States (a nonviolation claim). The United States requested further consultations with Japan on September 20, 1996, expanding the factual and legal basis of its claim. The consultations are pending.

Belgium—Measures Affecting Commercial Telephone Directory Services, complaint by the United States (WT/DS80). This request, dated May 2, 1997, was in respect of certain measures of the Kingdom of Belgium governing the provision of commercial telephone directory services. These measures included the imposition of conditions for obtaining a license to publish commercial directories and the regulation of the acts, policies, and practices of BELGACOM

N.V. with respect to telephone directory services. The United States alleged violations of Articles II, VI, VIII, and XVII of GATS, as well as nullification and impairment of benefits accruing to it under the specific GATS commitments made by the EC on behalf of Belgium. The consultations are pending.

Canada—Measures Affecting Film Distribution Services, complaint by the European Communities (WT/DS117). This request, dated January 20, 1998, was in respect of Canada's alleged measures affecting film distribution services, including the 1987 policy decision on film distribution and its application to European companies. The EC contended that these measures violated Articles II and III of GATS. The consultations are pending.

Canada—Certain Measures Affecting the Automotive Industry, complaint by Japan (WT/DS139). This request, dated July 3, 1998, was in respect of measures being taken by Canada in the automotive industry. Japan alleged that under Canadian legislation implementing the Agreement Concerning Automotive Products (Auto Pact) between the United States and Canada and related measures, only a limited number of motor vehicle manufacturers were eligible to import vehicles into Canada duty-free and to distribute the motor vehicles in Canada at the wholesale and retail distribution levels. Japan further alleged that this duty-free treatment was contingent on two requirements: a Canadian value-added (CVA) content requirement that applied to both goods and services, and a manufacturing and sales requirement. Japan alleged that these measures were inconsistent with Articles I:1, III:4, and XXIV of GATT 1994; Article 2 of the TRIMs Agreement; Article 3 of the Agreement on Subsidies and Countervailing Measures (SCM Agreement); and Articles I, II, VI, and XVII of GATS. Japan asserted that the measures also affected the distribution services of motor vehicles by allowing service suppliers of certain members to import motor vehicles duty-free and thus constituted "measures affecting trade in services" within the meaning of Article I of GATS. In the presence of the above advantage, the measures did not accord immediately and unconditionally "no less favorable treatment" to like service suppliers of other members, and thus were inconsistent with Article II of GATS. In addition, the measures entitled Canadian service suppliers, as manufacturers, to import motor vehicles duty-free, and did not accord no less favorable treatment to like service suppliers of other members, thus making them inconsistent with Article XVII of GATS. Under the measures, different levels of requirements were applicable to individual manufacturers for the two requirements referred to in "Measures at Issue," resulting in partial administration of those requirements. This was inconsistent with Article VI of GATS, which sets out that "each Member shall ensure that all measures of general application affecting trade in services are administered in a reasonable, objective, and impartial manner." On November 12, 1998, Japan requested the establishment of a panel. At its meeting on February 1, 1999, the DSB established a panel. Pursuant to Article 9.1 of the DSU, the DSB agreed that the panel would also examine the complaint by the EC in WT/DS142. India, Korea, and the United States reserved their third-party rights.

The panel concluded that Canada acted inconsistently with Article I:1 of GATT 1994 by according the advantage of an import-duty exemption to motor vehicles originating in certain countries, pursuant to the Motor Vehicles Tariff Order 1998 (MVTO 1998) and the Special Remission Orders (SROs), which advantage was not accorded immediately and unconditionally to like products originating in the territories of all other WTO members. The inconsistency of these measures with Article I:1 of GATT 1994 cannot be justified under Article XXIV of GATT 1994. Canada acted inconsistently with Article III:4 of the GATT 1994 by according less-favorable treatment to imported parts, materials, and nonpermanent equipment than to like domestic products with respect to their internal sale or use, as a result of application of the Canadian value-added (CVA) requirements as one of the conditions determining eligibility for the import-duty exemption on motor vehicles under the MVTO 1998 and the SROs and as a result of conditions concerning CVA requirements contained in certain Letters of Undertaking. In light of this finding, the panel did not find it necessary to make a finding on whether these conditions were inconsistent with Article 2.1 of the Agreement on Trade-Related Investment Measures (WT/DS139/R and WT/DS142/R, 10.90, 10.91, 10.131).

The European Communities had failed to demonstrate that Canada acted inconsistently with Article III:4 of GATT 1994 by applying ratio requirements under the MVTO 1998 and the SROs as one of the conditions determining eligibility for the import-duty exemption on motor vehicles.

Canada acted inconsistently with its obligations under Article 3.1(a) of the Agreement on Subsidies and Countervailing Measures (SCM Agreement) by granting a subsidy that is contingent in law upon export performance, as a result of the application of the ratio requirements as one of the conditions determining eligibility for the import-duty exemption on motor vehicles under the MVTO 1998 and the SROs.

The European Communities and Japan failed to demonstrate that Canada acted inconsistently with its obligations under Article 3.1(b) of the SCM Agreements by granting a subsidy that is contingent upon the use of domestic over imported goods, as a result of the application of the CVA requirements as one of the conditions determining eligibility for the import-duty exemption on motor vehicles under the MVTO 1998 and the SROs.

From the GATS standpoint this is a very complex and wide-ranging report that considered questions and claims relating, among other issues, to the applicability of GATS, the interface of GATT and GATS, the scope of Articles II, V, XVII, and XXVIII, the scope of measures affecting trade in services within the meaning of Article I of GATS, de facto discrimination, the origin of whole-sale trade service suppliers, ownership and control, vertical integration, and the commitments in Canada's GATS schedule.

The panel concluded that Canada acted inconsistently with Article II of GATS by failing to accord immediately and unconditionally to services and service suppliers of any other member treatment no less favorable than that it accords to like services and service suppliers of any other country, with respect to the granting of the import-duty exemption to a limited number of manufacturers/wholesalers of motor vehicles pursuant to the MVTO 1998 and the SROs. The inconsistency of these measures with Article II of GATS could not be justified under Article V of GATS. The panelists noted that Article V of GATS provides legal coverage for measures taken pursuant to economic integration agreements, which would otherwise be inconsistent with the MFN obligation in Article II. In their view, the extension of more favorable treatment to only a few service suppliers of parties to an economic integration agreement on a selective basis, even in situations where the maintenance of such measures may explicitly be provided for in the agreement itself, was not within the object and purpose of Article V (WT/DS139/R and WT/DS142/R, 20.271).

The panel stated that Japan had failed to demonstrate that the import-duty exemption granted pursuant to the MVTO 1998 and the SROs constituted treat-ment less favorable accorded to Japanese suppliers of wholesale trade services of motor vehicles than that accorded to like Canadian service suppliers, within the meaning of Article XVII of GATS.

The panel concluded also that Canada acted inconsistently with Article XVII of GATS by according treatment less favorable to services and service suppli-ers of other members, supplied through modes 1 and 2, than it accords to its own like services and service suppliers, as a result of the application of the CVA requirements as one of the conditions determining eligibility for the im-port-duty exemption on motor vehicles under the MVTO 1998 and the SROs.

Under Article 3.8 of the DSU, in cases where there is infringement of the obligations assumed under a covered agreement, the action is considered prima facie to constitute a case of nullification or impairment of benefits under that agreement. Accordingly, the panel concluded that to the extent that Canada had acted inconsistently with the provisions of the covered agreements, it had nul-lified or impaired benefits accruing to the complainants under those agreements. With respect to the conclusions regarding Canada's obligations under Articles I:1 and III:4 of GATT 1994, and Articles II and XVII of GATS, the panel recom-mended that the Dispute Settlement Body request that Canada bring its measures into conformity with its obligations under the WTO Agreement. The panel also recommended that the Dispute Settlement Body request that Canada withdraw the export subsidy within ninety days (WT/DS139 and WT/DS142, 11.1– 11.7).

The report of the panel was circulated to members on February 11, 2000. On March 2, 2000, Canada notified its intention to appeal certain issues of law and legal interpretations developed by the panel.

Canada submitted inter alia that the panel had erred in its interpretation of Articles I:1 of GATT 1994 and Articles I and II of GATS, and requested that the Appellate Body reverse the findings and conclusions of the panel and modify accordingly its recommendations (WT/DS139/5 and WT/DS142/5). The appeal is being considered by the Appellate Body. On April 28, 2000, the Appellate Body informed the DSB that the report in this appeal would be circulated to WTO members no later than May 31, 2000 (WT/DS139/6 and WT/DS142/6).

Canada—Certain Measures Affecting the Automotive Industry, complaint by the European Communities (WT/DS142). This request, dated August 17, 1998, was in respect of the 1965 Agreement Concerning Automotive Products between the Government of Canada and the Government of the United States; chapter 10 of the 1989 free trade agreement between Canada and the United States; the North American Free Trade Agreement (NAFTA); the 1998 Motor Vehicles Tariff Order; the special orders providing for the remission of customs duties on imports of automotive products made by specified manufacturers; the administrative memorandums relating thereto; other legislative provisions consolidated therein; and any implementing measures taken thereunder. The EC cited the same violations alleged by Japan, except Article XXIV of GATT 1994, which was cited by Japan but not by the EC. On January 14, 1998, the EC requested the establishment of a panel. At its meeting on February 1, 1999, the DSB established a panel. Pursuant to Article 9.1 of the DSU, the DSB agreed that the panel established in respect of the complaint by Japan (WT/DS139) would also examine this complaint. India, Korea, and the United States submitted arguments as third parties. The letter argued that GATS Article V was applicable in this case. The report of the panel (WT/DS/139/R and WT/DS142/R) addresses the complaints jointly.

In four cases with notable implications for services issues, the GATS provisions were not invoked by the member making the complaint. These cases are as follows.

Canada—Certain Measures Concerning Periodicals, complaint by the United States (WT/DS31). In its request for consultations dated March 11, 1996, the United States claimed that measures prohibiting or restricting the importation into Canada of certain periodicals were in contravention of GATT 1994

Article XI. The United States further alleged that the tax treatment of "split-run" periodicals and the application of favorable postage rates to certain Canadian periodicals were inconsistent with GATT 1994 Article III. The DSB established a panel on June 19, 1996. The panel found the measures applied by Canada to be in violation of GATT rules. The report of the panel was circulated to members on March 14, 1997. On April 29, 1997, Canada notified its intention to appeal certain issues of law and legal interpretations developed by the panel. The Appellate Body upheld the panel's findings and conclusions on the applicability of GATT 1994 to Part V.1 of Canada's Excise Tax Act, but reversed the panel's finding that Part V.1 of the Excise Tax Act was inconsistent with the first sentence of Article III:2 of GATT 1994. The Appellate Body further concluded that Part V.1 of the Excise Tax Act was inconsistent with the second sentence of Article III:2 of GATT 1994. The Appellate Body also reversed the panel's conclusion that Canada's "funded" postal-rate scheme was justified by Article III:8(b) of GATT 1994. The Appellate Body stated that the entry into force of GATS, as Annex 1B of the WTO Agreement, did not diminish the scope of application of GATT 1994. The Appellate Body agreed with the panel's statement that the ordinary meaning of the texts of GATT 1994 and GATS as well as Article II:2 of the WTO Agreement, taken together, indicate that the obligations under GATT 1994 and GATS can coexist and that one does not override the other.[70] The report of the Appellate Body was circulated to members on June 30, 1997. At its meeting on July 30, 1997, the DSB adopted the Appellate Body report and the panel report as modified by the Appellate Body. The implementation period agreed by the parties to be fifteen months from the date of adoption of the reports expired on October 30, 1998. Canada implemented the finding withdrawing the contested measure. Canada Post harmonized the commercial postal rates for domestic and foreign publications by reducing the foreign rate (approximately forty-three cents) to the Canadian rate (approximately thirty-eight cents) as of October 30, 1998.

Korea—Laws, Regulations, and Practices in the Telecommunications Procurement Sector, complaint by the European Communities (WT/DS40). This request for consultations, dated May 9, 1996, concerned the laws, regulations, and practices in the telecommunications sector. The EC claimed that the procurement practices of the Korean telecommunications sector (Korea Telecom and Dacom) discriminated against foreign suppliers. The EC also claimed that the Korean government had favored U.S. suppliers under two bilateral telecommunications agreements between Korea and the United States. Violations of GATT 1994 Articles I, III, and XVII were alleged. The 1992 Special Regu-

70. WT/DS31/AB/R, p. 20.

lation on the Accounting of Government-Invested Corporations requiring Korea Telecom to partly open its network equipment market to U.S. suppliers granted U.S. products an advantage, favor, or privilege that had not been accorded to like products originating in the European Communities. The European Communities therefore considered that this special regulation constituted a breach of Korea's obligations under Article I of GATT 1994. The second network operator in the Korean telecommunications market, Dacom, applied internal procurement rules that discriminated against foreign products. Article 5 of Dacom's "Working Rules for Materials Purchasing" provided that foreign purchasing should be undertaken only when the material was not available on the domestic market. The European Community wished to examine with Korea to what extent Dacom's purchasing policy and the government's role therein constituted breaches of Articles XVII and III of GATT 1994. On October 22, 1997, the parties notified the WTO Secretariat that they had agreed on a solution.[71]

Japan—Measures Affecting Consumer Photographic Film and Paper, complaint by the United States (WT/DS44). On June 13, 1996, the United States requested consultations with Japan concerning Japan's laws, regulations, and requirements affecting the distribution, offering for sale, and internal sale of imported consumer photographic film and paper. The United States alleged that the Japanese government treated imported film and paper less favorably through these measures, in violation of GATT 1994 Articles III and X. The United States also alleged that these measures nullified or impaired benefits accruing to the United States (a nonviolation claim). The United States requested the establishment of a panel on September 20, 1996, and it was established on October 16, 1996. The panel found that the United States did not demonstrate that the Japanese measures cited by the United States nullified or impaired, either individually or collectively, benefits accruing to the United States within the meaning of GATT 1994 Article XXIII:1(b); did not demonstrate that the Japanese distribution measures cited by the United States accorded less-favorable treatment to imported photographic film and paper within the meaning of GATT 1994 Article III:4; and did not demonstrate that Japan failed to publish administrative rulings of general application in violation of GATT 1994 Article X:1. The report of the panel was circulated to members on March 31, 1998. The panel report was adopted by the DSB on April 22, 1998. The case was completed.

Korea—Measures Affecting Government Procurement, complaint by the United States (WT/DS163/R). This dispute, dated February 16, 1999, was in respect of certain procurement practices of the Korean Airport Construction Authority (KOACA) and other entities concerned with the procurement of airport construction in Korea that were allegedly inconsistent with Korea's obligations under the Agreement on Government Procurement (GPA). These allegedly included practices relating to qualification for bidding as a prime contractor, domestic partnering, the absence of access to challenge procedures, and inadequate bid deadlines that were in breach of the GPA. The United States contended that KOACA and the other entities were within the scope of Korea's list of central government entities, as specified in Annex 1 of Korea's obligations in Appendix I of the GPA, and pursuant to Article I(1) of the GPA, applied to the procurement of airport construction. On May 11, 1999, the United States requested the establishment of a panel. At its meeting on June 16, 1999, the DSB established a panel. The EC and Japan reserved their third-party rights. The report of the panel was circulated on May 1, 2000. After considering the interpretation of the negotiating history of Korea's accession to the GPA, the panel concluded that the entities that had been conducting procurement for the Inchon International Airport construction project were not covered entities under Appendix I of the GPA and were not covered by Korea's obligations under the GPA (WT/DS163/R, 7.82, 7.83. 8.1). In considering the allegation of nonviolation nullification or impairment of benefits accruing to the United States, in the context of Article 26 of the DSU and the principle of *pacta sum servanda* as expressed in Article 26 of the Vienna Convention on the Law of Treaties of 1969, the panel referred to the doctrine of reasonable expectations of benefits. The panel noted that there was a particular obligation of transparency and openness on the offering party in negotiations on concessions under the GPA. These negotiations did not benefit from a generally accepted framework such as the Harmonized System with respect to goods or even the Central Product Classification in services. This duty did not relieve the other negotiating partners from their duty of diligence to verify the offers as best as they could. Under the circumstances the error of the complainant was no longer excusable, and only an excusable error can qualify as an error that may vitiate the consent to be bound by the agreement. For these reasons, the panel was of the view that the United States had not demonstrated error successfully as a basis for a claim on nonviolation nullification or impairment of benefits. The panel concluded that the United States had not demonstrated that benefits reasonably expected to accrue under the GPA, or in the negotiations resulting in Korea's accession to the GPA, were nullified or impaired by measures taken by Korea within the meaning of Article XXII(2) of the GPA (WT/DS163/R, 7.121, 7.125, 7.126, 8.2). The panel's report will have to be considered by the DSB.

Conclusions

The DSU rules and procedures may be invoked with regard to disputes over trade in services concerning the general obligations set out in Parts I, II, IV, V, and VI, in the GATS annexes, and with regard to the specific commitments set out in Part III of GATS and in the national schedules of GATS commitments. In future services negotiations members will have to give careful consideration to the sectors inscribed in their schedules and to the conditions and qualifications set out therein that are affected by the existing rules and regulations in force in the respective member countries. In the case of *European Communities—Regime for the Importation, Sale, and Distribution of Bananas* (WT/DS27/AB/R, 225), the Appellate Body noted that the EC had made a full commitment for wholesale trade services, with no conditions or qualifications, in its Schedule of Specific Commitments under GATS. Presumably the inscription in the Schedule of Specific Commitments of the European Communities of the licensing regime applicable to the operators—suppliers of wholesale trade services related to bananas—would have affected the findings and recommendations of the panel and the Appellate Body. A similar conclusion emerges from the report of the panel, Canada—Certain Measures Affecting the Automotive Industry (WT/DS/R/139 and 142, 10.297), in which the panel found that Canada had undertaken specific commitments in sectors affected by Canadian value-added requirements and that the limitations listed did not cover those requirements.

With regard to future services negotiations,[72] it should be noted that footnote 10 of Article XVII(1) of GATS recognizes that inherent competitive disadvantages may result from the foreign character of the relevant services or services suppliers. Article XVII(2) and (3) of GATS provides that a member may accord to services and services suppliers of any other member, treatment that is either formally identical to or formally different from that it accords to its own like services and service suppliers. Moreover, Article XVIII of GATS provides that members may negotiate commitments with respect to measures affecting trade in services not subject to scheduling under Articles XVI or XVII of GATS, including those regarding qualifications, standards, or licensing matters. This

---

72. On February 7, 2000, the General Council of the WTO decided, among other things, on the organization of the negotiations mandated in the WTO Agreements on Agriculture and Services, in the framework of special negotiating sessions of the Committee on Agriculture and the Council for Trade in Services, respectively. Special sessions of the Council for Trade in Services and the Committee on Agriculture have been scheduled for February and March 2000, respectively.

may broaden the scope of action of the DSU with respect to potential services disputes.

A review of the 192 complaints communicated to the WTO in accordance with the DSU confirms that a number of members who are also members of regional groupings, in particular free trade agreements, have brought some of their trade disputes to the WTO for consultation, adjudication, and settlement instead of taking them up in the framework of their regional agreements. The DSB cannot refuse to intervene as long as the dispute relates to the WTO agreements and is subject to the provisions of the DSU.[73]

There is a risk that the DSB will be called upon in the future to examine more complex issues in the services sector where a simple extrapolation of the interpretation of the provisions of GATT 1994 may not be adequate without prior agreement on the rules and principles. For instance, pursuant to the principle of reasonable expectations set out in GATS Article XXIII(3), or to some other concepts such as those concerning business practices set out in GATS Article IX, could services supplied through the Internet be considered to be covered by the provisions of GATS, the horizontal commitments or the specific commitments? Pursuant to the annex to GATS, could the DSB take up disputes concerning the termination or continuation of Article II (MFN Exemptions)? What are the rules and principles applicable to the fees, charges, and taxes levied on services included in the schedules of specific commitments? Does the consideration of disputes in services sectors require specialized expertise as provided in the Decision on Certain Dispute Settlement Procedures for GATS?[74] Or is the integration of the roster established under GATS into the Indicative List of Governmental and Non-Governmental Panelists satisfactory?[75] What are the consequences for GATS and other covered agreements of cross-retaliation under Article 22.3 (c) of the DSU? As services disputes become more numerous and more complex in the future, the answers to such questions will have important implications for the effectiveness of the WTO dispute-resolution process.

73. Canada—Measures Affecting the Importation of Milk and the Exportation of Dairy Products (WT/DS103), complaint by the United States. Argentina—Transitional Safeguard Measures on Certain Imports of Woven Fabrics of Cotton and Cotton Mixtures Originating in Brazil (WT/DS 190), complaint by Brazil.

74. S/L/2 dated April 4, 1995.

75. Article 4 of the Annex on Financial Services provides that panels for disputes on prudential and other financial matters shall have the necessary expertise relevant to the specific financial service under dispute. The Current Indicative List of Governmental and Non-Governmental Panelists established in pursuance of Article 8.4 of the DSU is reproduced in document WT/DSB/17.

PART TWO

Services Liberalization at the Regional Level

CHAPTER SIX

Mexico's Free Trade Agreements: Extending NAFTA's Approach

CARLOS PIÑERA GONZÁLEZ

THE URUGUAY ROUND NEGOTIATIONS on services that began in 1986 sparked Mexico's interest in services. In cooperation with the United Nations Conference on Trade and Development (UNCTAD) and the United Nations Development Programme (UNDP), the Mexican government carried out an extensive study on services in Mexico in 1988.[1] This analysis of the composition and characteristics of services in Mexico and their contribution to economic development helped the Mexican government to set objectives and establish an organizational system for participating in the multilateral negotiations on services and to begin the process of liberalization. Mexico has subsequently gained a great deal of experience in the liberalization of services trade, both unilaterally and through plurilateral and bilateral free trade agreements.

In the early 1990s, Mexico negotiated the North American Free Trade Agreement (NAFTA) with Canada and the United States, the first regional agreement among developed and developing countries. NAFTA came into force in January 1994. Since then, Mexico has negotiated five free trade agreements with seven Latin American countries: the Group of Three treaty with Colombia and Venezuela (1995); and bilateral free trade agreements with Costa Rica (1995), Bolivia (1995), Nicaragua (1998), and Chile (1999). All of these agreements contain provisions and disciplines similar to those of NAFTA and, including NAFTA, account for 87 percent of trade in services in the Western Hemisphere.

---

1. UNCTAD, SECOFI, and Government of Mexico, "Mexico, a Services Economy" (1991).

NAFTA: The Cornerstone

The NAFTA treaty has been the cornerstone of Mexico's approach to the liberalization of services trade. This chapter first examines and comments on the provisions of NAFTA and then discusses how the subsequent agreements that Mexico has negotiated modify or differ from the NAFTA approach.

In NAFTA, the chapters that apply to services trade are: Chapter XI (Investment), Chapter XII (Cross-Border Trade in Services), Chapter XIII (Telecommunications), Chapter XIV (Financial Services), and Chapter XVI (Temporary Entry of Business Persons). The next section describes the more significant aspects of each chapter. Following this description is a comparative analysis of the main principles and disciplines of the NAFTA-type free trade agreements Mexico has signed with Latin American countries.

All of the agreements negotiated by Mexico contain a specific and separate chapter on investment (or commercial presence) covering both goods and services. The provisions of the investment chapter are not discussed in this chapter. However, the principles of national treatment and most-favored-nation treatment for investment apply in the same way that they do for cross-border trade in services. Both NAFTA and the NAFTA-type agreements negotiated by Mexico guarantee the right of foreign direct investment for all service sectors covered by the agreements, without limits on the form, size, or equity of the investment, unless specified.

General Framework: Cross-Border Trade in Services

Chapter XII of NAFTA sets out the basic principles and disciplines applicable to cross-border trade in services. It covers, with limited exceptions, all service sectors and therefore applies to modes of supply 1, 2, and 4 of GATS: cross-border trade, consumption abroad, and movement of natural persons.[2]

BASIC PRINCIPLES: NATIONAL TREATMENT, MFN, AND LOCAL PRESENCE. The provisions on national treatment, most-favored-nation (MFN) treatment, and local presence are the basic principles on which the obligations on trade in services between or among the parties are founded. National treatment requires each member country to accord to service providers of any other member country treatment no less favorable than that it accords to its own service providers. On the basis of this principle, the parties undertake not to discriminate between

2. GATS defines the four modes of supply for trade in services as: (1) cross-border trade; (2) consumption abroad; (3) commercial presence; and (4) movement of natural persons.

national and foreign service providers. Under GATS, this obligation is specific, and countries are bound by this principle only in sectors or subsectors where they have made previous commitments, whereas in NAFTA this obligation automatically applies to all service sectors where there are no previous reservations.

The MFN provision requires each member country to accord to service providers of any other member country treatment no less favorable than that it accords to service providers of any other country. This principle is also one of the fundamental obligations contained in GATS, the aim of which is to extend to the parties to the agreement the benefits or preferences (or withdrawals of benefits) accorded to third countries.

The local-presence principle means that a service provider of any other member country shall not be required to reside in, establish, or maintain a representative office, a branch, or any form of enterprise in its territory as a condition for the provision of a service. This is an innovation by GATS. In GATS, the requirements regarding residence or any other form of representation as a condition for providing cross-border services—when applied in a nondiscriminatory manner—are not viewed as a trade restriction, while in NAFTA, by contrast, such requirements are considered a hurdle to market access and are thus liberalized.

NAFTA RESERVATIONS.   NAFTA allows each member country to establish reservations with respect to any legal provisions or other measures in force that do not conform to the principles explained above. The establishment of these reservations represents, moreover, a form of commitment adopted by the parties because they contain a description of the various legal conditions that surround the provision of services, the degree of existing liberalization, and the activities or sectors where restrictions remain.

Transparency is a key feature of a list of reservations. For instance, a reservation in a given annex should contain descriptive elements such as sector, classification, type of reservation (national treatment, MFN treatment, and local presence), and measure (laws and regulations that support the reservation). This information gives service providers a clear picture of the outstanding restrictions affecting services trade and can be referred to in the event of a dispute between the parties. On the basis of the national reservations described in the various annexes, it is possible to determine when a party may be in violation of the commitments in the agreement. A party that believes it has been injured may file for and initiate the proceedings provided for in the chapters on dispute settlement.

Since identifying measures at the state and provincial levels before the entry into force of the agreement was a very complex task, a two-year period was established for completing the list of reservations at the state or provincial level. Ultimately, however, this list was never completed.[3]

With respect to the modification of reservations, NAFTA allows members to renew or amend the measures listed, provided that such amendments or additions are not more restrictive than those previously in effect. Another innovation of NAFTA, which does not exist in any other previous agreement, is known as the "ratchet clause," which embodies a high level of commitment by the parties to maintain and even increase liberalization of their services sectors.

NONDISCRIMINATORY QUANTITATIVE RESTRICTIONS.   Each NAFTA member was obliged to provide a list of nondiscriminatory provisions in force that limit the number of service providers, or limit their operations, in a given service sector. The member countries may request consultations on these provisions in order to negotiate their liberalization or elimination.

Although GATS contains a similar rule, NAFTA establishes a different approach. Under GATS, nondiscriminatory restrictions are mixed with discriminatory restrictions in national schedules of WTO members, and both are treated as restrictions on market access. Under NAFTA, the two categories of restrictions are listed separately, which makes them easier for service providers to identify.

LICENSING AND CERTIFICATION.   In order to prevent unnecessary barriers to trade, NAFTA also contains provisions relating to procedures for the licensing and certification of professionals. In particular, each country is to ensure that licensing or certification is based on objective and transparent criteria, such as professional ability; is not more burdensome than necessary to ensure the quality of a service; and does not in itself constitute a restriction on the provision of a service.

The agreement innovates by requiring each party to eliminate, within two years of the date of entry into force, any citizenship or permanent residency requirement for the licensing or certification of professional service providers. Failure to comply with this obligation will entitle the other members to maintain or restore an equivalent requirement in the same service sector.

DENIAL OF BENEFITS.   The clause on denial of benefits enables a member country to deny the benefits of NAFTA to services provided by an enterprise of

---

3. It proved impossible to complete this list within the given time frame, and subsequently all measures at the state and provincial levels affecting services were grandfathered—that is, allowed to remain intact. Therefore they have not been liberalized under NAFTA.

another member country that is owned or controlled by a national of a non-member country and that does not carry out substantial business activities in the territory of a member country.

EXCEPTIONS. The provisions of the chapter on cross-border trade in services do not apply to areas covered by other chapters of the agreement, such as government procurement, subsidies, and financial services. They also do not apply to most air services, basic telecommunications, social services provided by governments, the maritime industry (except for some services between Mexico and Canada), and sectors reserved for the Mexican state or Mexican nationals under applicable legislation. Besides these exceptions, the chapter applies to all service sectors. However, the provisions of the separate chapters on government procurement and subsidies apply equally to services and goods.

ANNEX ON PROFESSIONAL SERVICES. The chapter in NAFTA on cross-border trade in services contains an annex (Annex 1210.5) that sets out the general provisions on cross-border supply of professional services. This annex contains three sections. The first has provisions to ensure that the competent authorities process applications for licensing and certification within a reasonable time frame. It also establishes criteria for development of professional standards in different areas (education, examinations, experience, conduct and ethics, professional development and recertification, scope of practice, local knowledge, and consumer protection). This section also states that the parties shall encourage the relevant professional bodies to develop mutually acceptable standards and criteria for licensing and certification of professional service providers and to submit recommendations on mutual recognition to the Free Trade Commission. The commission is to review those recommendations within a reasonable period of time to determine whether they are consistent with the provisions of the agreement. If the recommendations are approved, each party is to encourage its competent authorities to implement them.

The second section of the annex establishes special provisions relating to foreign legal consultants. The third section contains provisions on temporary licensing of engineers.[4]

4. In pursuit of these provisions, Mexico's professional associations formed the Mexican Committees on International Professional Practice (Comités Mexicanos para la Práctica Internacional de la Profesión, or COMPIs). Currently, the following professions have formed COMPIs: architects, actuaries, agronomists, accountants, lawyers, doctors, veterinarians, dentists, nurses, pharmacists, and psychologists. COMPIs were created in order for professional associations to establish contact with their counterparts in the United States and Canada with a view to negotiating joint documents containing recommendations for mutual-recognition agreements (MRAs) between these countries on the equivalence of credentials and licenses.

Telecommunications

NAFTA provides that public telecommunication networks or services shall be available under reasonable, nondiscriminatory terms and conditions to enterprises or persons that use them to conduct their businesses. The use of public networks includes provision of enhanced or value-added services and internal communications within companies. Under this chapter, the parties are to ensure that reasonable conditions prevail for access to and use of public networks. The provisions of the chapter on telecommunications do not apply to any measure relating to cable or broadcast distribution of radio or television programming, which are to have permanent access to and use of public networks and services.

In addition, the member countries are not required to authorize a person from another member country to operate or provide telecommunications networks or services, and they reserve the right to prohibit private network operators from providing public telecommunications networks or services.

This chapter also indicates that the licensing or any other permit procedure adopted by each country relating to the provision of enhanced or value-added services must be transparent, nondiscriminatory, and expeditious. Providers of enhanced telecommunications services from the three countries shall not be bound by the obligations generally imposed on providers of public telecommunications networks or services, such as the requirement that they provide those services to the public in general or justify their fees.

The chapter puts disciplines on the standards that may be applied to the connection of telecommunications equipment to the public networks. Such measures are to be applied only to the extent necessary to prevent technical damage or interference with public networks and services, prevent billing equipment malfunction, and ensure user safety and access. Furthermore, any technically qualified entity is to be permitted to test equipment that will be connected to public networks.

Financial Services

The principles set forth in the chapter on financial services apply to measures that affect the delivery of services by financial institutions (banking, insurance, and securities) and other financial services. Furthermore, each country defines its specific liberalization commitments, the transition period for adhering to the agreed principles, and its reservations regarding those principles.

The provisions in this chapter allow financial services providers of a member country to establish themselves in another member country to conduct banking, insurance, and securities operations and any other type of service that the host country deems financial in nature. Each country is to permit its residents to acquire financial services in the territory of another party and is not to impose new curbs on cross-border operations in any financial sector unless the country has specifically exempted a particular sector from this obligation.

Each country is to accord equal national treatment with respect to opportunities for competition, as well as MFN treatment to any financial services provider that operates in its territory. According equal competitive opportunities means that financial services providers of another party should not be placed at a disadvantage in relation to domestic financial services providers.

Regardless of any other provision of the agreement, the authorities of the member governments reserve the right to issue reasonable regulations intended to ensure the integrity and stability of the financial system. Under certain circumstances, the countries can also adopt measures to protect the balance of payments.

Temporary Entry of Business Persons

The NAFTA commitments adopted for expediting temporary entry of business persons who are nationals of any of the three countries do not establish a common market with freedom of movement for persons. Each member country retains the right to protect its labor market, to adopt any immigration policy it deems appropriate, and to protect the security of its borders.

The categories for which temporary entry of business persons shall be authorized are: business visitors, traders and investors, intracompany transferees, and certain categories of professionals who meet the minimum qualifications or who have equivalent credentials. A special working group will consider extending the provisions of this section to the spouses of business persons who have been granted temporary entry pursuant to the provisions of the agreement and to applicable provisions in each country.

The chapter also provides for recourse to the NAFTA dispute-settlement mechanism when another country engages in a pattern of practice that is incompatible with the provisions on temporary entry.

Mexico's Bilateral Treaties: The New Elements

When the NAFTA treaty was concluded in 1993, Mexico began intensive trade negotiations with its Latin American neighbors Colombia and Venezuela (forming the Group of Three), and bilaterally with Costa Rica and Bolivia. Free trade agreements with all of these countries came into force in January 1995.

At the end of 1996 Mexico began negotiations with Nicaragua and Chile that concluded in 1997. The agreement with Nicaragua entered into force in July 1998 and with Chile in August 1999.

The agreements Mexico negotiated with Colombia, Venezuela, Bolivia, Costa Rica, Nicaragua, and Chile deal with services in a manner very similar to that of NAFTA. In some cases, through negotiations, disciplines from GATS were included as well. Table 6-1 shows the year of entry into force of each agreement, together with the chapters and disciplines included.

Excluding the United States and Canada, the volume of trade accounted for by the Latin American countries involved in these agreements represents around 40 percent of the total volume of trade in services among developing countries in the Western Hemisphere.

Basic Principles

Table 6-1 shows that all the NAFTA-type agreements negotiated by Mexico include the basic principles of national treatment, most-favored-nation treatment, and local presence. The commitments established in each agreement are based on the same principles, the purpose of which is to eliminate discrimination between domestic and foreign service providers, as well as to extend the benefits of agreements that each party has negotiated with third countries, unless, as explained below, reservations are established for specific sectors.

Coverage

All the NAFTA-type agreements cover all service sectors except air transportation. However, aircraft repair and maintenance and specialty air services (such as air ticketing services, aerial sightseeing, photography, or fumigation services) are covered.

Reservations and Commitments

Each NAFTA-type agreement negotiated by Mexico contains an article that sets forth mechanisms to enable each party to maintain measures that do not conform to the basic principles. The wording and specifics of each article reflect the commitments adopted during each negotiation. Thus, for instance, in NAFTA, the Group of Three, and the agreements with Bolivia and Chile, a negotiating approach based on two annexes was used. One annex lists national laws and regulations for which reservations are applied to the basic principles.

The second annex lists activities or sectors to which countries may apply future measures that may be inconsistent with the provisions of the chapter.

In contrast, in the agreements with Costa Rica and Nicaragua, a single annex sets forth all existing nonconforming measures. No annex is included for future measures. Of the two approaches, the one pursued with Costa Rica and Nicaragua provides for a higher level of integration, since none of the parties may apply future measures that are inconsistent with the agreement.

In the agreement with Bolivia a two-annex approach was used. However, the annex listing unbound measures was only in force for two years, after which the activities listed in that annex became binding. Under this commitment, as of 1997, the agreement is to have only one annex, like the agreements with Costa Rica and Nicaragua.

Other Disciplines

Some agreements negotiated by Mexico, such as those with Costa Rica and Bolivia, include articles on safeguards and subsidies that are not found in NAFTA. Those articles provide, for instance, that:

The Committee shall determine the procedures for establishing disciplines relating to:
  a. Emergency safeguard measures; and
  b. Subsidies that distort trade in services.
  For the purposes of the foregoing paragraph, the work of the competent International Organizations shall be taken into consideration.

These provisions were included with the idea that it might be possible to develop rules on these issues more rapidly in forums other than GATS. However, owing to their complexity and characteristics, rules that apply to these issues have yet to be developed, and no progress has been made in these areas.

On the other hand, the various free trade agreements negotiated by Mexico do not have the same sectoral emphasis or cover the same issues. NAFTA, the Group of Three, and the bilateral agreements with Bolivia and Nicaragua are the more complete since they contain chapters on cross-border trade in services, financial services, telecommunications, and temporary entry of business persons; the agreement with Costa Rica does not include chapters on financial services and telecommunications, and the one with Chile does not include financial services. Both agreements contemplate the possibility of covering these chapters at a later stage.

Table 6-1. *Mexico's Free Trade Agreements: Disciplines Applicable to Trade in Services (Year of Entry into Force)*

NAFTA (1994) Cross-border trade in services, Chapter XII	Group of Three (1995) General principles on trade in services, Chapter X	Costa Rica (1995) General principles on trade in services, Chapter IX	Bolivia (1995) General principles on trade in services, Chapter IX	Nicaragua (1998) General principles on trade in services, Chapter X	Chile (1999) Cross-border trade in services, Chapter X
Art. 1201, Scope	Article 10-02, Scope	Article 9-02, Scope	Article 9-02, Scope	Article 10-02, Scope	Article 10-02, Scope
Article 1202, National treatment	Article 10-04, National treatment	Article 9-04, National treatment	Article 9-03, National treatment	Article 10-04, National treatment	Article 10-03, National treatment
Article 1203, Most-favored-nation treatment	Article 10-05, Most-favored-nation treatment	Article 9-03, Most-favored-nation treatment	Article 9-04, Most-favored-nation treatment	Article 10-03, Most-favored-nation treatment	Article 10-04, Most-favored-nation treatment
Article 1204, Level of treatment					Article 10-05, Level of treatment
Article 1205, Local presence	Article 10-06, Local presence	Article 9-05, Local presence	Article 9-05, Local presence	Article 10-05, Local presence	Article 10-06, Local presence
Article 1206, Reservations	Article 10-07, Consolidation of measures	Article 9-06, Consolidation of measures	Article 9-06, Consolidation of measures	Article 10-06, Consolidation of measures	Article 10-07, Reservations
Article 1207, Quantitative restrictions	Article 10-08, Nondiscriminatory quantitative restrictions	Article 9-07, Quantitative restrictions	Article 9-07, Quantitative restrictions	Article 10-08, Quantitative restrictions	Article 10-08, Quantitative restrictions
	Article 10-09, Future liberalization	Article 9-08, Future liberalization	Article 9-08, Future liberalization	Article 10-09, Future liberalization	Article 10-09, Future liberalization
Article 1208, Liberalization of nondiscriminatory measures	Article 10-10, Liberalization of nondiscriminatory measures	Article 9-09, Liberalization of nondiscriminatory measures	Article 9-09, Liberalization of nondiscriminatory measures	Article 10-10, Liberalization of nondiscriminatory measures	Article 10-10, Liberalization of nondiscriminatory measures
Article 1209, Procedures	Article 10-12, Procedures	Article 9-10, Procedures	Article 9-10, Procedures	Article 10-11, Procedures	Article 10-11, Procedures
Article 1210, Licensing and certification	Article 10-14, Licensing and certification	Article 9-12, Permit procedures and licensing		Article 10-13, Licensing and certification	Article 10-12, Licensing and certification
Article 1211, Denial of benefits	Article 10-15, Denial of benefits	Article 9-15, Denial of benefits	Article 9-13, Denial of benefits	Article 10-14, Denial of benefits	Article 10-13, Denial of benefits
Article 1212, Sectoral annex					
Article 1213, Definitions	Article 10-01, Definitions	Article 9-01, Definitions	Article 9-01, Definitions	Article 10-01, Definitions	Article 10-01, Definitions
Annex 1210.5, Professional services	Annex 1, Article 10-02, Professional services	Annex, Article 9-13, Professional services	Annex, Article 9-12, Professional services	Annex, Article 10-13, Professional services	Annex 10-12, Professional services

Appendix 1210.5-C, Civil engineers			
Annex 1212, Land transportation	Annex 2, Article 10-02, Transportation		Annex, Article 10-09, Elimination of barriers to land transportation flows
			Article 10-12, Limits on the supply of information
	Article 9-11, Disclosure of confidential information	Article 9-12, Recognition of professional credentials and licensing	
	Article 9-13, Recognition of professional credentials and licensing		
	Article 9-14, Commercial practices		
	Article 9-16, Exceptions		Article 10-15, Exceptions
	Article 9-17, Exceptions for security reasons		
Article 10-13, Technical cooperation	Article 9-18, Technical cooperation	Article 9-11, Technical cooperation	Article 10-18, Technical cooperation
	Article 9-19, Future work		Article 10-16, Future work
	Article 9-20, Relation to multilateral agreements on services	Article 9-15, Relation to multilateral agreements on services	Article 10-17, Relation to multilateral agreements on services
Article 10-03, Transparency		Annex 1, Article 9-06, Consolidation of measures	Article 10-07, Transparency
Article 10-11, Reciprocity and overall balance		Annex 2, Article 9-06, List of activities (Bolivia)	
			Article 10-14, Committee on Investment and Cross-Border Trade in Services

The Approach for Negotiations

Agreements negotiated under the NAFTA scheme feature a "negative list" or "top-down" approach, which includes the following elements:
—coverage of all service sectors, with limited exceptions;
—consolidation of measures upon entry into force of the agreement;
—annexes setting out reservations (nonconforming measures);
—a ratchet clause; and
—a phase-out calendar.
The following subsections elaborate on the most important elements of the approach to services liberalization contained in Mexico's NAFTA-type agreements.

Consolidation of Existing Measures

Through consolidation, the parties pledge to "freeze" their national laws that are applicable to the various service activities. In other words, they commit themsleves to consolidate the degree of liberalization that exists upon entry into force of the agreement and not to establish additional measures that restrict or limit that degree of liberalization.

On occasion, this concept is confused with the loss of sovereignty by national governments to regulate their service sectors. However, this provison on consolidation does not prevent countries from changing their legal framework or passing new laws for unregulated activities as deemed necessary. The only requirement under consolidation is that such changes must not reduce the degree of liberalization or the agreed level of commitment at the time of entry into force of the agreement.

Lists of Reservations or Nonconforming Measures

The majority of Mexico's free trade agreements contain two lists of reservations: a list of bound measures and a list of unbound or future measures.

The annex listing bound measures sets out the activities or sectors for which reservations are established to the basic principles for trade in services. Specified in this list are, for example, the reservations that one party maintains with respect to nationality requirements for providing a professional service, or the limits on foreign investment for a given sector, whereby a party, on the basis of its national law, establishes discriminatory treatment of foreign services providers. Including these restrictions in the list enables the member country to maintain them unless it makes some commitment to eliminate them.

The annex setting out unbound or future measures, as the name suggests, lists sectors and activities exempted from the provisions of the chapter and for which the parties may issue even more restrictive provisions than those in force when the agreement is signed. Although this annex is, in principle, contrary to the purposes of a free trade area, in most cases it is used to cover sectors that are extremely sensitive within the domestic economy and which the party in question is unable to consolidate. Sectors are also included in this annex as an outcome of the balancing of negotiations.[5] Nevertheless, the parties must restrict the annex of unbound measures to a limited number of sectors, since excluding many sectors from the coverage of a free trade agreement would be in breach of the provisions set out in Article V of GATS.

Under the negative list approach, those sectors not specifically included by a party in its annex of reservations are understood to be liberalized.

The Ratchet Clause

The principle behind the ratchet clause is that if a party amends its legal framework in a way that eliminates or reduces restrictions on a service sector or activity when the agreement is already in force, the party is automatically obligated to consolidate this new degree of liberalization with respect to members of the agreement. For instance, if a party lists in the bound measures annex a reservation that prohibits foreign investment in construction companies and later decides unilaterally to allow foreign investment of up to 49 percent in such companies, the new degree of liberalization is consolidated at that level. In other words, the party in question obligates itself to offer other parties to the agreement a level of liberalization for foreign investment in construction companies of up to 49 percent and cannot subsequently prohibit or lower that level of permitted foreign equity-holding. The ratchet clause makes consolidation a dynamic approach by preventing parties from moving backward in their liberalization policies.

When comparing the negative list approach with the positive list approach for the establishment of a free trade area, the former has the following advantages:

—Services providers enjoy increased transparency and certainty since restrictions applicable to the service sector as a whole are listed.

—Remaining nonconforming measures are known to the parties, thus paving the way for future negotiations to remove or further reduce them.

—Liberalization becomes a dynamic process.

5. However, special care should always be taken in the use of the annex on future measures, because a considerable number of sectors could potentially be left out, leading to a breach of the provisions on coverage contained in Article V of GATS.

—There is a commitment by the parties not to issue regulations that make trade in services more restrictive.

By comparison, the sector-by-sector negotiation principle espoused by the positive list approach lacks transparency regarding nonconforming measures that restrict trade in services, since there is no commitment to identify and list restrictions that apply to the service sector as a whole. Consolidation of existing measures only applies to bound sectors, thereby allowing a party to establish measures that further restrict trade in those sectors where it has not made commitments. The positive list approach does not consider a ratchet clause, thus allowing a party to go backward for liberalization measures implemented unilaterally.

Conclusions

The structural changes that took place during the 1980s reshaped the Mexican economy. During those years and even more so in the recent past, the economy experienced an important process of deregulation, as well as a thorough process of restructuring and modernization of the industrial sector, which together underpin a new development strategy.

Trade policy has been a key element of this new strategy, transforming a closed economy into an open, internationally competitive one, with the purpose of promoting a sustained growth of competitiveness and productive efficiency in the framework of multilateral, regional, and bilateral liberalization of trade.

The launch of the Uruguay Round of trade negotiations highlighted the need for a clear definition of the role of services in Mexico's development and how liberalization could help this sector gain strength. The search for this definition and the information-gathering process that subsequently took place became the cornerstone for Mexico's involvement in the services negotiations of the Uruguay Round.

The beginning of the NAFTA negotiations was a great challenge to Mexico since it made necessary the undertaking of a broad analysis of the service sector and its characteristics, advantages, and disadvantages, at both the global and sectoral levels, in order to carry out successful negotiations with the world's most important economy.

The experience that Mexico gained from the NAFTA negotiation evolved into an organizational model for future negotiations. With the purpose of defining negotiating positions, a formal structure for consultations between the public and private sectors was established. As a result of this, several studies were conducted both to evaluate the competitive position of a particular services sector and to discuss ways to increase its overall efficiency and competitiveness.

The free trade agreements signed by Mexico have always sought to ensure that the rules and disciplines applicable to trade in services offer certainty to service providers, stimulate trade and investment flows from and toward the domestic market, and adhere to the multilateral guidelines established in the international forums in which Mexico takes part.

The top-down mechanism based on negative lists has been the main guideline underlying Mexico's approach to liberalization of trade in services. This approach establishes a high level of commitment between the parties because it starts from the premise of consolidating existing measures for the entire service sector while allowing for reservations in areas where national law is incompatible with basic principles. The challenge of this approach is that it necessitates the identification of all national nonconforming measures before an agreement can be finalized. This identification is crucial, considering that all measures not set out in the relevant list of reservations are considered to be covered by the agreement and are therefore to be liberalized.

The listing of nonconforming measures offers transparency and certainty to service providers by setting out the legal conditions that apply to services trade; it also enables government to identify areas where restrictions may be removed or reduced to the benefit of the domestic economy, together with those that must be maintained for reasons of national interest. The content of the annex of reservations thus represents the elements of a country's domestic and investment policy and consequently establishes its basic negotiating position. Both Mexico and the countries with which it has undertaken trade negotiations will benefit in future trade negotiations from having already performed the identification of nonconforming measures.

A little over a decade after Mexico began its liberalization process, and only six years after it did so in the services sector, there is strong evidence that this policy has helped boost the overall efficiency of the sector and enabled the supply of higher-quality services to the domestic market at internationally competitive prices.

Services liberalization has been a key element in helping to cushion Mexico against international financial crises, especially the crisis of 1995, when the export of goods and services was able to soften the impact of economic adjustment by redirecting part of the country's productive capacity toward international trade. This would not have been possible without the preferential access set forth in the trade agreements signed by Mexico—especially NAFTA—or the foreign direct investments that such agreements have attracted into the country.

CHAPTER SEVEN

Services in MERCOSUR: The Protocol of Montevideo

MARÍA-ANGÉLICA PEÑA

THIS CHAPTER EXPLAINS AND COMMENTS on the commitments that have been adopted by the four member states of MERCOSUR (Argentina, Brazil, Paraguay, and Uruguay) on trade in services, and also discusses other relevant negotiated instruments in MERCOSUR (the Southern Cone Common Market). Some of these agreements have already been concluded, and others are being negotiated.

The chapter discusses how MERCOSUR members have approached problems related to existing commitments under the umbrella of the WTO General Agreement on Trade in Services (GATS), as well as those discussed in the Free Trade Area of the Americas (FTAA) process, the Conference on Global Trade in Services and the Americas, and the World Services Congress, both held during 1999.

Objectives of the Montevideo Protocol on Trade in Services

Article 1 of the Treaty of Asunción, the founding document of MERCOSUR, signed in Asunción, Paraguay, on March 26, 1991, provides that:

This common market shall involve:
—The free movement of goods, services and factors of production between countries through, *inter alia*, the elimination of customs duties

and non-tariff restrictions on the movement of goods, and any other equivalent measures.

In its framework, the treaty lays out the procedures originally adopted to complete the first step toward the liberalization of trade in goods between the member states, but makes no mention of how to accomplish the same objective for services. Later, in December 1994, the member states of MERCOSUR adopted the Treaty of Ouro Preto, which set out the institutional structure of MERCOSUR.

At the beginning of 1996, and on the basis of these provisions, officials began drafting a set of disciplines that would create the legal framework for proceeding with the complete liberalization of trade in services among the four member states, in compliance with Article 1 of the Treaty of Asunción. The Ad Hoc Group on Services was created for this purpose, under the oversight of the umbrella entity, the Common Market Group, whose mandate is to elaborate the framework for services on the basis of several principles that had been determined politically from the outset. This resulted in the adoption of the Protocol of Montevideo on Services in December of 1997, the goal of which is to promote free trade in services in MERCOSUR.

The instrument was to be developed according to the normative framework of GATS (of which all four MERCOSUR countries are members) and with a similar methodology, but the agreement reflected the willingness of the members to deepen their intra-MERCOSUR commitments. Thus, the members expected to launch a process that would make possible the establishment of disciplines of an automatic and obligatory nature, adequate to fulfill the agreed-upon goals within a reasonable time frame. These disciplines would also allow the gradual adaptation of member states that were starting out with dissimilar conditions as concerns their internal regulations for the various services sectors. The process was to be imbued with the principles that have guided MERCOSUR from its very beginning, namely gradualism and pragmatism.

In addition, as already enshrined in other instruments of MERCOSUR, trade in services was to comply with the objectives set out in the preamble to the Protocol of Montevideo:

Reaffirming that in accordance with the Treaty of Asunción the Common Market implied, among other commitments, the free movement of services in the expanded market;

Recognizing the importance of liberalizing trade in services for the development of the economies of the Members of MERCOSUR, for the

deepening of the Customs Union and for the progressive structuring of
the Common Market;

Considering the need for the less developed countries and regions of
MERCOSUR to enjoy a growing participation in the services market,
and the need to promote trade in services on the basis of reciprocity of
rights and obligations;

Willing to enshrine within a common instrument the rules and principles for trade in services between the Members of MERCOSUR, with a
view to expanding trade in conditions of transparency, equilibrium, and
progressive liberalization.

Universal Coverage

In accordance with the multilateral disciplines of the WTO, the protocol
took into consideration, as a second objective, the fulfillment of the mandate of
Article V of GATS in relation to coverage. The sectoral coverage is to be universal and to encompass all services sectors as prescribed in Article 1 of the
Treaty of Asunción. Liberalization of measures restricting trade in all these
service sectors is to be achieved within ten years after the protocol enters into
force by ratification by three of the four member states. At that time, the outcomes of each successive annual round of negotiations would be automatically
incorporated, thereby respecting the principle of gradualism.[1]

The Protocol of Montevideo applies to the provision of a service; the purchase, payment, or use of a service; access to services that are offered to the
public in general by order of the member states, and the use of those services
for the provision of a service; and the presence, including commercial presence, of persons of a member state in the territory of another member state for
the provisions of a service.

The four modes of service provision were thus defined as in GATS:

1. from the territory of one member into the territory of any other member;

2. in the territory of one member to the service consumer of any other
member;

3. by a service supplier of one member through commercial presence in the
territory of any other member; and

---

1. Nonetheless, the political will of member states has been to continue the negotiations to
liberalize services. The first round of negotiations is expectd to culminate before the summit of
June 2000 in Argentina. The second round will likely end in December 2000. These successful
rounds of negotiations would help to achieve the objectives set out in the Protocol of Montevideo
sooner than the specified ten years. Of course the results of these negotiations will most likely not
be implemented until the protocol is ratified by the MERCOSUR member governments.

4. by a service supplier of one member through the presence of natural persons of a member in the territory of any other member.

The measures affected by the disciplines of the protocol were defined in similar fashion:

(a) "Measures by Members" means measures taken by:

(i) central, state, provincial, regional, municipal or local governments and authorities; and

(ii) non-governmental bodies in the exercise of powers delegated by the governments or authorities mentioned under (i).

In fulfilling its obligations and commitments under the Agreement, each Member shall take such reasonable measures as may be available to it to ensure their observance by state, regional, provincial, municipal, and local governments and authorities and non-governmental bodies within its territory.

(b) "services" includes any service in any sector except services supplied in the exercise of governmental authority;

(c) "a service supplied in the exercise of governmental authority" means any service which is supplied neither on a commercial basis, nor in competition with one or more service suppliers.

The following, inter alia, are obligations of a general nature: most-favored-nation treatment; market access; national treatment; establishment of specific commitments; transparency; recognition; and origin for trade in those services included in the denial of benefits.

Most-Favored-Nation Treatment

This principle is absolute in the MERCOSUR Agreement, and there is no possibility of introducing exemptions to it. (In contrast, Article II of GATS allows exceptions to the MFN principle for a period of ten years.) Each state shall accord immediately and unconditionally to services and service suppliers of any member treatment that is no less favorable than that it accords to like services and like service suppliers of any other member or of third countries.

Market Access and National Treatment

Market-access provisions are similar to those contained in GATS. In the listing of restrictions that cannot be maintained or adopted by the members of MERCOSUR, there is no provision that limits the inputs destined for the supply of services, given that in MERCOSUR trade in goods is covered by other instruments (the Treaty of Asunción and the Protocol of Ouro Preto).

National Treatment is also conceptually similar to that of GATS.

Establishment of Specific Commitments

It is established that in the listing of specific commitments members may invoke exceptions to the provisions of market access and national treatment if there exist nonconforming measures or measures that violate these provisions.

The measures that are nonconforming with *both* Article IV (Market Access) *and* Article V (National Treatment) must be listed in the column relating to Article IV. In this case, the entry will also be considered a condition or a restriction to Article V. It is also established that the lists of specific commitments will be annexed to the protocol and become an integral part of it.

Transparency

The MERCOSUR Agreement and GATS treat transparency similarly. MERCOSUR is currently going through an exercise in transparency in an effort to respond to the concerns of each member about the commitments adopted by another member. The members have also begun gathering information related to the regulations of each member on investment, the movement of persons (migration), and professional services.

The Trade Commission of MERCOSUR is in charge of receiving the relevant information. Members are to provide the information to the Trade Commission.

Recognition

Article XI on recognition has two particularities, both aimed at promoting advancement in this area through a demonstration effect. First, it contains the first provision in the MERCOSUR text to encourage a kind of bilateralism. Article XI establishes:

When a Member recognizes, unilaterally or by way of an agreement, the education, experience, licenses, matriculation records or certificates obtained in the territory of another Member or any country that is not a member of MERCOSUR:

(a) nothing in this Protocol shall be construed to require this Member to recognize the education, experience, matriculation records or certificates obtained in the territory of another Member; and

(b) the Member shall accord to any other Member an adequate opportunity to (i) demonstrate that the education, experience, licenses, and certificates obtained in its territory should also be recognized; or (ii) to conclude an agreement or treaty of equivalent effect.

Second, the protocol also establishes a rather novel provision that has stimu-
lated meetings of professional associations from the four member countries in
a number of areas, although no recognition agreements have yet been approved:

Each Member commits itself to encourage the competent bodies in their
respective territories including, *inter alia*, those of a governmental nature, as well as professional associations and colleges, in cooperation
with the competent bodies of the other Members, to develop mutually
acceptable rules and criteria for the exercise of activities and professions
pertinent to the area of services, through the granting of licenses, matriculation records, and certificates to the suppliers of services, and to
propose recommendations on mutual recognition to the Common Market Group.

Once the recommendation referred to in the previous paragraph has been
received, "the Common Market Group shall examine it within a reasonable
period to determine its consistency with this Protocol. Based on this examination, each Member commits itself to charge its respective authorities, where
necessary, to implement the provision passed down by the competent
MERCOSUR agency within a mutually agreed period."
Education ministers have adopted the "Memorandum of Understanding on
the implementation of an experimental accreditation mechanism for the recognition of university degrees, in the countries of MERCOSUR."
This framework has given rise to a pilot project that comprises the professions of architect, agronomist, geologist, and engineer. In 1999 the Board of
Architecture, Agronomy, Geology, and Engineering Professional Entities for
MERCOSUR Integration (Comisión de Integración de la Arquitectura,
Agrimensura, Agronomía, Geología e Ingeniería para el MERCOSUR, CIAM)
adopted a resolution on the temporary exercise of a professional service by
foreign architects, agronomists, geologists, and engineers. This resolution allows for the reciprocal recognition of these professionals by the four member
countries.

Determination of Origin

In the chapter on denial of benefits, which determines the beneficiaries of
the agreement, preference was given to a position leading to greater opening.

This allows MERCOSUR to stimulate the entry of foreign investment and the transfer of technology in order to enhance the level of excellence in the offering of regional services.

Thus the definition of "legal person of another Member" signifies "a legal person that is constituted or organized in accordance with the legislation of the other Member, that has its head office in the territory of that Member and engages or plans to engage in substantial commercial activities in the territory of that or any other Member."

Liberalization Program

A significant difference between the MERCOSUR Agreement and most other existing agreements in the Western hemisphere covering trade in services has to do with the liberalization objectives set out in the Protocol of Montevideo.

Article XIX states the following in relation to the negotiation of specific commitments:

1. In fulfillment of the objectives of the present Protocol, the Members will conduct successive rounds of negotiations with the aim of completing, within a maximum period of ten years from the entry into force of this Protocol, the Liberalization Program for trade in services within MERCOSUR. The negotiating rounds shall be carried out annually and will have as their main objective the progressive incorporation of sectors, subsectors, activities, and modes of service supply into the Liberalization Program of the Protocol, as well as the reduction or the elimination of the negative effects of measures on trade in services, as a way of ensuring effective access to markets. The aim of this process is to promote the interests of all participants, on the basis of mutual advantages, and to attain a global equilibrium of rights and obligations.

2. The process of progressive liberalization shall be guided in each round through negotiations aimed at increasing the level of specific commitments adopted by Members in their lists of specific commitments.

Modification or Suspension of Commitments

The Protocol of Montevideo lacks a safeguard clause. Only in Article XX is there any mention of modifying or suspending specific commitments in the lists of commitments during the ten-year transition period, until the envisioned complete liberalization of trade in services is achieved. In this aspect, it repeats what already exists in other instruments of MERCOSUR. The safeguard clause will also be absent from the provisions on trade in goods at the end of the transition period once the Protocol of Ouro Preto enters into force.

Article X says:

1. Each Member can, during the implementation of the Liberalization Program referred to in Part III of the present Protocol, modify or suspend specific commitments included in its list of specific commitments.

This modification or suspension shall be applicable starting from the date on which it is established, in respect of the principle of no retroactivity, in order to preserve the acquired rights.

2. Each Member will make recourse to the current regime only in exceptional cases, and on condition that when it does so, it shall notify the Common Market Group and present before it the facts, reasons, and justifications for said modification or suspension of commitments. In such cases, the Member in question will carry out consultations with the Member or Members that consider themselves to be affected, in order to reach a consensual understanding of the specific measure to be applied and the period when it will be in force.

The Institutional Framework of MERCOSUR for Services

The legal framework for trade in services refers to the institutional framework of MERCOSUR and the responsibilities established in the area for each entity of MERCOSUR.

The Common Market Council is tasked as follows: "The Common Market Council will approve the results of the negotiations with respect to specific commitments, as well as to any modification and/or suspension thereof."

And the Common Market Group has the following responsibilities:

"Negotiation in the area of services within MERCOSUR is the responsibility of the Common Market Group. In what concerns the present Protocol, the Common Market Group will have the following functions:

(a) initiate and supervise the negotiations provided for in Article XIX of the Protocol (Negotiation of Specific Commitments). To this effect, the Common Market Group will establish the scope, criteria, and instruments for carrying out the negotiations on specific commitments;

(b) receive the notifications and the results of the consultations with respect to the modification and/or the suspension of specific commitments as provided for in Article XX (Modification or Suspension of Commitments);

(c) fulfill the functions determined in Article XI (Recognition);

(d) evaluate periodically the evolution of trade in services in MERCOSUR; and

(e) carry out any other tasks that the Council of the Common Market determines for it in the area of trade in services.

2. To give effect to the functions determined above, the Common Market Group will constitute an auxiliary body and will regulate its composition and method of functioning.

Finally, the Trade Commission has the following responsibility:

1. Without prejudice to the functions referred to in the previous articles, the Trade Commission of MERCOSUR will be in charge of the application of the present Protocol, with the following functions:

(a) receive the information that, in accordance with Article VIII (Transparency) of this Protocol, will be notified to it by the Members;

(b) receive information from Members with respect to the exceptions provided for in Article XIV (Exceptions related to security);

(c) receive information from Members in relation to the actions that could lead to abuse of dominant position or practices that distort competition, and bring it to the knowledge of the national bodies responsible for the application of the Protocol for the Defense of Competition;[2]

(d) oversee the consultations and the complaints brought by Members in relation to the application, interpretation, or non-fulfillment of the present Protocol and of the commitments adopted in the lists of specific commitments, applying the mechanisms and procedures applicable in MERCOSUR; and

(e) carry out any other tasks that the Common Market Group determines for it in the area of services.

Dispute Settlement

The disputes that might arise between members concerning the application, interpretation, or nonfulfillment of commitments established under the Protocol of Montevideo are to be solved in accordance with the dispute-settlement procedures and mechanisms applicable in MERCOSUR (the Protocols of Brasilia and Ouro Preto).

2. The four countries have representatives on the recently created Committee for the Defense of Competition.

Future Regulations

In the MERCOSUR Protocol on Services, provisions exist to deal in the future with the question of new service activities, as well as with the possibility of regulating sectors that at present are covered by regulations that are dissimilar among the four member countries.

Liberalization under MERCOSUR

The decision that the complete liberalization of trade in services shall be brought about in a progressive manner is of great importance. Countries will be able to gradually fulfill the principles of Article IV (Obligations and General Disciplines for Market Access) and Article V (National Treatment) of the Protocol of Montevideo. This, together with the principle of positive lists and the obligation to conduct annual rounds of negotiations toward the complete liberalization of trade in services in ten years, makes it possible for even the smallest and most vulnerable countries to establish temporary restrictions on market access. They might do so in order to prepare their most sensitive or most deregulated sectors for a broader market.

To this discussion must be added the explicit provisions of paragraphs 3 and 4 of Article XIX (Negotiation of Specific Commitments) of the Protocol of Montevideo:

> In developing the Program of Liberalization, differences in the level of commitments adopted will be recognized, taking into consideration the specifics of certain sectors and respecting the objectives indicated in the next paragraph.
>
> The process of liberalization shall respect the right of each Member to regulate and to introduce new regulations in their territories in order to fulfill the objectives of national policies with respect to the services sector. Such regulations may regulate, *inter alia*, the areas of national treatment and market access, as long as they do not annul or impair the obligations derived from this Protocol and from the specific commitments.

Exceptions

The Protocol of Montevideo allows for the possibility of general exceptions and exceptions related to security that are very similar to the provisions contained in GATS. The only difference is that this category of measures must be communicated to the Trade Commission of MERCOSUR.

Annexes to the Protocol of Montevideo and Specific Commitments
(Decision C.M.C. No. 8/98)

Since the finalization of the Protocol of Montevideo in December 1997, the members resolved that the protocol would not be sent for legislative approval until the texts of the sectoral annexes and the lists of initial specific commitments had been completed, which was agreed in Buenos Aires in June of 1998 through Decision C.M.C. No.9/98.

Because the specifics of some services sectors require special treatment, MERCOSUR members felt it necessary to adopt annexes addressing financial services, land and water transport, air transport, and the movement of natural persons.

ANNEX ON FINANCIAL SERVICES. This annex contains provisions regarding "services supplied in the exercise of governmental authority of the member states," "transparency and the disclosure of confidential information," "prudential measures," and "harmonization."

ANNEX ON LAND AND WATER TRANSPORT SERVICES. This annex provides a temporary exemption from the application of the protocol to these services, given the prior existence of regional agreements in this area. The annex states specifically:

The provisions of the present Protocol will not apply on a temporary basis to each one of the bilateral agreements on transport in force or signed before the entry into force of this Protocol.

The Common Market Group during the third year after the entry into force of the present Protocol, and once a year afterwards, shall examine and weigh the progress achieved in pursuit of bringing the instruments referred to above in conformity with the objectives and principles of this Protocol.

ANNEX ON AIR TRANSPORT SERVICES. This annex applies to the measures that concern trade in regular and nonregular air transport services. A regional agreement existed before the Protocol of Montevideo, and for the moment it is preserved.

The annex says specifically:

With respect to regular and exploratory subregional air services on routes different from the regional routes that are effectively operated under the terms of the bilateral Agreements on Air Services maintained between the Member States, the provisions of the agreement on Sub-regional Air Services signed in Fortaleza, Brazil, on 17 December 1996 apply, complemented by the lists of commitments resulting from the Program of Liberalization.

The annex also sets a deadline for completing the necessary revisions and modifications:

The Common Market Group, in the first three years from the entry into force of this Protocol, shall revise the present Annex on the basis of proposals made by the air transport specialists who represent the four Member States, with a view to deciding on any necessary modifications, including those aspects relevant to the scope of application, in line with the principles and objectives of this Protocol.

ANNEX ON THE MOVEMENT OF NATURAL PERSONS SUPPLYING SERVICES. This annex is similar to that which exists under GATS, with an addition: "For the regulation of a specific situation of a work-related nature, which affects natural persons who are services suppliers of a Member, or natural persons of a Member employed by a services supplier of a Member, the laws of the place of execution of the services contract shall apply."

LISTS OF INITIAL SPECIFIC COMMITMENTS. MERCOSUR members made initial specific commitments in services that indicated a deepening of the lists of commitments that each country had previously established under the WTO, and from which each one of the four states already benefited by virtue of their membership in the multilateral organization. These new lists represent an emblematic first step upon which the members will have to build once the Protocol on Services enters into force, following its adoption by the legislatures of the four countries.

The commitments refer to various sectors, including financial services, communications, professional services, and others.

When the first list was drawn up in 1998, both Argentina and Uruguay included commitments on professional services only in the column on national treatment, starting from a horizontal commitment that indicates the restrictions of both countries with respect to access to their markets in this services sector.

Once the conditions set out in the horizontal commitment have been fulfilled, both countries will be in a position to offer national treatment. This was an unorthodox but expedient approach.

LAUNCHING THE FIRST ROUND OF NEGOTIATIONS. Although the Protocol of Montevideo has not been approved by the legislatures of at least three countries and is therefore not yet in force, the Common Market Group launched the first round of services negotiations at the Summit of Río de Janeiro in December 1998. The outcome of this round is to be incorporated into the internal statutes of the countries as soon as the protocol enters into force.

The Common Market Group also created the Services Group as an auxiliary organ in charge of carrying out the negotiations in this area. The Services Group will continue to exist until the liberalization process is complete. Resolution No. 73/98 sets out the composition, procedures, and instruments of the Services Group.

Service-Related Issues under MERCOSUR

MERCOSUR's agenda also includes other service-related issues, all of which apply horizontally to goods as well as to services. They are currently at different stages of the MERCOSUR negotiating process and either have already become or will become new regulations or protocols. The issues that are mentioned in the Protocol of Montevideo will also legally apply to services and these are described below.

The Defense of Competition

The four members of MERCOSUR approved the Protocol for the Defense of Competition covering monopolies and exclusive service suppliers on December 17, 1996 (Decision 18/96); covering goods and services, it is a norm that applies generically to monopolistic enterprises, abuse of power, and other monopolistic activities. The Committee for the Defense of Competition, like other issue-specific committees of MERCOSUR, was created as the entity that oversees consultations in this area.

Payments and Transfers and the Balance of Payments

The Protocol of Montevideo on Services contains no provisions covering payments and transfers or the balance of payments, since these are enshrined in the overall process of harmonization within MERCOSUR.

The issue of payments and transfers is followed by Subgroup No. 4 on financial matters, under the umbrella of the Common Market Group. In addition, the four MERCOSUR countries are members of the Agreement on Payments and Transfers of the Latin American Integration Association (LAIA).

General problems related to the balance of payments are dealt with in periodic meetings among economics ministers and central bank presidents. In addition, Decision C.M.C. No. 7/99 created the Group for the Coordination of

Macroeconomic Policies at the vice-ministerial level to monitor macroeconomic indicators and work out solutions to problems related to the balance of payments.

Investment

MERCOSUR members have drafted the Protocol of Colonia (Decision 11/93) to cover the promotion and mutual protection of investments among members. The Protocol of Buenos Aires (Decision 11/94) covers the promotion and protection of investments from states that are not members of MERCOSUR. These two investment protocols are still awaiting legislative endorsement in the countries of MERCOSUR and are not yet in force.

Consumer Protection

MERCOSUR has not yet concluded the negotiation of an instrument to address consumer protection. Discussions are taking place in Technical Committee No. 7 under the oversight of the Trade Commission of MERCOSUR. The rules to be developed will cover both goods and services.

Subsidies and State Monopolies

Issues related to subsidies and state monopolies are being negotiated at this writing early in the year 2000. Both topics are being addressed by Technical Committee No. 4 under the topic "public policies that distort competition."

Government Procurement

The topic of government procurement is being negotiated in the ad-hoc Group on Government Procurement under the oversight of the MERCOSUR Common Market Group, which received the mandate to elaborate a legal instrument that establishes common disciplines in this area, covering both goods and services.

Conclusions

Like all the commitments established under MERCOSUR, the Protocol of Montevideo for Trade in Services opens the way for a gradual liberalization of services trade within the region. The process has great potential, and if the political will continues to be maintained, it should result in the complete liberalization of trade for all service sectors at the end of ten years.

Because the protocol is based on the principle of gradualism, as much with respect to new regulations as to their gradual incorporation into the lists of commitments, it will allow countries to adapt to new circumstances as they arise.

The institutional structure of MERCOSUR, already elaborated for trade in goods, offers certainty to service operators through a dispute-settlement regime that favors consultations and conciliation among the parties, offers possibilities for establishing bilateral solutions to solve problems rapidly, and incorporates a process of arbitration for working out problems.

The recent set of rules adopted in relation to the defense of competition should also contribute to the stability of the system. In addition, efforts under way in the area of recognition of licenses and degrees should provide a vehicle for the creation of trade in services sectors that are heavily regulated.

MERCOSUR members, aware of the need to continue clarifying the application of the disciplines on trade in services, are making considerable effort to improve transparency and information-sharing about laws and regulations that apply to service sectors. Efforts are also being undertaken to enhance the clarity of the services nomenclature, while also taking account of progress in this area under the WTO. Similarly, it is expected that results will be available shortly in what concerns the more flexible treatment of horizontal commitments related to the movement of natural persons.

Finally, there is the possibility of linking the Services Group, an auxiliary organ of the Common Market Group, and the Investment Commission of the Working Subgroup No. 4, Financial Matters, which is also overseen by the Common Market Group. Such a collaboration would be premised on the link that exists between investment and mode 3 of service supply (in which one member supplies services through its commercial presence in the territory of another member), as defined by GATS and the Protocol of Montevideo.

Dealing with the issue of services in MERCOSUR is a dynamic process with enormous potential for promoting the growth of the service sector and improving its competitiveness within the four member economies.

CHAPTER EIGHT

Integration in Central America and the Liberalization of Services Trade

ALVARO R. SARMIENTO

THE CENTRAL AMERICAN COMMON MARKET (CACM) is the outcome of one of the first processes of economic integration in the Americas. In December 1960, the countries of the region signed the General Treaty of Central American Economic Integration, a legal instrument whose objective is the creation of a common market and a customs union among its members.[1]

In the first stages of the treaty negotiation process, trade in services was included exclusively from a sectoral perspective. Specifically, the 1960 agreement envisioned granting national treatment to the construction sector, in particular to the enterprises dedicated to building regional infrastructure.[2] At the same time, the agreement offered freedom of movement to the transit of goods that originated in the region and national treatment to the land-based road transport sector that carried those goods.

Later, in June 1962, the same countries signed the Convention on the Exercise of Post-Secondary Professions and the Recognition of Post-Secondary Studies. The instrument has been ratified and is currently in force in all of the countries of Central America except Nicaragua.

---

1. The members of the CACM are Guatemala, El Salvador, Honduras, Nicaragua, and Costa Rica.
2. "The Contracting Parties shall grant the same treatment as that accorded to national companies, to the companies of the other signatory States that engage in the construction of roadways, bridges, presses, irrigation systems, the distribution of electricity, housing and other works that contribute to the development of the Central American economic infrastructure." Article XVI of the General Treaty (www.sieca.org.gt).

After twenty-five years of ups and downs that affected regional integration and intraregional trade, including natural phenomena, oil crises, and civil wars, commercial exchanges within the region have been on the rebound since the second half of the 1980s, growing from U.S.$500 million in 1984 to almost U.S.$2,400 million in 1998.[3]

In the 1990s the Central American countries undertook a review of the status of the integration process. This review produced, among other things, the Protocol of Guatemala on August 17, 1995, which addresses, among other things, issues related to trade in services. Specifically, the protocol acknowledges the need to harmonize national laws in banking, insurance, and capital markets.[4] Following the same sectoral approach, the protocol reiterates the need to liberalize the transit of goods originating in Central American countries and to harmonize national policies that are relevant to public services and infrastructure.

The Participation of Central America in Multilateral Services Negotiations

The year 1995 represents an important departure point for the Central American region in the area of services. Since then, all the countries in the region have been members of the World Trade Organization (WTO) and have adopted commitments through the General Agreement on Trade in Services (GATS). Although they were "baptized" in the area of services during the Uruguay Round negotiations, under GATS the Central American countries undertook new commitments on market access and national treatment.

In particular, countries made commitments in areas including services supplied to companies (business services), communications services (value-added telecommunications services such as mobile telephony, private networks, and teleconferencing); financial services; air transport services (aircraft repair and maintenance); and tourism services. The Central American countries made the largest share of their market-access and national-treatment commitments in the area of tourism, specifically hotel services, lodging, tour guides, food services, travel agencies, and tour operators. Table 8-1 provides a summary of the GATS commitments by the CACM members.

Although the results of the Uruguay Round are considered a starting point in the multilateralization of trade in services, the additional GATS sectoral nego-

---

3. SIECA (1999).

4. "In the services sector, the Member States agree to harmonize, *inter alia*, their legislation in the areas of banking, financial, exchange and insurance entities." Article XXX of the Protocol of Guatemala to the General Treaty of Economic Integration (www.sieca.org.gt).

Table 8-1. *Specific Commitments of Central American Countries in GATS, by Sector*[a]

Sector[b]	Guatemala	Honduras	El Salvador	Nicaragua	Costa Rica
Business services	X	X	X	X	X
Communication services, telecommunications			X	X	
Education services					X
Environmental services			X		
Financial services	X	X	X	X	
Social and health services					X
Travel and tourism services	X	X	X	X	X
Transport services					
Road		X			
Air	X	X	X	X	
Rail				X	

Source: SIECA/USAID, PROALCA Project, Central America: Trade in Services, no. 1 (February 1998).

a. To conserve space, the specific commitments have been aggregated. Results of the negotiations on basic telecommunications services and financial services completed in 1997 are not included in the table.

b. The name of the sector or subsector is not necessarily the same as the one that was included in the official list.

tiations on financial services and basic telecommunications represented a true challenge for the countries of the region. On February 15, 1997, the negotiations on basic telecommunications at the WTO ended after three years. Sixty-nine countries that represent 90 percent of global telecommunications income adopted commitments to improve the liberalization of this important sector. From Central America, only El Salvador and Guatemala participated. El Salvador expanded the list of services from its original offer in the Uruguay Round (on mobile telephony) and increased its commitments on basic telephony. It introduced commitments for the transborder supply of telecommunications services. El Salvador has also adopted commitments for opening basic telecommunications services to competition in all segments of the market (local, long distance, and international), including voice telephony, the transmission of data, locators, and cellular telephony mobile services (see table 8-2).[5] Although Guatemala participated in the negotiations, the country was unable to sign the Fourth Protocol. The Fourth Protocol of GATS contains the schedules of specific commitments and a list of exceptions concerning basic telecommunications negotiations in the WTO. Nonetheless, Guatemala submitted new opening commitments on telecommunications, specifically concerning telephony,

5. SIECA/USAID, PROALCA Project, *Central America: Trade in Services*, no. 2 (1999).

Table 8-2. *Central American Commitments on Banking Services in the WTO Negotiations*[a]

Country	Activity[b]
El Salvador	Lending of all types
	Other financial services
Honduras	Acceptance of deposits and other repayable funds from the public
	Provision of credit except factoring
	Provision, transfer, and processing of financial information
Nicaragua	Acceptance of deposits and other repayable funds from the public
	Lending of all types
	All payment and monetary transfer services
	Guarantees
	Money market instruments
	Foreign exchange
Costa Rica	Acceptance of deposits and other repayable funds
	Lending of all types
	Provision, transfer, and processing of financial information
	Financial lease services with an option to purchase

Source: SIECA/USAID, PROALCA Project, Central America: Trade in Services, no. 2 (1999).

a. Because of space limitations, we indicate only some of the specific commitments. The official list of commitments may be viewed on the WTO website (www.wto.org).

b. The name of the activity is not necessarily the same as that registered in the official offers.

telex, fax, private networks, paging, mobile cellular telephony, and satellite services.[6]

In the financial services sector, on December 12, 1997, the second round of multilateral negotiations concluded with the participation of seventy members of the WTO. Together they represent 95 percent of global income in this sector. Four countries from the region (El Salvador, Honduras, Nicaragua, and Costa Rica) participated in this negotiation, and Costa Rica made its first offer in this sector. In banking, commitments were adopted for the provision of loans, the submission and transfer of financial information, and the acceptance of deposits and other funds. El Salvador eliminated the 50 percent limit on the participation of foreign capital in banks and financial companies. In insurance, Honduras guaranteed market access in all insurance subsectors. Honduras also made commitments in banking related to the acceptance of deposits and other reimbursable funds from the public.

Faced with a new round of multilateral negotiations beginning in 2000, the joint position on tourism of Honduras, El Salvador, and the Dominican Repub-

6. GATS/SC/36/Suppl.1/Rev. 1 of November 29, 1999.

lic, as set out before the 1999 WTO trade ministerial meeting in Seattle, reflects a common strategy to ensure that the tourism providers in these countries have effective market access to global distribution systems and electronic reservation systems. Their position paper calls for the elimination of significant obstacles to trade in tourism, in particular transportation and travel distribution, including wholesale services and group travel services.[7]

Free Trade Agreements with Third Countries

Another significant catalyst for including trade in services in the intraregional agenda was the negotiation and conclusion of free trade agreements with countries that are not members of the CACM. From 1995 through 1999, the Central American countries, together and bilaterally, negotiated and concluded NAFTA-type free trade agreements with Mexico, the Dominican Republic, and Chile.[8] Those agreements include separate chapters that cover transborder trade in services and the provision of services through commercial presence.[9] They were the first agreements by Central American countries to include the liberalization of services.

The first free trade agreement (FTA) signed by a Central American country was the agreement between Costa Rica and Mexico. It has had a decisive influence on the "mode" with which other Central American countries, specifically Chile and the Dominican Republic, subsequently approached their commercial negotiations in services. The legal texts on services and investment clearly follow the framework adopted by the North American Free Trade Agreement (NAFTA), incorporating the concepts of national treatment, most-favored-nation treatment, and nonobligatory local presence. This approach follows the negative list or "top-down" approach to liberalization, in contrast to the positive list or "bottom-up" framework adopted by GATS. However, the investment chapter for Central America and Chile is not NAFTA-inspired. Obliga-

7. The submission to the WTO on tourism by those three countries specifies in paragraph 3.1: "adequate measures will be adopted to prevent anti-competitive practices in the tourism cluster, including by suppliers of air transport services and travel distribution systems (including travel agencies, tour operators, tour wholesalers, computer reservation systems, and global distribution systems), either individually or jointly." It further specifies in paragraph 5.2 and 5.3: "each Member shall ensure that the tourism service suppliers of any other Member have access to Global Distribution Systems/Computerized Reservation Systems according to transparent, reasonable, and objective criteria, and on a non-discriminatory basis." See WT/GC/W/372. S/C/W/127, October 14, 1999, which can be found at www.wto.org.

8. Mexico–Costa Rica (1995); Mexico-Nicaragua (1998); Central America–Dominican Republic (1998); and Central America–Chile (1999).

9. Although this is true, one cannot affirm strictly that the investment chapter in these agreements is equivalent to the mode of service provision through commercial presence. But for convenience it is understood that this mode of service provision is covered by the investment chapter.

tions in investment will be those signed by each Central American country in its bilateral investment treaty with Chile

To date, there are not sufficient data to assess the commercial effects of these agreements on third parties. However, it is anticipated that the short- to medium-term effects will be minimal, since the liberalization provisions in the majority of cases and sectors only foresee the consolidation of the status quo, or the obligation to not increase discrimination in services trade.

The commercial negotiations by the members of the CACM with third countries have been handled differently in each case. The countries of the region decided to negotiate jointly with both the Dominican Republic and Chile. In the multilateral negotiations in the WTO and the Free Trade Area of the Americas (FTAA), the positions of the CACM members are coordinated. In contrast, the negotiations between Mexico and Costa Rica and between Nicaragua and Mexico were conducted bilaterally, and jointly in the case of Guatemala, Honduras, and El Salvador (the "Northern Triangle").

This flexible approach has allowed for different speeds of market opening. Nonetheless, it is important to analyze the potential effects of this approach in the medium and long term on the process of regional economic integration. The reality is that the countries of the CACM have adopted liberalizing commitments with third countries without having a regional agreement on services among themselves. The lack of a regional agreement will probably translate into a gap in the integration process, since the most-favored-nation clause in the commitments adopted with third countries could, one way or another, obligate the members to accord automatically to extraregional partners all the benefits and advantages that the CACM members might wish to grant to each other through a regional agreement. Thus, the CACM countries might well adopt a more reserved position when the time comes to make concrete progress on services liberalization at the regional level.

This panorama suggests that it is necessary to reconsider the order of priorities in Central America's commercial policy, since continuing to conclude these agreements with third countries before having a regional agreement may create inconsistencies and anomalies that could negatively affect the process of economic integration.

Putting Services on the Regional Agenda

The adherence of all the countries of the region to the WTO with the subsequent adoption of commitments in and through GATS, as well as the modernization of the instruments of regional economic integration, have provided the optimum environment for the introduction of this "new" issue on the Central American trade agenda. In particular, the Council of Ministers in charge of economic integration instructed the Secretaria de Integración Económica Centroamericana (SIECA) to incorporate trade in services into its work plan beginning in 1995. SIECA drew up a short-, medium-, and long-term strategic program, whose objective is to facilitate, for the countries of the region, the incorporation of trade in services into the subsystem of economic integration. This strategy was based on three concrete elements:

—The Central American Inventory of Measures That Affect Trade in Services. This inventory is a database of all the legal and administrative measures, sectoral or horizontal, that could affect and impede intraregional trade in services in the countries of the region.

—Monographs about the telecommunications, road transport, banking, and insurance sectors. Their purpose is to present a realistic description and analysis of the service sectors that could be of greatest importance to regional integration.

—The design and implementation of an information and training program for the public, regulatory, private, and academic sectors. The objective of this program is to create an awareness of the principal trends in the liberalization of trade in services in the WTO and the FTAA. Another important objective is to create a critical mass of civil servants and operators in the public, regulatory, and private sectors who can support the processes of negotiation and commercial opening.

One of the principal obstacles to negotiation and trade liberalization in services is the gap between the complex legal instruments in these areas and the significance that they have in commercial and operational terms for the business people and the regulators who actually engage in such trade. For this reason, since 1996, SIECA has organized local and regional meetings with important service providers from the banking, insurance, professional services, transport, and telecommunications sectors to share the principal results of multilateral, bilateral, and regional negotiations from a business perspective and to prepare these components of society for a continuous process of commercial opening. Likewise, SIECA organized workshops with the technical committees of the Central American Monetary Council and the Regional Technical Commission on Telecommunications to discuss the liberalization of the financial and telecommunications sectors and how regional forums could facilitate the process of liberalization.

A Future Regional Agreement on Trade in Services?

During 1999 the Central American countries made significant progress in the design of a Central American agreement on trade in services and investment, which could, if finalized, be the first regional instrument to liberalize trade in services. Although the negotiations have not yet been concluded, it is anticipated that the governments in the region will follow the legal framework of the free trade agreements they previously adopted with Mexico, the Dominican Republic, and Chile—that is, a NAFTA-style framework using negative lists as the basis for liberalization. This means providing nondiscriminatory national treatment to the services and providers of services in the region, listing the reservations to this treatment in the sectors that require them, and setting a deadline for the elimination of those reservations. It is anticipated that the agreement will include specific provisions for the area of professional services, a sector with extensive commercial potential.

Commercial Practice: The Underlying Basis for a Regional Agreement

Though the formal inclusion of trade in services within the CACM will be a long process, commerce and trade in the service sector of the economies of the region have existed for several years and, as may be expected, are ahead of the negotiation and signing of trade agreements. The following are selected examples of services integration "in practice" in the region:

—Since 1995, Salvadoran and Guatemalan financial groups have merged in order to deal with the process of liberalization and, more generally, globalization.

—Salvadoran business groups have concluded investments in the financial and hotel sectors in Costa Rica and Honduras.

—Large Costa Rican, Salvadoran, and Guatemalan retail distribution corporations have invested in Honduras and Nicaragua in an attempt to position themselves in this service sector.

—The 1999 privatization of the Empresa Telefónica de Guatemala (TELGUA) includes the participation of investors from Honduras and El Salvador.

—In the air transport sector, the Salvadoran enterprise Transportes Aéreos Centroamericanos (TACA) acquired the other flag carriers, creating one of the most important airlines in Latin America.

—One of the largest credit card companies in the region belongs to a financial group from Nicaragua, which provides services in the five countries of the CACM.

—A stock exchange house from Nicaragua has branches throughout the region.

—Several banks offer the "Central American Cheque," with which it is possible to make payments in any of the five member countries' currencies using one account and checkbook.

Given that this business dynamic has come about without the support or the tutelage of a "regional agreement on trade in services and investment," it would be worthwhile to ask the following question: What would have been the commercial, financial, wealth-generating, and employment effects in Central America had a regional instrument provided a legal framework for the liberalization of trade in services several years ago? The Central American region should seriously consider relying on a legal instrument that would be coherent with both the formal and the informal processes of economic integration. The primary objective of trade agreements is of course to provide conditions that spur greater commercial exchanges and thereby foster the economic and social development of their members.

Services not only constitute the backbone of international trade, by serving as direct support for the production of goods (financial services, banking, insurance, transport, and telecommunications); they also are one of the fundamental variables in the competitiveness of nations. The Central American presidents have committed themselves to improving the competitiveness of the region and sustainable development through a project that utilizes the concept of "industry clusters."[10] One of the main outcomes of this work undertaken has been the identification of clusters that hold the greatest competitive potential for the Central American economy: tourism, agribusiness, textiles and apparel, and electronic services. These economic sectors were chosen as the most likely catalysts and engines of growth for enhancing the region's participation in the global markets.

Nevertheless, developing clusters in the region without facilitating the free and nondiscriminatory exchange of services could prove to be almost impossible. The tourism and agribusiness clusters are particularly dependent on services (efficient telecommunications and access to information distribution systems in tourism; research services, genetics, certified laboratories, and the like in agribusiness). Developing separate research and development structures in each Central American country in order to compete internationally in agribusiness would seem to be countereconomic. Instead, the liberalization of

---

10. "Industry clusters" is a concept developed by Michael Porter. The Central American presidents committed themselves to this project in the Resolution of the Fifteenth Summit of Central American Presidents, Guacimo, Costa Rica, 1994.

trade in services—and specifically professional and business services—is likely to have a more significant impact on the goal to convert Central America into a highly competitive region.

The Consolidation of the Status Quo in Central America

Assuming that the legal instrument being designed and implemented is useful, one would expect new intraregional trade and investment to be created. But views on this topic vary. The application in Central America of a legal instrument that was designed to be implemented by parties whose economies are asymmetric (such as those of Mexico and the United States) may not be the best choice. In theory, then, setting the consolidation of the status quo as a goal could have no effect on trade.

This discussion should not be interpreted as taking sides in the "classical" and endless dilemma regarding the methods of liberalization in services and whether this should be accomplished through negative or positive lists.[11] Rather, I recommend that the CACM introduce specific commitments to substantially liberalize trade in services and investment before external factors such as negotiations in the FTAA or with third countries make the framework for preserving and strengthening a common market obsolete. The time factor is very important. Without reasonable and immediate deadlines for offering services and service providers national treatment and full access to markets, all the efforts in this area could be rendered useless.

Conclusions

—The process of economic integration in Central America will be difficult to sustain without the immediate incorporation of a legal instrument covering both trade in services and investment.

—The consolidation of the status quo should not become the objective of the negotiation. Independently of the model that a Central American agreement on trade in services and investment should follow, countries will need to agree on concrete commitments for trade liberalization.

—The incorporation of service regulators and business entities within the negotiating process is critical and must be supported by training programs and the distribution of information.

11. There are two main approaches to the process of liberalization in trade in services: the positive list approach, used in GATS, where the commitments refer to specific sectors to be liberalized and the areas in which there are no commitments are not liberalized; and the negative list approach, where the members to the agreement commit themselves to liberalize all the sectors except those included on a list of reserved sectors.

—The multilateral services negotiations under the WTO, as well as those of the FTAA, must be viewed as a clear opportunity to obtain concrete benefits in all sectors that will facilitate the development of competitive industry clusters as identified by the regional program on competitiveness in Central America.

References

Foreign Trade Ministry of Costa Rica. *Free Trade Area between the Central American Governments and the Government of Chile (Tratado de Libre Comercio entre los Gobiernos de Centroamérica y el Gobierno de la República de Chile).* Part IV. Costa Rica.

———. *Free Trade Agreement between the Government of the Republic of Costa Rica and the Government of Mexico (Tratado de Libre Comercio entre el Gobierno de la República de Costa Rica y el Gobierno de los Estados Unidos Mexicanos).* Chapters IX, X, and XIII. Costa Rica.

———. *Free Trade Area between the Central American Governments and the Government of the Dominican Republic (Tratado de Libre Comercio entre los Gobiernos Centroamericanos y el Gobierno de la República Dominicana).* Chapters IX, X, and XI. Costa Rica.

INCAE/Harvard University. 1998. "Central America in the 21st Century: An Agenda for Competitiveness and Sustainable Development." Working Paper. Costa Rica.

Mattoo, Aaditya. 1997. "National Treatment in the GATS: Corner-Stone or Pandora's Box?" *Journal of World Trade* 31, no. 1.

Secretaria de Integración Economía Centroamericana (SIECA). 1999. *Centroamérica el Comercio de Servicios,* Boletín no. 2.

———. 1999. *General Agreement of Economic Integration in Central America (Tratado General de Integración Económica Centroamericana).* Guatemala.

———. 1999. *Protocol to the General Agreement of Economic Integration in Central America (Protocol of Guatemala) (Protocolo al Tratado General de Integración Económica Centroamericana (Protocolo de Guatemala).* Guatemala.

———. 1998. *Centroamérica el Comercio de Servicios,* Boletín no. 1.

———. 1997. *El Comercio de servicios, enfoque para su liberalización en el mercado común centroamericano en los sectores bancario, telecomunicaciones, transporte terrestre y seguros.* Guatemala.

———. 1994. The XV Summit of Central American Presidents. Guácimo, Limón, Costa Rica (August 20).

———. 1987. *Centroamérica Inventario de Medidas que afectan el Comercio de Servicios.* Guatemala.

———. 1999. *Statistical Bulletin,* no. 7.3 (June).

Stephenson, Sherry M., and Francisco Prieto. 1999. "Multilateral and Regional Liberalization of Trade in Services." In Miguel Rodriguez Mendoza, Patrick Low, and Barbara Kotschwar, eds., *Trade Rules in the Making.* Brookings.

World Trade Organization. 1994. "General Agreement on Trade in Services." *Uruguay Round Legal Texts.* Geneva, Switzerland (April).

CHAPTER NINE

Andean Community Decision 439 on Services Trade

MARÍA ESPERANZA DANGOND

IN PURSUING THE GENERAL OBJECTIVE of promoting balanced and harmonious economic development, the Andean integration process has gone through several stages since the 1969 Cartagena Agreement. Over the years, the members of the Andean Community (Bolivia, Colombia, Ecuador, Peru, and Venezuela) have adjusted the content and mechanisms of the Cartagena Agreement in an attempt to facilitate their participation in the complex world of international economic relations.[1]

Thus the concept of inward-looking integration that dominated the group a few years ago has given way to a new scheme of open regionalism, which allows countries to rely on an inward-looking subregional integration process. Recognition by member governments that the Andean Community is an important tool to this end has strengthened the integration process and helped the community achieve and even exceed some of the objectives set forth in the 1969 Cartagena Agreement.

The five nations that constitute the Andean Community (which together have a population of more than 105 million people in a territory of 4.5 million square kilometers and a gross domestic product [GDP] of U.S.$285 million) multiplied their intraregional exports forty-eight times over between 1970 and 1998 (from U.S.$111 million to U.S.$5,333 million). A common external tariff (CET)

---

1. The Andean Group, founded by the Cartagena Agreement in 1967, metamorphosed into the Andean Community through the signing of the Trujillo Protocol in June 1997.

has been in force since February 1, 1995.[2] Foreign investment grew from U.S.$1,200 million in 1990 to U.S.$10,610 million in 1998. Within the community, all transportation services have been liberalized.

The Andean process seeks to transcend the purely economic and trade aspects of integration. The establishment of a Common Andean Market by 2005 is a goal to which all respective presidents have stated their commitment. To achieve the goals of Andean integration, the Cartagena Agreement through the Trujillo Protocol calls for developing an advanced liberalization program; harmonizing economic and social policies; coordinating national legislation in those areas where the process so requires; and taking action in the fields of services, physical and border integration, science, technology, and social development.

As part of the integration process there are ongoing efforts to harmonize economic tools and policies, such as rules to prevent and curb distortions in, among other things, competition, determination of origin, technical and sanitary standards, and customs valuation. Common foreign investment and intellectual property regimes are under discussion.

At successive summits, the Andean presidents have stressed the importance of defining the criteria that will bring about a closer coordination of macroeconomic policies, in particular monetary, exchange, tax, and fiscal deficit policies.[3] In addition, the Andean Council of Ministers of Foreign Affairs has adopted guidelines for a common foreign policy aimed at providing Andean Community members with a stronger international presence and fostering rapprochement with other integration processes in Latin America and the Caribbean.

Ministers and national authorities for science and technology have pledged to allocate, as soon as possible, 1.5 percent of the GDP in each member country to the development of science, technology, and innovation. Furthermore, they have set out an Andean work program that includes initiatives on the implementation and deepening of cooperation among scientific, research, and technological development centers in the region and with other countries.

Before 1998, the Andean countries had adopted measures to liberalize several specific service sectors. Generally, these measures are related to the development of trade in goods, and most target the area of transport. They include the elimination of restrictions on shipping, the introduction of an "open-skies"

---

2. Peru does not yet apply the CET; Bolivia and Ecuador have been granted special treatment.

3. To that end, the Advisory Committee, which consists of representatives of the Ministries of Finance, central banks, and economic planning bodies, has agreed to intensify its efforts to harmonize policies in the areas of major macroeconomic variables; price stability and equilibrium; fiscal policy; banking regulation; accounting and stock exchange standards; taxation; and investment.

policy for air transport, freedom of transit on the Andean road system for international overland transport, and open border-crossing points.

In 1998 the Tenth Council of Andean Presidents, held in Guayaquil, Ecuador, reiterated the importance of free trade in services and referred to the establishment of a market for the free movement of services no later than 2005. Decision 439 was subsequently adopted by the Andean Community Commission on June 11, 1998, to regulate the services liberalization process for the region.

The Importance of Services Trade in the Andean Region

In the Andean Community, the services sector has consistently made up, on average, over 50 percent of the GDP for each of the countries and for the region as a whole. Table 9-1 shows that trade in services between the Andean Community and the rest of the world reached U.S.$39 billion in 1997, with U.S.$13 billion for services exports and U.S.$26 billion for services imports. This figure represented 13.5 percent of regional GDP that year. Services exports of the Andean Community in 1997 amounted to 26 percent of goods exports by all member countries, and services imports equaled 63 percent of goods imports.

Commercial services exports, which totaled 68 percent of all services exports in 1997, increased at an average annual rate of 10 percent between 1992 and 1997. In fact, services exports almost doubled after 1994, reaching U.S.$8,502 million in 1997. Imports of commercial services showed a similar trend during the same period, almost doubling between 1990 and 1997 (to reach U.S.$13,274 million). Among the four categories of commercial services shown in table 9-2 (transport, telecommunications, travel, and other services), telecommunication services show a surplus trade balance; transport and other services show a net deficit and a widening gap. The net trade balance for tourism has been improving.

Decision 439 on Services

On June 11, 1998, the Andean Community Commission adopted Decision 439, establishing the general framework of principles and rules for the liberalization of trade in services in the Andean Community region. Member countries now have an effective framework in place for moving toward the creation of an Andean Common Market for services. Decision 439 has been incorporated into domestic legislation of the Andean countries under conditions of direct application and supranationality, pursuant to the community legal system.

Table 9-1. *Ratio of Services to GDP for the Andean Community, 1993–98*
Percent

Country	1993	1994	1995	1996	1997	1998
Bolivia	56.3	56.6	55.1	53.5	54.3	53.9
Colombia	51.3	52.4	53.2	54.8	54.0	54.4
Ecuador	50.3	45.7	46.5	51.2	48.8	50.0
Peru	57.2	55.0	54.9	50.0	52.4	51.2
Venezuela	55.5	55.7	57.7	50.8	57.1	63.2

Source: General Secretariat of the Andean Community.

Based upon the general objectives of progressively liberalizing regional trade in services in order to create an Andean common market for services and strengthening and diversifying the services market, Decision 439 provides for the elimination of restrictive measures within the region and the harmonization of national policies where appropriate. Decision 439 defines the modes of supplying services as GATS does: (1) cross-border supply, from the territory of one member country to the territory of another; (2) through consumption abroad, or the supply of services in the territory of one member country to the consumer of another member country; (c) through commercial presence, or the supply of services through the establishment of the service provider of a member country in the territory of another member country; and (d) through movement of natural persons, or the supply of services by natural persons of a member country in the territory of another member country.

The Andean Agreement on Services applies to all service sectors and all four modes of supply, except services provided in compliance with government powers, service procurement by government entities or public bodies of member countries, and air transport services. For the latter, the agreement defines separate specific treatment, including the elimination of discrimination. The question of service procurement by government bodies and official entities is being studied and is to be provided for in a Decision to be adopted no later than January 1, 2002. Should this Decision not be adopted by then, the national-treatment principle set forth in Decision 439 for government purchase of services is expected to enter into force immediately. The Andean countries have made progress in liberalizing intraregional air transport and have implemented an open-skies policy (see discussion in the next section).

Decision 439 incorporates the principles of market access and national treatment upon which the Andean liberalization process has been defined. It also includes the general principles of most-favored-nation treatment and transparency, as well as the commitment to consolidate the status quo. Criteria for the recognition of titles, licenses, and authorizations to provide services will be

Table 9-2. *Balance of Commercial Services Trade in the Andean Community,*
1990–97
Millions of dollars

Sector	1990	1991	1992	1993	1994	1995	1996	1997
Transportation	−947	−1,655	−1,745	−1,615	−1,305	−1,646	−1,552	−2,007
Communications	178	222	272	288	291	324	318	246
Travel	−654	−801	−1,023	−1,497	−990	−652	−978	−763
Other	−849	−1,043	−1,482	−1,189	−1,420	−1,753	−1,838	−2,248

Source: General Secretariat of the Andean Community.

developed through a future decision to be adopted by the Andean Community
Commission. Work is also under way to allow the free movement and temporary presence of service providers and their employees pursuant to whatever
decision is made by the Andean Council of Foreign Ministers in this matter.
The principles and commitments mentioned above apply to measures implemented by any member country affecting trade in services, regardless of whether
such measures are implemented at the national or subnational level.

Article 6 of Decision 439 requires each member to provide market access to
services and service providers of other member countries through any of the
four modes of supply. Article 8 states that each member is to accord services
and service providers of other members treatment that is no less favorable than
that accorded to their own like services and service providers.

On the issue of most-favored-nation treatment, Decision 439 establishes that
each member shall provide services and service providers of other members
with treatment that is no less favorable than that accorded to like services and
service providers of any other country, whether or not it is a member of the
Andean Community. This principle applies generally, immediately, and unconditionally. The only exemption is for advantages provided to neighboring
countries in contiguous border areas, with a view to facilitating the exchange of
services that are produced and used locally.

The principle of transparency provides for timely disclosure and notification of any general measure affecting trade in services to the Andean Community General Secretariat.

A commitment to consolidate the status quo is set out in Article 10, whereby
members agree not to increase the degree of inconsistency between measures
in force as of June 17, 1998 (the date of entry into force of Decision 439) and
market-access and national-treatment commitments.

Similar to provisions contained in the Cartagena Agreement with respect to
trade in goods, Decision 439 provides for exceptions to the liberalization of
trade in services—for example, to protect morality or preserve public order and

to protect the life or health of people, animals, and plants. Such measures, however, are to be applied in compliance with the objective they pursue; they shall not be used to protect national services or service providers or be implemented in such a way that they become an unnecessary barrier to regional trade in services or a tool to discriminate against any Andean Community services or service provider in favor of another Andean or non–Andean Community member country.

The liberalization process as provided for in the Andean Decision is to be based upon an inventory of the domestic measures of each member country that affect the principles of market access and national treatment. Such an inventory is to be incorporated into the community legal system no later than July 1, 2000. The measures listed in the inventory are to be phased out through yearly rounds of negotiations to be held until the end of the process in the year 2005, at which time all the measures should be eliminated.

The Andean agreement also provides for deepening the liberalization and harmonization of regulations in specific service sectors. To this end, Article 15 stipulates that, based on studies conducted by the General Secretariat, the Andean Community Commission shall adopt relevant sectoral decisions. The agreement also establishes that when two or more members agree to streamline or deepen the liberalization of specific service sectors or subsectors, the resulting benefits shall be extended immediately and unconditionally to other countries whose regulation is at a similar level and to the rest of the Andean Community members through negotiations.

Chapter VI (Complementary Issues) of Decision 439 establishes general measures providing for the development of the service sector in member countries in compliance with their domestic regulations until a community regulation is adopted.

In the area of competition, the agreement calls for members to prevent and penalize competition-distorting practices, in particular the abuse of a dominant position in the services market. The competition policy instrument set out in Decision 285 also applies to services. In addition, a draft decision is being studied to promote free competition in trade in goods and services in the region. It is foreseen that members will ensure that the measures implemented to promote and foster trade in services do not undermine competition within the regional market. The implementation of a community regime covering incentives to trade in services is also expected.

In order to ensure effective liberalization of trade in services in the region, Decision 439 prevents members from imposing restrictions to international transfers that may affect the fulfillment of commitments, except for those restrictions that are necessary to counter balance-of-payments difficulties. In the case of external financial or balance-of-payments difficulties or threats thereof, a member is entitled to use measures applied to third countries to handle intraregional services trade as well. These measures must be necessary, nondiscriminatory, transitional, and consistent with the Articles of Agreement of the International Monetary Fund (IMF) and shall be previously authorized by the General Secretariat; or, in case of an emergency, the Secretariat must be notified of the special measures within five days following their adoption. Should this happen, the decision creates an administrative procedure that allows the General Secretariat to determine the merits of the measures adopted by a member country.

Andean Decision 439 provides for special treatment for Bolivia and Ecuador. This principle stems from the Cartagena Agreement and, in the case of services, provides these two countries with more time and temporary exemptions to comply with their obligations as agreed upon during the negotiations.

In the area of rules of origin, Decision 439 provides that, to be entitled to the benefits resulting from liberalization, the services provider must be a natural person who is a permanent resident of any member, or a company that has been incorporated or is authorized or domiciled pursuant to the domestic legislation and that conducts substantial business in the territory of any member or by means of cross-border supply through direct provision from the territory of any of the members. Article 24 of this Decision provides for the participation of the General Secretariat in determining the origin of a service provider about whose residency or incorporation a member country may harbor doubts.

Sectoral Decisions on Services

Article 5 requires that service sectors and subsectors governed by decisions in force at the time Decision 439, or any amendment thereof, enters into force shall be governed by such decisions and be supplemented by Decision 439. This includes sectoral decisions adopted with a view to strengthening or harmonizing rules in service sectors or subsectors (Article 15).

When Decision 439 was adopted in 1998, a number of sectoral decisions on services were already in force. Most were in the area of transport, elaborated in response to a substantial increase in intraregional trade in goods, which prompted member countries to develop rules to govern certain service sectors. Andean agreements for the transport sector have been developed since 1972, when Decision 56 established free transit in order to permit international overland transport to be conducted reciprocally by authorized agents. The Andean legal framework later adopted rules for the regulation of air cargo and shipping services, tourism, and telecommunications.

After Decision 439 was adopted, the Andean Community Commission is-sued Decisions 462 and 463 on telecommunications and tourism, respectively. These decisions updated previous efforts and provided for sectoral develop-ment programs. The Andean Community is currently studying a number of draft community Decisions regarding financial services and recognition of pro-fessional titles, authorizations, and licenses that may apply to the provision of services in the member countries.

Overland Transport

In 1997 the Andean Community Commission adopted Decisions 398 and 399 on international overland transportation of people and freight, with a view to creating conditions to facilitate such services among members. These Deci-sions included such basic principles as freedom of operation, market access, national treatment, transparency, nondiscrimination, equal legal treatment, free competition, and most-favored-nation treatment. They apply to international overland transport conducted on the roads and at the border-crossing points that make up the main Andean Road System; members may also authorize additional border-crossing points.

The supply of international overland transport services, as well as the ve-hicles in an operator's fleet, must be previously authorized both by the country of origin and by the country where the service is to be provided. With respect to passenger transportation, Decision 398 calls for the relevant authorities to agree on routes, frequencies, and itineraries.

Shipping

With a view to improving, expanding, and modernizing infrastructure ca-pacity and the supply of transport services and supporting the improvement of trade competitiveness, Decision 288 was adopted in March 1991 to eliminate freight reserve requirements. Free access was established for freight originat-ing and remaining in the region to be transported on ships owned, chartered, or operated by shipping companies from member countries or third countries. As a result of this decision, members were required to eliminate any restrictions on chartered vessels, the allocation of routes within the region, and the replace-ment of systems to establish or authorize freight with simple tariff registration procedures. Access to regional cargo that is transported by shipping companies from a country or a group of countries outside the region is subject to the prin-ciple of reciprocity.

Decision 314, passed in February 1992, comprises policies to develop the merchant marine in member countries whose goal is to harmonize shipping policies and improve the competitiveness of this sector.

Air Transport

Decision 297, adopted by the Andean Community Commission in 1991, was an important milestone in the liberalization of intraregional air transport. This Decision allows for the implementation of a twofold open-skies policy. First, it provides for the free exercise of the third, fourth, and fifth freedoms of the air in scheduled combined flights for passengers, cargo, and mail (or exclusively for passenger or cargo flights), under the general principle of multiple designation.[4] Second, in the case of nonscheduled services for passengers, cargo, and mail from the region, it provides for automatic authorization by national entities to national companies from member countries. The concepts of scheduled and nonscheduled flights were defined in Decision 360 of 1994 in compliance with the guidelines of the International Civil Aviation Organization (ICAO).

As for air transport between countries in the region and third countries, since 1992, Decision 360 has required members to grant fifth freedom air traffic rights for scheduled flights, as agreed to in bilateral and multilateral negotiations and subject to the principles of equity and adequate compensation.

Through the Andean Air Transport Policy, members agreed that all operating permits, bilateral agreements, and other administrative procedures in force among them shall abide by the principles of unrestricted intraregional trade provided that they are in the community's interest and promote fair competition; such principles aim to ensure high-quality and efficient international air transport services.

Multimodal Transport

Andean Community regulations also govern multimodal transport—that is, the transportation of goods from one location to another by at least two differ-

---

4. Decision 297 defines freedoms as follows.

—First freedom: the right to fly through the territory of another country without landing.

—Second freedom: the right to land in another country for noncommercial purposes.

—Third freedom: the right to, in another country, disembark passengers and unload cargo and mail that had embarked and been loaded in the territory of the country of which the carrier is a national.

—Fourth freedom: the right to, in a country, embark passengers and load cargo and mail that are to be flown to the territory of the country of which the carrier is a national.

—Fifth freedom: the right to, in a country other than that of which the carrier is a national, embark passengers and load cargo and mail that are to be flown to another country in the subregion or outside it, which is also not the country of which the carrier is a national.

ent modes and pursuant to a single transportation contract. Decisions 331 and 393 define the responsibilities, rights, and obligations of the multimodal transport agent and promote the development of multimodal transport throughout the region.

Telecommunications

With respect to telecommunications, Decision 395 establishes general conditions for commercial use of the orbit-spectrum resource by authorized companies. Such conditions have to do with the establishment, operation, and management of Andean satellite systems. Decision 429 authorizes the Empresa Multinacional Andina (ANDESAT S.A.) to use the orbit-spectrum resource corresponding to the Simón Bolívar Satellite System for commercial purposes. It is scheduled to begin operations in 2002.

The Andean Community Commission adopted Decision 462 in May 1999, which provides a schedule for the liberalization of all telecommunications service sectors and modes of supply (except radio and television broadcasting), in accordance with the principles identified in Decision 439. The liberalization process is to be organized in two stages. Beginning on January 1, 2000, restrictions imposed on all telecommunications services were eliminated, except for those on basic local telephony, national and international long-distance calls, and ground mobile telephony. Beginning on January 1, 2002, liberalization will be extended to all other telecommunications services (again, except for radio and television broadcasting). Bolivia and Ecuador are to follow a special schedule, pursuant to the treatment accorded to these two countries in the Cartagena Agreement as a whole and Decision 439 in particular. According to this schedule, Bolivia will include its data-carrying and transmission packet switching services by November 27, 2001, and Ecuador will later determine and communicate the date on which it will liberalize trade in local telephony, national and international long-distance calls, and data-carrying services, including the lease of wireless lines and circuits, telegraph, and telex.

Decision 462 also contains provisions regarding, among other issues, interconnection rules, use of public telecommunications networks and services, and recognition of enabling titles and authorizations to provide services among member countries.

Tourism

Decision 463, adopted by the Andean Community Commission in May 1999, establishes a system to develop and integrate the Andean region in the area of tourism. The regime applies to all tourist services and covers three aspects: liberalization and harmonization of measures implemented by member countries; identification and implementation of tourist development programs of community interest; and facilitation measures for tourists. As for liberalization, the regulation seeks to eliminate all measures that are not consistent with the principles of national treatment and market access, under the general principles and commitments set forth in Decision 439.

The decision provides for the implementation of permanent programs, projects, and actions for tourism promotion and investment, as well as for technical, economic, social, and environmental cooperation. Programs and projects are to be identified by the respective tourism authorities in the member countries and are to be based upon economic, commercial, social, and environmental criteria. Priority is to be given to projects aimed at the development of intraregional tourism and tourism in border areas. The Decision also calls for the elimination of barriers to tourism by no later than December 31, 2002.

Conclusions

The Andean framework for the liberalization of regional trade in services, as set out in Decision 439, is an ambitious one. Although the regulatory framework of the Andean Community for the liberalization of trade in services is based on the same principles as those included in other mutilateral and regional agreements (transparency, nondiscrimination, most-favored-nation treatment, and national treatment), its ultimate goal is the complete liberalization of trade in services in the Andean region and the creation of a Common Market among members. Andean member countries have also committed themselves to harmonize their regulatory policies in all relevant services sectors.

While recognizing that Article V (Economic Integration) of the WTO General Agreement on Trade in Services (GATS) lacks clarity in the formulation of a number of its requirements, the Andean statute would appear to have no problem meeting the conditions set forth in this article through the far-reaching objectives for services liberalization it contains.

In order for the integration process to achieve the goals set forth in the Andean Community's Decision on the liberalization of trade in services, the inventory of measures affecting trade in services must be completed as stipulated so that it can be used as a basis for gradually eliminating all measures that restrict trade in services. Equally important is the parallel process of developing a competitive services market through the promotion of competition rules and an adequate regulatory infrastructure.

Appendix 9A. *Services-Related Decisions of the Andean Community*

Decision	Description
Decision 277	Overland transport; Andean Road System
Decision 288	Shipping; freedom of access for cargo originating in and bound for the subregion
Decision 290	Overland transport; Andean third-party insurance policy for the agent
Decision 297	Air transport; integration regime
Decision 314	Shipping; freedom of access for shipped freight and policies to develop the Andean Group merchant marine
Decision 320	Air transport; multiple designation
Decision 331	Multimodal transport
Decision 360	Air transport; amendment to Decision 297
Decision 361	Air transport; amendment to Decision 320
Decision 390	Shipping; amendment to Decision 314, "Freedom of access for shipped freight and policies to develop the Andean Group merchant marine"
Decision 393	Multimodal transport; amendment to Decision 331
Decision 395	Telecommunications; commercial use of the orbit-spectrum resource, operation and management of satellite systems by Andean companies
Decision 398	Overland transport; international ground passenger transportation
Decision 399	Overland transport; international ground transportation of goods
Decision 429	Telecommunications; Andean Community authorization to the Empresa Sistema Satelital Andino Simón Bolívar
Decision 439	General Framework of Principles and Measures to Liberalize Trade in Services in the Andean Community
Decision 462	Telecommunications; integration and liberalization of trade in telecommunications services in the Andean Community
Decision 463	Tourism; development and integration of tourism in the Andean Community
Decision 467	Overland transport; Regime of Infringements and Penalties in International Ground Transportation of Goods

CHAPTER TEN

Services in the Caribbean: Protocol II on Establishment, Services, and Capital

PAMELA COKE HAMILTON

CARIBBEAN COMMUNITY AND COMMON MARKET (CARICOM) countries, recognizing the vast opportunities for expansion of services trade in the rapidly changing environment of the past decade, have undertaken a comprehensive liberalization of intra-CARICOM trade in services through the signing and provisional application of Protocol II in 1998.[1]

Interest in the liberalization and expansion of services trade also arises from the fact that the services sector has played a dominant role in the economies of most CARICOM countries over the past thirty years, contributing in particular to gross domestic product (GDP), employment, and the export earnings of member states. In 1997 services constituted 57 percent of the GDP for Jamaica and 52 percent for Trinidad and Tobago, whose major export earnings had previously been goods, bauxite and crude oil, respectively. These figures, when compared with the world average of 61 percent, reflect the significance of this sector to the economies of these countries. In some countries of the Organiza-

The views expressed in this paper are solely those of the author and do not represent the views of the Caribbean Regional Negotiating Machinery (RNM) or the member states of CARICOM.

1. CARICOM comprises the fourteen Caribbean countries, namely Antigua and Barbuda, the Bahamas, Barbados, Belize, Dominica, Grenada, Guyana, Haiti, Jamaica, St. Kitts and Nevis, St. Lucia, St. Vincent and the Grenadines, Republic of Suriname, and Trinidad and Tobago. The Bahamas does not participate in the common market, and Haiti is not yet a full member.

tion of Eastern Caribbean States (OECS) the contribution of services is estimated to exceed 60 percent of GDP.[2]

The services sector has also made significant contributions to the foreign exchange earnings within CARICOM countries. Table 10-1 provides an overview of the foreign exchange earnings by goods and services in selected Caribbean countries.

The increasing importance of the services sector in the Caribbean is largely attributable to the enormous growth in tourism since 1995 (see table 10-2). The Bahamas, Haiti, Jamaica, and Trinidad and Tobago have seen a steady increase in foreign exchange earnings from services, with services trade outstripping merchandise trade for the first time in Jamaica in 1997. Until then, bauxite constituted Jamaica's single largest export earner; however earnings from tourism now surpass export earnings from that sector.[3]

The contribution of the services sector to employment in the Caribbean region has been very significant, particularly for women. This fact is extremely important given the number of female–headed households in the region. The services sector has surpassed industry and agriculture to provide the majority of employment opportunities in CARICOM countries. The main sources of employment are the tourism sector, telecommunications and data-processing, finance and insurance, and entertainment.

Background to Protocol II

In 1989 at the Tenth Meeting of the Conference of Heads of Government of the region, the heads of government of the CARICOM countries reiterated their commitment to achieving regional unity. This commitment was enshrined in the Declaration of Grand Anse in which CARICOM member states agreed to move beyond a common market toward a deeper level of economic integration, which would result in the creation of the CARICOM Single Market and Economy (CSM&E). The most important components of the CSM&E as posited are the free movement of all factors of production, including goods, services, capital, and skilled labor, as well as the harmonization of monetary policies throughout the region.

The creation of this seamless single economic space required, however, the amendment of the Treaty of Chaguaramas, which established the legal exist-

2. The OECS members are Antigua and Barbuda, Dominica, Grenada, St. Kitts and Nevis, St. Lucia, and St. Vincent and the Grenadines.
3. In the first half of 1999 Jamaica earned U.S.$758.5 million from services exports, of which tourism accounted for U.S.$503.5 million, or 66 percent of foreign exchange earnings in the services sector. In addition the sector accounted for 76.9 percent of GDP in 1998.

Table 10-1. *Foreign Exchange Earnings by Goods and Services in Selected Caribbean Countries*
Millions of U.S. dollars

Country	1995		1996		1997		1998	
	Goods	*Services*	*Goods*	*Services*	*Goods*	*Services*	*Goods*	*Services*
Bahamas	225.3	1,544.3	249.7	1,578.1	246.2	1,593.5	362.9	1,586.3
Barbados	245.3	913.3	286.7	960.1	287.5	1,013.6		
Guyana	495.7	133.5	575.0	138.8				
Haiti	152.8	104.1	169.9	159.4	205.5	173.6	299.4	179.9
Jamaica	1,796.0	1,612.8	1,721.0	1,624.5	1,700.0	1,714.6	1,613.0	1,770.3
Trinidad and Tobago	2,456.1	342.6	2,565.0	463.2	2,542.0	546.6		

Source: Inter-American Development Bank (1999).

Table 10-2. *Direct Foreign Exchange Earnings from Tourism*
Millions of U.S. dollars

Destination	1993	1994	1995	1996	1997
Bahamas	1,304.0	1,332.6	1,346.2	1,450.0	1,415.9
Barbados	528.0	597.6	661.8	684.9	717.0
Belize	70.0	71.4	77.6	83.6	88.0
Haiti	30.0	27.0	56.0	58.0	57.0
Jamaica	942.0	973.0	1,068.5	1,100.0	1,131.0
Trinidad and Tobago	81.1	87.3	72.6	108.1	192.6

Source: Caribbean Tourism Organization (1999).

ence of the Caribbean Community in 1973. Amendments were necessary because the treaty, in its existing configuration, contained provisions that presented obstacles to the successful integration of markets for capital, services, and labor and the creation of a single economic space. In order to manage the process of revising the treaty and enabling a smooth transition to a single market and economy, the heads of government established the Inter-Governmental Task Force (IGTF) in October 1992, charged with supervising the implementation of the decision to establish the CSM&E.

The IGTF decided to conduct the revision process through a series of protocols that would revise the provisions of the treaty on an incremental basis. This decision was made against the background of a report by the West Indian Commission that the major weakness of the CARICOM integration movement was the lack of implementation of decisions by the heads of government over the years. The IGTF felt that an incremental approach to the revision process would enable member states to see progress over a shorter time period. As a result of this decision nine protocols have been drafted, and two have become provisionally applicable for member states, one of which is Protocol II.

Provisions of Protocol II

The protocol governing the treatment of services in CARICOM is formally known as Protocol II: Establishment, Services, Capital. It was issued in July 1997 and entered into force provisionally on July 4, 1998, replacing either completely or partially Articles 28, 35, 36, 37, 38, and 43 of Annex V of the Treaty of Chaguaramas. The protocol represents the single most important advance in the movement toward the creation of the CARICOM Single Market and Economy through the conferment of the right of establishment, the right to provide services, and the right to move capital by any CARICOM national in

the community. It is envisioned that these rights will operate to equate the
CARICOM economies to a single economic space. Protocol II prohibits the
introduction of new restrictions on the provision of services and strengthens
the disciplines when such restrictions are imposed. It has also significantly expanded the commitments of member states to allow the free movement and
provision of services, the unfettered establishment of enterprises by community nationals, and the free movement of capital and skilled labor.

The most important elements of Protocol II can be summarized as follows:

—the provision guaranteeing national treatment to all members of
CARICOM;

—the removal of existing restrictions on the free movement of services, the
right of establishment, the right to move capital, and the free movement of
labor (subject to country exclusions); and

—the obligation not to impose any new restrictions once the protocol enters
into force.

Scope of Application

Article 35 of Protocol II provides that this agreement shall apply to the right
of establishment, the right to provide services, and the right to move capital
throughout the community. The article, however, contains a general exception
that excludes from coverage those activities that involve the "exercise of governmental authority." The term "activities involving the exercise of governmental authority" has been defined for the purposes of the agreement as those
activities conducted neither on a commercial basis nor in competition with one
or more economic enterprises. These include, but are not limited to, the activities of the central bank of a member state, social security plans, national security, and the maintenance of public order.

Article 36, paragraph 4, defines the provision of services in a manner similar to the General Agreement on Trade in Services (GATS) to include the supply of services

—from the territory of one member state into the territory of another member state;

—in the territory of one member state to the service consumer of another
member state;

—by a service supplier of one member state through commercial presence
in the territory of another member state; and

—by a service supplier of one member state through the presence of natural
persons of a member state in the territory of another member state.

National Treatment

One of the basic principles of an agreement on services is the provision of national treatment among all parties to the agreement; in other words, member states are not allowed to discriminate against a nonnational service provider in favor of local service providers. Article 38 of Protocol II clearly establishes that there shall be no discrimination among member states on the grounds of nationality and mandates that the Community Council establish rules to prohibit such activity. This provision is to apply to all sectors unless countries make specific reservations to be exempted from compliance.

Article 35b prohibits the implementation of new restrictions on the basis of nationality, and as a corollary Article 35c mandates the removal of all restrictions on the right of establishment. In addition, Articles 36 and 36a provide for the nondiscriminatory removal of restrictions on the provision of services and the prohibition of new restrictions on a discriminatory basis.

Treatment of Monopolies

Article 35a allows member states to maintain certain exclusions or restrictions on the right of establishment in any industry or sector if it is determined that such exclusions are required to protect the public interest. Such a determination may result in the creation or maintenance of either a government monopoly or a private sector monopoly. The imposition of such restrictions, however, must not be implemented in a discriminatory manner among member states and is subject to the agreed rules of competition established under Protocol VIII, which seeks to address anticompetitive practices within the community.

Denial of Benefits

This clause determines who will be eligible to benefit from the preferential access granted in the agreement. Under this provision, member states may deny the benefits of the agreement to a national of another member state under specified circumstances. Under Article 35b, paragraph 5, Protocol II clearly defines who shall be considered a national of a member state for the purposes of the agreement. It requires that a service provider shall be regarded a national if the person:

1. is a citizen of the state; or
2. has a connection with the state that entitles him to be regarded as a national in keeping with the relevant laws of the member state (such as a naturalized citizen or permanent resident); or

3. is a company that has its registered office and central administration in the member state and carries on substantial activity within the community. Such a company must be substantially owned and effectively controlled by persons mentioned in subparagraphs 1 or 2. A company is "substantially owned," according to the agreement, when more than 50 percent of the equity interest is owned by nationals, and it is "effectively controlled" when nationals have the power to name a majority of the directors or otherwise legally direct the actions of the company.

Recognition and Equivalency

This concept addresses the issue of member states granting recognition to the qualifications received by nationals of another member state. Providentially, as a result of common historical experience, the member states of CARICOM all participate and contribute to the functioning of the University of the West Indies as well as other recognized institutions in the region, which provide access to nationals of all member states. This cooperation has served to ease, to some extent, the rigors associated with the establishment of common standards and measures for accreditation, mutual recognition of qualifications, and the establishment of equivalency in qualifications among nationals for service providers from Caribbean states.

Some problems do exist, however, and the inclusion of Article 35e in Protocol II was specifically designed to address the difficulties faced by CARICOM nationals in the free movement of labor. This provision provides for the creation of a framework for the implementation of the comprehensive policy, agreed by the heads of government of CARICOM, on the free movement of CARICOM nationals in a single market and economy. It is envisaged that the provisions of this article will facilitate access to and engagement in nonwage earning activities as well as the movement of skilled persons eligible under Protocol II.

Free Movement of Persons

The most significant aspect of Protocol II is the expansive provision for the free movement of university graduates, other professionals, and skilled persons and occupations. No other regional agreement includes such a wide-ranging policy on the free movement of nationals among countries of their region. It is a revolutionary aspect of the services agreement, and if successful will serve to approximate the provisions of the European Union in the CARICOM region on the movement of labor. It would consequently surpass all other arrangements in the Western Hemisphere with respect to the free movement of persons. The primary elements of the policy covering the free movement of CARICOM nationals are:

1. *Free movement of university graduates, other professionals, and skilled persons and occupations as follows:* graduates of the University of the West Indies, the University of Guyana, and the University of Suriname; graduates of other recognized institutions in the region; graduates of institutions outside the region; duly accredited media workers; sports persons, musicians, and artists; treatment of hucksters/higglers; treatment of workers in the tourism and entertainment industries; skilled persons eligible under Articles 35d and 36a of Protocol II.

2. *Freedom of travel and exercise of a profession:* elimination of a need for passports for travel within the region; facilitation of ease of entry without bureaucracy at immigration points; elimination of the requirement for work permits for CARICOM nationals.

3. *Other supporting measures:* the harmonization and transferability of social security benefits; mechanisms for certifying and establishing equivalency of degrees and accrediting institutions; completion of a skills register; coordination of social policies; development and promotion of a public education program on the policy of free movement.

Thus far, eleven member states of CARICOM have enacted legislation on the free movement of university graduates within the region.[4] Table 10-3 presents a summary of the status of the implementation by member states of domestic legislation based on the Skilled CARICOM Nationals Law, which was developed to implement the provisions outlined above.[5]

Removal of Restrictions on Services Trade

Article 36a of Protocol II provides for the removal of restrictions on the provision of services and for the elimination of discriminatory restrictions on the provision of services by nonnationals. This includes the removal of restrictions that take the form of domestic regulatory practices and procedures, as well as discrimination against the entry of nonnationals. If a service supplier seeks to provide services by establishing a commercial presence, Article 35d

4. The governments of Montserrat and Suriname are in the process of preparing to implement legislation on the free movement of university graduates, but at this writing the process is not complete.

5. The Bahamas has opted not to be a member of the CARICOM Single Market and Economy and as such will not implement at this time the CARICOM policy on the Freedom of Movement of Skills and Labor as envisaged by the model legislation entitled the "Free Movement of Skills Act." In reality, however, many CARICOM nationals are employed in the Bahamas.

Table 10-3. *Status of the Implementation by Member States of Domestic Legislation Based on the Skilled CARICOM Nationals Law, 1999*

Member state	Legislation enacted	Additional steps required
Antigua and Barbuda	Legislation has been enacted. Act No. 3 of 1997 (Caribbean Community Skilled Nationals Act)	
Barbados	Immigration Act Chapter 190 has been amended by the Immigration (Amendment) Act, 1996, to give effect to the relevant decision.	
Belize	Legislation has been enacted.	
The Bahamas	No legislation has been enacted.	The government has indicated that it will not participate in the arrangements for the free movement of skilled persons at this time.
Dominica	Legislation has been enacted. Act No. 30 of 1995 (Caribbean Community Skilled Nationals Act)	
Grenada	Legislation has been enacted. Act No. 32 of 1995 (Caribbean Community Skilled Nationals Act)	
Guyana	Legislation has been enacted. Act No. 6 of 1996 (Caribbean Community Free Entry of Skilled Nationals Act)	
Jamaica	Legislation has been enacted. Act No. 18 of 1997 (Caribbean Community Free Movement of Skilled Persons Act)	
Montserrat	No legislation has been enacted.	National consultations on the policy and law are being held.
St. Lucia	Legislation has been enacted. Act No. 18 of 1996 (Caribbean Community Skilled Nationals Act)	
St. Kitts and Nevis	Legislation has been enacted.	Regulations and administrative arrangements need to be completed.
St. Vincent and the Grenadines	Legislation has been enacted. Act No. 4 of 1997 (Caribbean Community Skilled Nationals Act)	
Republic of Suriname	No legislation has been enacted.	Draft law will be sent through relevant legal entities, then ratified by the president.
Trinidad and Tobago	Legislation has been enacted. Act No. 26 of 1996 (Caribbean Community Skilled Nationals Act)	The act must be promulgated in order to take effect.

Source: CARICOM Secretariat (1999).

prohibits the maintenance of any administrative practices or procedures that would impede the exercise of the rights of establishment. It also prohibits restrictions on all managerial, supervisory, and technical personnel and on branches, subsidiaries, and agencies of parent companies operating within CARICOM member states.

Significantly, this article also requires that member states do not obstruct access by enterprises in obtaining land, buildings, or other real property required for the conduct of their business. This provision is extremely important because numerous CARICOM countries maintain restrictions on the purchase of real property in their own countries. Many require that such purchases be made in partnership with a national of that member state, with the latter having majority ownership in the property. The implementation of this provision therefore will require the repeal of any existing Alien Landholding Legislation that prevents CARICOM nationals from acquiring land in a member state.[6]

Movement of Capital and Current Transactions

Articles 37, 37a, and 37b prohibit the introduction of any new restrictions on the movement of capital and payments connected with such movement and on current payments and transfers and require the removal of any restrictions that exist. The authorization for the movement of capital shall be provided on a nondiscriminatory basis.

Safeguards

Article 37c provides for the adoption of restrictions, including quantitative restrictions on imports, the right of establishment, the right to provide services, and the right to move capital, in the event of serious balance-of-payments and external financial difficulties, or the threat thereof, within a member state. These restrictions, however, may not be applied in a discriminatory manner either among member states or against member states in favor of third parties. In addition, the government imposing safeguard restrictions should at all times seek to minimize damage to the interests of another member state and must not take steps that exceed those necessary to alleviate the problem.

6. Many of the very small islands within CARICOM do, however, have valid concerns regarding the ownership of property by nonnationals because it is possible that in a very short period of time the majority of an island's land mass could be owned by others living outside the country. It is perhaps likely that countries with such concerns could seek an exception to the implementation of this provision on the basis of security considerations.

The imposition of restrictions must be temporary and not longer than a period of eighteen months and phased out progressively as the situation improves. Paragraph 3 of Article 37c allows member states to accord priority to those activities that are essential to the maintenance of economic stability. Such restrictions, however, are not to be maintained for the purpose of protecting a particular sector in contravention of the treaty. The inclusion of this provision under the safeguards clause reflects the sensitivity of the CARICOM region to the realities of small economies, which are highly dependent on a narrow range of products and extremely vulnerable to fluctuations in the wider world economy.

Paragraphs 5, 6, and 7 provide for periodic consultations among member states to assess the balance-of-payments situation and assist countries in overcoming the problems associated with external financial difficulties.

Restrictions to Resolve Difficulties or Hardships Arising from the Exercise of Rights

The provision of Protocol II for resolving difficulties or hardships is not present in any other regional agreement on services. Article 38a allows member states to apply restrictions on the exercise of rights granted under Protocol II if the exercise of such rights creates serious difficulties in any sector of a member state. In addition, member states may impose restrictions if the exercise of rights occasions economic hardship in a region of the community (such as the OECS states). It is not clear how the latter formulation will operate or whether one country will be able to seek the imposition of restrictions on behalf of other member states of the subregion.

Article 38a also requires member states to notify the competent organ of the intention to impose restrictions before applying those restrictions; if it is unable to do so, member states must immediately notify the competent organ of the application of the restrictions. The competent organ shall then make a determination about the appropriateness of the restrictions and whether they should be maintained. If the restrictions are maintained, the organ shall determine the adequacy of the program submitted by the member state and the period in which the restrictions should continue.

Although Article 38a seeks to place limitations on the ability of a member state to use this provision, unlike the Safeguards and Waiver of Obligations clauses, there is no set time limit within which such restrictions must be removed. Thus it is possible to envision the protracted implementation of protective measures for a sector within a member state or within a subregion of the community in contravention of the treaty.

Waiver of Obligations to Grant Rights

Article 38b allows a member state to apply to the Community Council for a waiver of the requirement to grant any and all rights under Protocol II. The application for the waiver must be made before the establishment of a program to remove restrictions on rights, must identify the rights in respect of which the waiver is required, must justify the circumstances requiring such a waiver, and must indicate the time period for which the waiver is required. However, a waiver allowing member states to maintain such restrictions cannot be maintained for a period exceeding five years.

Exceptions

Protocol II includes the general exceptions for the maintenance of limitations on the rights granted in the treaty to protect public morals, maintain public order and safety, protect human, animal, or plant life, or secure compliance with the laws of a member state. Article 38b (ter) allows the maintenance of restrictions to protect the national security interests of each member state.

Special Provisions for Less-Developed Countries

Article 38c allows the member states or competent organs of the community to take into consideration the special needs and circumstances of the less-developed countries in the removal of restrictions on the exercise of rights under this agreement.[7] Special provision for the less-developed countries is strongly rooted in the history of CARICOM, which has always attempted to take into account different conditions among members and to minimize unequal benefits between members.

Some Missing Elements

Protocol II is a comprehensive agreement that grants a much wider range of rights to member states of the CARICOM region than is granted in any other regional agreement in the Western Hemisphere. This is particularly true for those provisions governing the movement of workers and nationals of CARICOM, which should literally create a single economic space for the provision of services among member states. Despite the comprehensive nature of

7. Less-developed countries are Antigua and Barbuda, Belize, Dominica, Grenada, St. Kitts and Nevis, St. Lucia, and St. Vincent and the Grenadines.

the agreement, however, some significant elements are missing and will need
to be addressed in order to ensure its effective implementation.

Most-Favored-Nation Clause

Protocol II, unlike any other agreement for the liberalization of trade in services, does not contain a provision granting most-favored-nation (MFN) treatment to all CARICOM member states. The MFN principle would require that a
trading partner within the agreement be treated no less favorably than any other
member of the agreement and in addition, no less favorably than a third party to
which rights are granted in a member state. The implications of an absence of
an MFN clause become evident when assessing the commitments entered into
by CARICOM member states in other services agreements such as GATS, as
well as any future commitments that a CARICOM member state may undertake in an agreement with a third party. It is accepted that all commitments
entered into within the framework of GATS are immediately applicable to all
CARICOM member states given the fact that the MFN clause is a foundational
principle of the agreement.

The lack of an MFN clause within Protocol II means that no CARICOM
member state is obligated to grant equal rights of access to all other CARICOM
member states for any trade concession granted to a third party. In addition, it
means that a member state, in the course of an agreement with a third party, is
obligated to immediately accord to the third party all the benefits deriving from
Protocol II unless that member state specifically includes an exception covering Protocol II.[8]

It is important, therefore, that specific language on MFN be included in
Protocol II in order to ensure that CARICOM member states benefit from
extraregional agreements entered into by one of its members. It should also be
required that a CARICOM state entering into such negotiations seeks an exception for the regional agreement on trade in services under Protocol II.

Process of Liberalization

Another missing element in Protocol II is the absence of a clearly defined
approach to the services liberalization process within CARICOM. All other
regional agreements on services address this issue, clearly outlining the scope

8. The CARICOM Council on Trade and Economic Development (COTED) has undertaken
extensive discussions on the MFN issue. COTED will be addressing this aspect in future discussions on Protocol II. Also see Protocol IV of the CARICOM Treaty—Trade Policy.

of liberalization, progressive or limited, and the approach to be taken to achieve such liberalization. The determination of the approach to liberalization will have direct implications for the methodology utilized to identify the existing restrictions and measures affecting trade in services among CARICOM member states.

The negative list approach to services liberalization, adopted by the majority of regional trade agreements in the Western Hemisphere, will require much more intensive work at the outset, given the lack of readily available information on restrictions on services trade within CARICOM. However, in the long run, the adoption of the negative list approach would better serve the region in its effort to achieve greater liberalization. It would also maximize the CARICOM region's ability to take advantage of the provision of services in new and emerging sectors such as electronic commerce and other developments in the technological revolution.

It is important that CARICOM clearly outline, as a supplement to Protocol II, the modality for regional liberalization in the services sector. This is a crucial juncture for decisionmaking, because consultants are presently gathering information on the restrictions and measures affecting intra-CARICOM trade to support the implementation of Protocol II. In the absence of a clear process, the collection and compilation of such information may be rendered useless in successfully implementing the agreement and in preparing CARICOM countries for participation in wider negotiations such as those under the Free Trade Area of the Americas (FTAA) and the World Trade Organization (WTO).

Conclusions

The prospects for growth and development presented by the liberalization of the services sector in CARICOM are immeasurable and have the potential to catapult the region from a high dependence on agriculture to grasping the enormous opportunities in this dynamic environment. The new areas of electronic commerce and revolutionary telecommunications advances present the region with an unparalleled opportunity to take advantage of trade in services that require no significant overhead and can be conducted from virtually anywhere in the world.

Protocol II: Establishment, Services, Capital (1998) represents one of the most significant steps taken by the CARICOM member states to create a single economic space within the region. The concept of a region without internal borders should be realized through the implementation of the provisions for the free movement of persons, in particular university graduates and other professionals, skilled persons, and occupations. In addition, the agreement allows unrestricted freedom of travel through the removal of requirements for passports and other administrative requirements.

The services sector should greatly benefit from the free movement of natural persons specified in Protocol II. Increased labor mobility will likely help to solve the problem of a skilled-labor shortage in member countries and reduce their dependency on sources outside the community. However, much effort still needs to be made to make effective the movement of natural persons, professionals, and skilled labor within the region. All CARICOM countries need to pass the necessary legislation to enact it. National laws should be uniform in treatment of natural persons, professionals, and skilled labor. Common educational certificates should be established.

Protocol II also places CARICOM in a strong position to negotiate as a group in the negotiations on services taking place in the FTAA and WTO context. It should allow the region to work from a common foundation and to collect the necessary information on the existence of restrictions and measures affecting trade in services in order to inform the commitments undertaken multilaterally.

CARICOM has begun to examine those service sectors in which countries may enjoy a comparative advantage, such as professional services, entertainment services, movement of natural persons including skilled labor, telecommunications services, and health and tourism services, among others. In so doing, CARICOM will be able to identify and seek commitments from other participating member states in those areas that are advantageous to the region.

CARICOM still needs to clearly define the process of liberalization that it intends to pursue in order to implement the protocol. There remains a great deal of division among member states over the advantages and disadvantages of the positive- and negative list approaches to services liberalization. This matter will need to be resolved before concrete progress can be made in the implementation of Protocol II.

Despite the remaining challenges, however, there is no denying the significant potential contribution of liberalization of the services sector to the economies of CARICOM. This sector presents innumerable opportunities, including the possibility of dramatically expanding export opportunities for the region and increasing growth indicators in a region that has experienced much dislocation over the past decade.

References

CARICOM Secretariat. 1997. *Protocol Amending the Treaty Establishing the Caribbean Community: Protocol II: Establishment, Services, Capital.* Georgetown, Guyana.

————. 1999. *The Development of the Single Market and Economy.* Georgetown, Guyana. (June).

Gill, Henry S. 1997. "The Services Sector in CARICOM: The State of Analysis and Suggestions for an Agenda." Paper presented at "United Nations Development Programme (UNDP) Caribbean Regional Development Project." (August).

Hamilton, Pamela Coke. 1998. "Background Paper on CARICOM in the FTAA Services Agreement." Prepared for the CARICOM Regional Negotiating Machinery (CRNM) (October).

————. 1999. "The CARICOM Single Market and Economy: Overview and Potential Implications for Labour." Prepared for the Jamaica Employers Federation and Jamaica Trade Union Congress. (September).

Planning Institute of Jamaica. 1999. "The Importance of Trade in Services for CARICOM Economies and Prospects for Future Development." A paper presented at "Commonwealth Caribbean Workshop on Opportunities and Challenges." Basseterre, St. Kitts and Nevis. (September 30–October 2).

World Bank. 1996. *Caribbean Countries, Prospects for Services Exports from the English-Speaking Caribbean.* Report No. 15301—CRG. Washington, D.C. (May).

WTO. 1994. *General Agreement on Trade in Services (GATS).* Geneva, Switzerland.

PART THREE

Challenges and Conclusions

Liberalizing Trade in Services:
A Developing-Country Perspective

EDUARDO LIZANO

SINCE THE 1950s the liberalization of international trade in the global economy has advanced very rapidly. Thanks to successive rounds of negotiations, countries have substantially reduced such obstacles as customs duties on traded goods; as a result, international trade has grown in real terms faster than global production. Throughout this process, as protectionist policies repeatedly failed, the negotiating position of developing countries has changed significantly. Poor nations, reluctant in the beginning to open their markets, have gradually changed their position and are today stronger advocates of market opening than the richer countries.

Smaller and less-developed countries are in urgent need of achieving greater integration within the international economy. Whether this process is called globalization, opening, or internationalization, there is no doubt about the importance of accelerating and expanding trade with the outside world. Small markets simply do not provide the best conditions for achieving an optimum division of labor, scale economies, and capital accumulation or for adopting new technologies. In *The Wealth of Nations*, Adam Smith discussed the close relationship between economic development and market size and made it clear that without international trade the possibility of reaching higher levels of economic development is very limited. Although international trade is a necessary condition for development, it is not sufficient by itself. Each country must create institutions and satisfy certain prerequisites in order to meet the challenges and take advantage of the opportunities of globalization.

Previously, many developing countries favored the opening of developed-country markets but preferred to keep their own closed (following the famous import-substitution doctrine), but this idea has ceased to carry much weight. Developing countries have realized that protectionism prejudices their competitive position and, as a consequence, prevents them from reaping the benefits of international trade.

Although developing countries have made important advances, there is still a long way to go. With this in mind, the following two observations are in order:

—Protectionist tendencies are not fading; on the contrary, in some countries they are experiencing a revival. Recent examples abound in highly developed nations, as in the case of steel in the United States and that of bananas in the European Union, which represent, without doubt, poor examples for developing countries. Therefore, these countries must intensify efforts and not lower their guard, since failing to advance in the sphere of globalization would signify a step backward, as it would encourage incipient protectionist forces.

—The trade policy agenda is not finalized and it is abundant. Anne Krueger has recommended the following next steps for trade policy, some of which are particularly important for developing countries: implement the commitments undertaken in the Uruguay Round; continue reducing tariffs; accelerate market opening for agricultural products; deepen and broaden market opening for trade in services; strengthen the institutional system of the World Trade Organization (WTO); and exclude labor and environmental issues from future WTO negotiations.

Services and Economic Development

Within this general frame of reference, the issue of services has become more prominent in the past few years, for several reasons. The value of global services production has been growing faster than the production of goods; therefore, the world economy cannot ignore trade in services. As a consequence, the issue of services has gained an ever more determining role in multilateral trade negotiations.

The cost of services as a percentage of the unit cost of production for goods and primary producers has reached a high ratio. As such, the costs of transportation, financial services, insurance, packaging, communications, legal services, education, computer services, accountancy services, and other services have quickly grown in importance and in their proportion of output. Thus the availability, quality, and cost of services influence more and more the competitive position of developing countries in international markets. Hence the heightened interest on the part of those countries in reducing costs in this sector, which will allow them to participate more actively in international trade.

In most developing countries, the cost of services inputs as a proportion of final products is frequently significantly higher than in developed countries, in large part because of the protectionism that still characterizes their markets. By diminishing the cost of services, these countries could improve the competitive position of their exports in international markets, thereby reducing their export costs. Bigger world markets for a wide array of services would also open the possibility for developing countries of finding niches for the export of some services that would help them diversify and increase their share in international trade.

The liberalization of trade for certain services, such as financial services, attracts important contingent benefits. In fact, the local financial sector, faced with external competition, must focus on improving its efficiency (by diversifying services) and productivity (by reducing costs of production); improve transparency, including providing better access to and quality of information; adopt more modern techniques for risk administration; diversify financial operations for various economic agents (companies, depositors, investors); and encourage the stability of the financial sector through the liberalization of trade in financial services.

In sum, the liberalization of trade in services would have marked positive effects for developing countries. An improved competitive position for goods exports and a reduction in the cost of services would raise the possibility of opening up new export niches and ultimately foster economic growth.

Obstacles to Liberalizing Trade in Services

If the opening of services markets brings with it obvious advantages, why are governments advancing so slowly in this area? Why were developing countries so opposed to the liberalization of trade in services in the past? The following four factors are at least part of the answer.

—The pressure of interest groups in service sectors is very significant and varies enormously. The interests of local services producers are very different from those of the national regulators, to whom all too often not enough importance is paid.

Regulators are concerned that the liberalization of trade in services would cause them to lose a significant share of their discretionary powers, as well as their power more generally. For this reason, many regulators are firmly opposed to opening up trade in services. Their objections become particularly complicated when the service providers are the national state-owned enterprises. In those cases unions of public employees sometimes form a third interest group opposed to the liberalization of trade in services.

—Authorities and providers in developing countries have frequently noted that their capacity to compete successfully with services providers from developed nations is very limited, and many believe it to be impossible in many instances because they lack business expertise or national competitiveness. They therefore insist on opening the domestic market very slowly to international competition. These fears are similar to those that predated them, when goods markets were beginning to open up to international competition. Those fears by and large turned out to be unfounded.

—Frequently, the opposition to liberalization is a negotiating position of the poorer countries. They tend to give priority to the further opening of goods markets, such as the market for agricultural products, over the opening of services markets. As a result, the asymmetry of commitments made by different countries, as well as the criteria of "reciprocity" and "compensation," are permanently on the negotiating table. The liberalization of trade in services thus becomes an integral part of their general negotiating strategy. The more restricted and time-sensitive the agenda—that is to say, the more "sectoral"—the more difficult it is for the participating countries to reach agreement within the give-and-take (offer and request) scenario—that is, the more difficult it is to balance the costs and benefits.

—The vertiginous technological progress that today characterizes the production and trade of many services, in particular those related to communications, is also a factor that makes many developing nations prefer to advance slowly, while waiting to better identify and respond to the challenges and opportunities of the opening of services markets.

Negotiating Agenda

In the services negotiations at the multilateral and regional levels, developing countries face the complex challenge of participating in the elaboration of the agenda and of participating in a new or revised services agreement, an opportunity that they should use to full advantage. These negotiations are very important for developing countries. As is well known, the broader the markets, the better the possibilities for development, especially for smaller economies. Therefore, great emphasis should be placed on global negotiations under the WTO umbrella as well as on the regional agenda at the broadest level of the Western Hemisphere. Ideally, these negotiations should move quickly in order to generate positive results in a not too distant future. If this does not happen, the result will be uncertainty and lack of confidence on the part of smaller countries with respect to the functioning of international markets.

Developing countries cannot continue down the path of unilateral opening of services markets. Although this generates tangible economic benefits, it is not viable politically. Just as these countries need to open their markets in order to improve their efficiency and competitiveness, they also require access to external markets so as to fully benefit from their comparative advantages. Thus developing countries must pursue both multilateral and regional services negotiations with the understanding that although unilateral opening is an important component of their foreign trade policy it has limitations that cannot be ignored.

Smaller countries should consider bilateral trade agreements very carefully. Although these agreements open up access to export and import markets, they nonetheless pose two significant problems. The first is the possibility of raising costs by rechanneling trade flows from more-competitive to less-competitive countries, also known as trade "diversion." Second, the costs of administering several bilateral trade agreements simultaneously are considerable and growing. When the clauses contained in each of them differ, for example those regarding rules of origin, the customs administrations of smaller countries become very complicated. For these and other reasons, the pursuit of bilateral trade agreements should be considered only in exceptional cases.

Broader regional agreements present other possibilities. The Free Trade Area of the Americas (FTAA), for example, currently being negotiated within the American continent, offers important advantages. First, unlike bilateral agreements, regional agreements do not "divert" trade and they have lower administrative costs. Second, regional agreements generally provide access to more markets than bilateral agreements do. Third, regional agreements, if negotiated properly, can lay the groundwork for international negotiations under the WTO. They provide experience that smaller economies can use in the multilateral WTO negotiations. Fourth, regional agreements, as their name indicates, require agreement among only a few countries, rather than dozens, as in the case of the WTO. Thus it is probably less difficult to advance regionally than globally.

Active participation in regional agreements must be perceived as a complement to multilateral trade negotiations. The FTAA, in particular, represents a significant opportunity for smaller countries. The agenda must be broad enough to allow a trade-off of interests among participants so as to give countries adequate room to maneuver.

The interest of developing countries lies especially in the areas of agriculture, manufactured goods, and trade in services. The latter, however, should not be negotiated without simultaneously discussing other issues that are closely related. In other words, the "sectoral" focus in services should not be at the top of the negotiating agenda. In particular, sectoral negotiations should not take place before a normative framework for services trade is either completed (under the WTO) or elaborated (under the FTAA). A general framework is needed to balance the costs and benefits of the negotiation, so that in the end each participating country benefits from the agreement.

Conclusions

Developing countries need to keep the following observations in mind when negotiating trade agreements on services issues.

—The economic advancement of developing countries depends to a considerable degree on the success of trade negotiations in goods and services, whose main goal is to reduce barriers to international trade and to broaden access to foreign markets.

—Negotiations over the liberalization of trade in services must be made in the context of a broad agenda that also includes other issues of acknowledged relevance, such as agriculture.

—The pace at which developing countries can advance in opening services markets will be influenced by interest group pressures, among them those of national service suppliers, regulators, and unions.

—The current WTO services negotiations and those at the regional level in the Western Hemisphere offer significant opportunities for developing countries if they are able to define and implement an agenda that reflects their needs and interests.

Reference

Krueger, Anne. 1999. "The Developing Countries and the Next Round of Multilateral Trade Negotiations." Working Paper 2118. Washington: Trade Development Research Group, World Bank.

The GATS, Subregional Agreements, and the FTAA: How Much Is Left to Be Done?

FRANCISCO JAVIER PRIETO

THE DEVELOPMENT OF NORMS AND DISCIPLINES aimed at promoting the progressive liberalization of services is a relatively new phenomenon in the multilateral as well as in the regional and bilateral realms. Although this development has occurred simultaneously with the process of unilateral liberalization undertaken by many countries, including those of Latin America and the Caribbean, the majority of existing agreements have not yet generated an effective liberalization of services trade. The commitments made in these agreements have been limited to providing more transparency of the conditions in which trade takes place and, in the best of cases, providing greater juridical certainty for service providers. Nonetheless, the existing agreements have yet to fulfill an important task: that is, to advance the liberalization of services in such a way that these and any future reforms will be anchored in international commercial agreements that contain binding obligations for liberalization and reforms aimed at the gradual elimination of all barriers to trade in services.

Two types of agreements have guided the development of disciplines in services in the countries of the Western Hemisphere: those that took their inspiration from the 1995 General Agreement on Trade in Services (GATS) under the World Trade Organization (WTO), and those whose structure is similar to that of the 1994 North American Free Trade Agreement (NAFTA). This chapter begins with an analysis of the limitations and shortcomings of these two types of agreements, as well as the improvements achieved in the new subregional agreements inspired by them. It then attempts to identify the tasks that

217

should guide the development of hemisphere-wide disciplines in services within the framework of the Free Trade Area of the Americas (FTAA) negotiations. In addition, it examines two alternative schemes for services liberalization that in some ways are hybrids of the two paradigms mentioned above but that at the same time improve on those paradigms: the "General Framework of Principles and Norms for the Liberalization of Trade in Services in the Andean Community" and the "Protocol of Montevideo on Trade in Services in the Southern Cone Common Market (MERCOSUR)."

The North American Free Trade Agreement

The North American Free Trade Agreement (NAFTA), signed by Mexico, Canada, and the United States of America, took effect in January 1994. It represents an ambitious effort by these countries to enhance the obligations and enlarge the economic space created in 1989 between Canada and the United States. Among its goals, NAFTA sought to allow the direct provision of services in the markets of the member countries by way of disciplines contained in Part V of the agreement (Investments, Services, and Related Issues) and more specifically in Chapters 12 (Cross-Border Trade in Services); 13 (Telecommunications); 14 (Financial Services), and 16 (Temporary Entry for Business Persons).

Several important subregional agreements on services concluded by the countries of the Western Hemisphere have been inspired by this treaty. Those agreements have worked out disciplines and obligations that closely follow the rules on services contained in NAFTA.[1] For various reasons, the business world and several governments believed that the structure of NAFTA, as well as its rules on services, would lead more rapidly than the GATS model to transparency and a stable juridical-normative framework for international transactions in services, as well as more effective liberalization of trade in services. Over 85 percent of the trade in services conducted by countries in the hemisphere is subject to commitments in NAFTA-like agreements.

One feature that supports the greater liberalizing capacity of NAFTA-type agreements is that its regulatory principles and obligations are general rather than specific. That is to say, they apply immediately to all cross-border services transactions. Even though NAFTA allows for the establishment of reservations,

---

1. See especially Organization of American States, Trade Unit, "Provisions on Trade in Services in the Trade and Integration Agreements of the Western Hemisphere" (FTAA OAS/IDS/ECLAC Tripartite Committee, October 1999); as well as Francisco J. Prieto and Sherry M. Stephenson, "Multilateral and Regional Liberalization of Trade in Services," in Miguel Rodriguez Mendoza, Patrick Low, and Barbara Kotschwar, eds., *Trade Rules in the Making* (Brookings, 1999).

these must be based on existing nonconforming measures (laws, norms, and regulations) and must be listed in the respective annex under the threat of being automatically dismantled, a characteristic that reinforces its transparency objectives. Since NAFTA does not permit raising the level of nonconformity described in the agreements, the treaty legally guarantees certain minimum conditions for the operations of service providers.

NAFTA-type agreements are distinguished by the quality and greater scope of the liberalizing principles they contain. In addition to the most-favored-nation (MFN) treatment and national-treatment provisions, the agreements contain obligations with respect to no local presence requirements, quantitative restrictions, and specific rules for moving toward the mutual recognition of licenses and certificates for professional services as well as for the temporary entry of business persons. In countries with deficiencies in the national regulation of services, NAFTA-type agreements favor the development of quality standards, which guarantee the competency of technicians and professionals and protect the interests of consumers.

NAFTA-type agreements also include a provision on ratcheting, which does not exist in any other services agreement and which introduces a high level of commitment that helps consolidate liberalization. If a party amends its legal framework in a way that eliminates or reduces restrictions on a service sector or activity, the ratchet clause obligates the party to offer this higher degree of liberalization to the other members as well. This dynamic approach prevents backsliding and enhances liberalization.

NAFTA-type agreements on services also aim to liberalize trade in services between residents of different countries, and as such they cover three of the four modes of supply: (1) cross-border trade, (2) consumption abroad, and (4) temporary movement of providers. The disciplines that apply to transactions between residents of the same country (mode 3) are contained in a separate chapter (Investment) and are the same for both goods and services. Thus the bias in favor of adopting commitments that require service providers to have a commercial presence is effectively eliminated.

Despite the apparently greater liberalizing tendency of NAFTA, this type of agreement also has features that do not advance liberalization. Among the most significant limitations of NAFTA-type agreements, the following may be noted:

—the exclusion of important services activities from the disciplines of the agreement through their inclusion in the Annex on Reservations on Future Measures;[2]

2. NAFTA-type agreements admit general reservations by way of which entire sectors or subsectors may be excluded from the obligations of the agreement through their inclusion in the corresponding annex.

—the inability of its members to comply adequately with the rules on transparency, in particular subfederal or provincial measures;

—the erosion of MFN obligations;

—the absence of a deadline for the elimination of nonconforming measures;

—the lack of commitments for the future incorporation of the sectors and subsectors excluded from the obligations of the agreement;

—contradictions between the concept of ratcheting and commitments related to the elimination of nationality requirements and permanent residence in the provision of professional services; and

—difficulties in achieving mutually advantageous outcomes and an adequate balance of rights and obligations between the parties.

The WTO General Agreement on Trade in Services

The second major type of agreement on trade in services is represented by the General Agreement on Trade in Services (GATS) of the WTO. This agreement is of critical importance for two reasons: first, because it provides the multilateral framework that sets out the conditions economic integration agreements must fulfill in order to be compatible with multilateral WTO disciplines; second, because it has inspired the establishment of an integration agreement among an important group of countries in the Western Hemisphere.

GATS was the first step in integrating the service sector into the multilateral disciplines of the WTO and in promoting the progressive liberalization of services trade throughout the world. However, when the Uruguay Round ended (in 1994), several issues under GATS still remained unresolved: some critical sectoral issues (basic telecommunications, financial services, maritime transport, and air transport); issues linked to mode 4, the provision of a service by a member temporarily in the territory of another member, in particular the operational aspects of the "Appendix on the Movement of Natural Persons Supplying Services"; and questions related to the GATS regulatory structure for specific areas (government procurement, safeguard action, and subsidies).

Some of the outstanding issues on sectoral negotiations have been resolved since GATS was established in 1995, particularly those related to financial services and basic telecommunications. However, other issues have gradually been added to those included in the so-called built-in agenda, thereby slowing the goal of progressively liberalizing trade in services. Moreover, Part IV of the agreement establishes the procedures for achieving progressive liberalization, and GATS Article XIX, subparagraph 1, specifically, reads:

In pursuance of the objectives of this Agreement, Members shall enter into successive rounds of negotiations, beginning not later than five years from the date of entry into force of the WTO Agreement and periodically thereafter, with a view to achieving a progressively higher level of liberalization. Such negotiations shall be directed to the reduction or elimination of the adverse effects on trade in services of measures as a means of providing effective market access. This process shall take place with a view to promoting the interests of all participants on a mutually advantageous basis and to securing an overall balance of rights and obligations.

The next section identifies those areas that call for a concerted effort by participants to make significant progress toward the liberalization of trade in services in the GATS 2000 negotiations. Reforms and improvements should, ideally, be addressed within the multilateral framework on which GATS is based. However, liberalization initiatives at the broad regional level such as the FTAA offer a second-best option for improving on the multilateral institutional framework.

Areas for Improvement in GATS

The weaknesses of the current GATS architecture are being increasingly acknowledged by WTO members.[3] The commitments undertaken by the parties to the agreement do not provide adequate sectoral coverage and do not adequately address the possible modes of supply. Furthermore, the overwhelming majority of measures listed in the GATS schedules of WTO members reflect, at best, the status quo, or else establish conditions and limitations that do not reflect the real level of the liberalization of domestic services industries.

GATS Classification Systems and Coverage

Classification systems should provide clear and precise terminology that enables an unequivocal identification of the activities that fall under the specific disciplines of the trade agreement. The diversity of services and the constant emergence of new services renders work in this respect quite complex. The relative newness of international trade in services partly accounts for the lack of clarity in the existing classification systems. The advancement of liber-

---

3. Also refer to the chapters by Geza Feketekuty and by Kalypso Nicolaïdis and Joel Trachtman in this volume.

alization will require clearly defining the scope of the commitments to be undertaken by each party to an agreement.

GATS members use two main sources to specify their commitments on trade in services. One is the Central Product Classification (CPC) system, which was prepared provisionally by the United Nations for improving national accounts and is still under review. The second is the Service Sector Classification List, a summarized list based on the CPC prepared by the former General Agreement on Tariffs and Trade (GATT) Secretariat.[4]

The WTO Secretariat itself has pointed out the deficiencies of the classification systems, and the Organization for Economic Cooperation and Development (OECD) has proposed ways to supplement and expand the subcategories of services in areas such as environmental services. These documents make manifest how deficiencies in the classification systems can lead to major trade divergences when it comes to specifying and interpreting the scope and depth of the commitments undertaken by the parties.[5] Both classification systems, however, provide incomplete coverage and ambiguous definitions. Recognizing this, the NAFTA countries have developed their own classification system for all industrial activities included in the agreement, the so-called NAICS (North American Industrial Classification System).

It is important for the disciplines to be comprehensive and applicable to all services. Exclusions, such as that of air transport, must end. Air transport is increasingly important both for the internationalization of many other services (such as professional services and tourism) and as a supplement to trade in perishable goods (such as fruits and flowers).

The question of electronic commerce (e-commerce) also needs to be addressed. Members of the multilateral trade system appear somewhat confused about how to deal with e-commerce on the international agenda and how to solve specific problems related to this issue. Although proposals have been made to draw up separate disciplines for e-commerce, there is considerable ambiguity and confusion about its appropriate location on the international trade agenda.[6]

4. See also *UN Central Product Classification*, Version 1.0 (New York: United Nations Statistical Division, 1998); Service Sector Classification List, Doc. MTN.GNS/W/120 (Geneva: GATT Secretariat); Bureau of Economic Analysis, U.S. Government, "Services Classification," Issues Paper 6 (March 1994), p. 2; International Monetary Fund, *Balance of Payments Manual*, 5th ed. (Washington, 1993); OECD Statistical Directorate, "A System of Health Accounts for International Data Collection," Part I: "Principles and Methods," Doc. STD/NA/RD(98)4.

5. See World Trade Organization, "Preparing for the GATS 2000 Negotiations," communication from Switzerland, Doc. S/C/W103 (March 23, 1999).

6. There is a need to establish common multilateral e-commerce standards that do not imply any reduction of consumer protection in the member countries. This could be achieved along

In my view, e-commerce is not substantially different from more traditional service industries, especially distribution and transportation. It would therefore seem desirable to include e-commerce as a category of services in the service classification list of activities. Like traditional services such as transport and distribution, e-commerce makes it possible to advertise, trade, transport, and even distribute goods and services to the end consumer. This service can be used either as a distribution and transportation channel or in association with other transport services such as air and land transport. Modification of GATS to deal explicitly with e-commerce would probably require the extension—and improvement—of existing disciplines, particularly Articles VI (Domestic Regulation), VIII (Monopolies and Exclusive Service Suppliers), IX (Business Practices), XIV (General Exceptions), and XIV bis (Security Exceptions) to address specific problems such as technical standards, protocols, and other matters related to the development and handling of electronic documentation.

Organizing service industries into clusters of interconnected services may be necessary in order to improve the negotiating modalities and the classification system used by GATS. The effectiveness and efficiency of the internationalization of specific services usually depends on a bundle or cluster of related services. A cluster may be defined as a main service or *service node* and several interconnected services, which together allow the main service to operate efficiently.

Identifying the services to be included in a given cluster could be done in close consultation with industry. An example is passenger air transport. To operate efficiently, this service node needs to be accompanied by other services such as food catering, computer reservation systems, ticket sales, aircraft repair and maintenance, and technical and professional services. E-commerce is another example. E-commerce is a service node that relies on a related cluster of services, including courier services, air cargo transportation, customs agents, wholesale and retail distribution services, and others.

Defining Trade in Services on the Basis of Modes of Supply

The internationalization of services differs considerably from the internationalization of goods. Two forms of international services are usually identified: one involves cross-border transactions, and the second involves establish-

with the decision of the European Parliament to vote in favor of establishing a single standard, equally applicable throughout the fifteen countries of the European Union (EU), for the distance sale of financial services by telephone, by mail, or through the Internet, in line with the project proposed by the European Commission.

ing a commercial presence. Cross-border trade is similar to trade in goods in that it involves trade between residents of different countries. A commercial presence is established when a service provider operates in the same country as the purchaser. Because commercial presence may require international movement of the factors of production on a permanent basis, it is conceptually analogous to the treatment accorded to foreign direct investment.

Cross-border trade involves—among other activities—using transportation based on telecommunication systems (telephone; fax; e-mail; e-commerce for consultancy services; databases; the sale of software, music CDs, and books) in a manner quite similar to the methods used for trade in goods by air, land, and maritime transport. However, cross-border trade in services also takes place when transactions involve the temporary movement of consumers to the country of residence of the supplier (for example, for tourism, health care, or education) or the temporary movement of the supplier to the country of residence of the consumer (for professional, technical, and specialized services, entertainment, and promotional services).

Commercial presence, however, requires the "permanent" relocation of the factors of production, including capital and human resources. It is primarily used to provide services that require direct and sustained contact between suppliers and consumers. Such is the case with many financial services (customer banking); distribution services (large department stores, supermarkets, and the like); domestic transport services (urban and interurban, air, land, and maritime transport); and chains of movie houses, fast-food outlets, hotels, and restaurants. Commercial presence may vary substantially depending on the type of legal entity authorized as well as on the requirements of international capital movements. Thus, commercial presence may range from a partnership based on franchising, to establishing representative offices, opening up branch offices, establishing affiliates, or purchasing an existing company.

The mutually exclusive definition of the four modes of supply in the current architecture of GATS has produced numerous ambiguities. In many service industries it is difficult—and perhaps even impossible—to use a single mode of supply to conduct trade. Governments may find it equally difficult to identify the measures that affect only one mode of supply while at the same time allowing the introduction of changes to such measures for other modes of supply that are not bound. This arbitrary separation renders ambiguous the commercial significance of the measures listed by the member countries in their national schedules.

Furthermore, the inclusion of commercial presence as a mode of supply has tended to cause an imbalance in the commitments undertaken by GATS members. The current use of four modes of supply introduces a bias against the undertaking of commitments in "cross-border trade in services" and favors the adoption of commitments under mode 3, "commercial presence."[7] Indeed, a significant number of WTO members have felt more inclined to undertake commitments under this mode of supply.[8] Various assessments of the GATS commitments indicate that there is a higher concentration of commitments in mode 3. Commitments under the other three modes of supply are usually intended to make effective the commercial presence commitments. The result is considerable confusion among trade negotiators as well as among individuals who are expected to benefit from its results—that is, service industries and consumers.

Finally, there appears to be no justification for establishing separate and distinct disciplines for the treatment of direct foreign investment aimed at producing goods and investment aimed at the supply of services. GATS has turned out to be a fairly appropriate framework for establishing disciplines to regulate the treatment of foreign investment in services.[9] However, there is still no comprehensive multilateral agreement for investment. As long as this is true, the possibility of making faster progress in the liberalization of cross-border trade in services is reduced.

Provisions on Transparency

The heterogeneous nature of GATS measures affecting trade in services underscores the importance of improving their transparency. This is a key element in making a user-friendly GATS for the business community.

Current provisions on transparency in GATS Article III are quite limited in this respect. The only requirements are that members establish inquiry points (such as an office that provides information on regulatory aspects of trade in services) and notify Geneva of amendments in measures listed in their national schedules. These obligations are insufficient to provide greater transparency with respect to measures affecting trade in services.

Exhaustive notification procedures are not necessary, would be impossible for countries to follow, and would also offer no operational advantages to the users of the resulting information. Not all measures have the same ability to obstruct trade in services, and different measures have different effects on dif-

7. A document of the WTO Secretariat even describes the agreement on services as "Rules for Growth and Investment."
8. WTO, "Structure of Commitments for Modes One, Two, and Three," Note by the Secretariat, Doc. S/C/W99 (March 3, 1999); and "Presence of Natural Persons (Mode Four)," Doc. S/C/W/75 (December 8, 1998).
9. For further discussion of this issue, refer to the chapter on investment by Pierre Sauvé in this volume.

ferent services. Some ideas are proposed below for ranking approaches on the basis of their relative impact on trade in services.

Discrimination among Members: MFN Exemptions

Most-favored-nation treatment has been defined as the cornerstone of the multilateral trading system and the key piece in all the WTO agreements. Unconditional adherence to this obligation is perceived as the best way to prevent undue use of economic and political pressure among member countries and also as the fastest and most efficient way to multilateralize the commitments exchanged by members.

The Annex on Exemptions to the MFN obligations of GATS Article II sets forth "the conditions under which a Member, at the entry into force of this agreement, is exempted from its obligations under paragraph 1 of Article II." Likewise, paragraph 2 establishes that "Any new exemptions applied for after the date of entry into force of the WTO Agreement shall be dealt with under paragraph 3 of Article IX of that Agreement." Although the Annex establishes that, "In principle, such exemptions should not exceed a period of ten years," both the number of exemptions listed—especially by developed countries—and the numerous cases in which exemptions are listed for an indefinite duration raises concerns about the full implementation of the MFN obligation. If this obligation is not met, the main purpose of the multilateral trade system will be weakened, and its credibility among countries adversely affected by exemptions will also be reduced.

Limiting "Free Riders" and Negotiating Modalities

Aspects of GATS that induce WTO members to assume substantive commitments in favor of the liberalization of services need to be strengthened. Accordingly, means should be sought to prevent members from benefiting from commitments exchanged by other members that do not contribute significantly to the efforts to advance the nondiscriminatory liberalization of services.

Maximizing the benefits of free trade could be brought about by modifying the structure of the existing agreement to make market access (Article XVI), national treatment (Article XVII), and additional commitments (Article XVIII) part of the general obligations of the agreement.

This change could be facilitated by the adoption of commitments on the basis of clusters of related services. In many cases, undertaking commitments in a specific service activity may not be effective or commercially significant if the commitment is not accompanied by additional commitments related to other activities that supplement the service in question. Background papers prepared by the WTO Secretariat point out that the marketing of many services such as audiovisual services, education and health care services, business services, and transportation services may be negatively affected by a lack of liberalizing commitments in distribution services or information networks.[10]

The adoption of a liberalization scheme based on clusters would allow GATS members to establish their commitments according to groups of services that reflect their specific trade interests. Their aspirations would thus be protected through the exchange of concessions. At the same time, members could list reservations to the existing measures that do not conform with market-access and national-treatment obligations. Countries could then undertake commitments in clusters of their choice (creating a positive list of clusters) and at the same time maintain the existing nonconforming measures they intend to keep (creating a negative list of nonconforming measures).

Another aspect of GATS negotiating modalities is related to the provisions of Article XIX (Progressive Liberalization). Article XIX establishes that progressive liberalization shall be achieved in successive rounds of negotiations, the first of which should take place five years after the date of entry into force of the agreement, and periodically thereafter. The weakness of this provision is that it does not contemplate methods for further liberalization in the periods between negotiating rounds. The introduction of an approach similar to the "ratchet effect" included in other trade agreements would allow for progress in binding measures subject to liberalization in the time that elapses between one round and the next.[11]

Negotiating liberalization of trade in services is also challenging because of the complex mixture of nontariff measures that make it difficult to determine the degree of liberalization in a given service market. Although the multilateral system has dealt effectively with the major nontariff barriers affecting trade in goods and has made progress in identifying and ranking these obstacles and reducing their undesired effects on trade flows, this is not the case for services.

Several efforts are under way to categorize and even quantify the commercial impact of the measures affecting trade in services. The World Bank and the

10. See especially the Notes prepared by the WTO Secretariat to the Council on Trade in Services: Accountancy Services (S/C/W/73); Advertising Services (S/C/W/47); Air Transport Services (S/C/W/59); Architectural and Engineering Services (S/C/W/44); Audiovisual Services (S/C/W/40); Computer and Related Services (S/C/W/45); Construction and Related Engineering Services (S/C/W/38); Distribution Services (S/C/W/37); Education Services (S/C/W/49); Energy Services (S/C/W/49); Energy Services (S/C/W/52); Environmental Services (S/C/W/46); Financial Services (S/C/W/72); Health and Social Services (S/C/W/50); Land and Transport Services Part 1 (S/C/W/60); Land and Transport Services, Part 2 (S/C/W/61); Legal Services (S/C/W/43); Maritime Transport Services (S/C/W/62); Postal and Courier Services (S/C/W/39); Telecommunication Services (S/C/W/74); Tourism Services (S/C/W/51), Geneva.

11. See North American Free Trade Agreement, Chapter XII.

Australian government's Productivity Commission are leading these efforts.[12] A similar effort could be made for services, grouping these with the biggest impact on trade flows in specific categories or subcategories of services. The WTO Secretariat has provided support for the identification of measures affecting trade in services. The material collected in twenty-two sectors and the documents distributed by several member countries in these same sectors may help in this respect.[13]

Loopholes That Impair Commitments: "What You See Is Not What You Get"

Trade in services underscores the significance of issues such as consumer protection, market stability, level of specialization, technical proficiency and professional responsibility of service providers, national security, health protection, protection of law and order, and the prevention of fraudulent practices.[14] Some of these concerns are reflected in Article VI (Domestic Regulation), Article XIV (General Exceptions), and Article XIV bis (Security Exceptions). However, the current wording of Article VI leaves room for arbitrariness and discrimination in establishing the requirements and procedures for certification, technical standards, and licensing requirements, especially in the rendering of professional, technical, and specialized services.[15] Given that these requirements and procedures do not fall within the scope of Article XVI (Market Access) and Article XVII (National Treatment), the commercial significance of a commitment that includes the term "none" in both columns may be totally obscured because there are no transparent, appropriate, nondiscriminatory requirements and procedures regarding qualifications, technical standards, and licensing.[16]

It is therefore important to make effective the provisions of GATS Article VI(4) establishing that "the Council for Trade in Services shall, through the

12. Greg McGuire, "Australia's Restrictions on Trade in Financial Services," Staff Research Paper (Canberra, Australia: Productivity Commission, November 1998); S. Claessens and T. Glaessner, "Internationalization of Financial Services in Asia" (Washington: World Bank, 1998).

13. See especially Organization for Economic Cooperation and Development, "Survey of Measures Affecting Trade in Professional Services in the OECD Area," Doc. S/WPPS/W/4 (Paris).

14. See especially WTO, "Background Notes by the Secretariat" on different professional services: Accounting (S/C/W 73); Architecture and Engineering (S/C/W/44); Legal Services (S/C/W/43); Educational Services (S/C/W/49), Geneva.

15. WTO, "International Regulatory Initiatives in Services," Note by the Secretariat, WTO S/C/W/97 (March 1, 1999).

16. See also WTO, "Preparing for the GATS 2000 Negotiations," communication by Switzerland, Doc. S/C/W/103 (March 22, 1999).

appropriate bodies it may establish, develop any necessary disciplines to ensure that measures relating to qualification requirements, technical standards, and licensing requirements do not constitute unnecessary barriers to trade in services." The current wording of this article is ambiguous about the final goal of this provision. On the one hand, it is part of the general obligations of the agreement since it establishes the objective of achieving harmonized systems for accreditation, licensing, and technical standards. But this obligation is qualified by Article VI(5), which limits the scope of the provision exclusively to sectors that are the subject of specific commitments.[17]

Abundant material for developing harmonized disciplines and criteria under Article VI(4) has been compiled by the Working Group on Accountancy Services (particularly in the "Disciplines on Domestic Regulation Applicable to Accountancy Services"),[18] in the regulatory disciplines contained in the GATS Annex on Telecommunications, in the "Reference Paper" on regulatory principles for Basic Telecommunications (adopted April 24, 1996), and in the Annex on Financial Services in the paragraphs referring to prudential issues. Together, they could form the basis for multilateral agreements and plurilateral codes that would ensure an acceptable degree of nondiscriminatory liberalization and adequately safeguard issues linked to consumer protection, market stability, technical proficiency, and the professional responsibility of service providers.[19]

Nationality or permanent residence requirements for service suppliers in practice as well as in the national schedules also deny access to certain markets. One way to encourage the progressive eradication of such measures would be to remove, as a general obligation, nationality or permanent residence as a requirement for qualification, technical standards, and licensing procedures. The establishment of the no local presence requirement is also a desirable goal. Disciplines may also be needed to address other inequities, such as double taxation and social security.

Defending Fair and Loyal Market Competition

As progress is made in introducing free-market policies, making regulatory systems more flexible, and advancing the exposure of domestic economic activities to international competition while confining the state to subsidiary ac-

---

17. WTO, "Article VI:4 of the GATS: Disciplines on Domestic Regulation Applicable to All Services," Note by the Secretariat, Doc. S/C/W/96 (March 1, 1999).

18. WTO, "Document WTO S/L/64 (October 14, 1998).

19. On this subject, see also the provisions of the agreement between Australia and New Zealand entitled "Closer Economic Relations."

tivities, better institutional schemes to ensure adequate functioning for markets become even more essential.

This reality is particularly significant for services, where natural monopolies continue to operate in large sectors. Some of the problems that make it imperative for regulations to encourage competitive conditions in markets include restrictive trade practices, the relative imbalance between big companies and poorly organized consumer groups (such as the users of many services), and the inefficiencies that may result from difficulties in identifying critical links in the complex network of interconnected services.

The current GATS provisions are insufficient in this respect. Although Article IX on business practices acknowledges that "certain business practices . . . may restrain competition and thereby restrict trade in services," it merely calls for member countries to enter into consultation with a view to eliminating such practices and to giving these matters "sympathetic consideration." Unlike other GATS articles, Article IX contains no commitment to draw up multilateral and mandatory disciplines in this important matter.

Meager Progress on the Movement of Natural Persons

Commitments achieved in services provided through the temporary presence of natural persons are extremely limited. This weakness reduces the appeal of GATS, especially for developing countries, which have a limited financial capability to establish a commercial presence in other countries. The ability to make direct foreign investment continues to be concentrated among a small number of developed countries. However, thanks to increasingly lower costs in international transport, improved controls for supervising foreign citizens in the countries, enhanced fluency in world communications, and a growing and homogeneous demand for standardized goods and services from different markets, big opportunities are opening up for countries with qualified human resources willing to provide low-cost services.

Unfortunately, this situation has not been translated into the results achieved through GATS to date. The limited commitments in this field are restricted to intracompany personnel movements and to top-level executives, with little progress in the provision of professional services and much less—or none at all—in the provision of technical and specialized services. This circumstance calls for easing the temporary entry of service suppliers into the markets of GATS member countries, a move that would not only generate badly needed resources and foreign currency for the supplying countries but also provide consumers in importing countries with more abundant, more varied, and less costly services. Once more, regional agreements might throw some light on how to approach needed reforms in this field. Regional agreements have been able to preserve the stability of their member countries' labor markets and their freedom to implement their own immigration policies and regulations. And they have also succeeded in creating the conditions to facilitate the international movement of service suppliers to their mutual benefit.

The precarious status of the current "Annex on Movement of Natural Persons Supplying Services under the Agreement" and the difficulties that the GATS Working Group has encountered in making progress on this subject should not discourage the search for efficient solutions. The current asymmetry among countries' provisions and regulations governing obligations on commercial presence should facilitate the development of rules that would ease the restrictions on the temporary entry of service suppliers and not threaten individual countries' immigration policies. The adoption of speedy business visa systems and clear definitions of international service providers are only two examples.

Imprecisions and Deficiencies in Provisions on Economic Integration

One of the basic principles of the multilateral trade system, since its beginnings, has been to allow pairs or groups of member countries to move more quickly in enhancing their mutual economic integration than multilateral agreements allow. The expectation is that these more advanced bilateral and regional integration agreements will eventually be consolidated and adopted by a global integration system. The inclusion of Article XXIV of GATT in the original text of this agreement is one accomplishment toward that end.

Implementing economic integration has not been easy. The Uruguay Round of multilateral trade negotiations addressed this issue again and improved the provisions of the original articles in the "Understanding on the Interpretation of Article XXIV of the General Agreement on Tariffs and Trade of 1994."[20] The subject has caused concern in the services area among several members of the WTO, who underscored the need to supplement and improve GATS Article V (Economic Integration) and Article XXVII (Denial of Benefits), both of which determine the conditions for granting mutual preferences for services trade to members of economic integration agreements.[21]

---

20. WTO, "The Results of the Uruguay Round," pp. 32–35.
21. On improving GATS Article V, see "Systemic Issues Arising from Article V of the GATS," communication from Hong Kong–China, Doc. WT/REG/W/34 (February 19, 1999), WTO. For a detailed discussion of the application of GATS Article V to economic integration agreements, see the chapter by Sherry M. Stephenson in this volume.

Weak Provisions on Increasing the Participation of Developing Countries

GATS Article IV (Increasing Participation of Developing Countries) includes some provisions intended to facilitate developing-country participation "*inter alia*, through access to technology on a commercial basis" and "the improvement of their access to distribution channels and information networks." However, in most cases, developing countries have been unable to take advantage of the possibilities apparently offered by these provisions. They would need to make major, creative efforts to ensure that they comply with the purpose stated in the article. One solution might be to identify service clusters that give real commercial meaning to commitments as well as liberalization in the movement of natural persons.

Two Alternative Models of Subregional Integration in Services: Lessons for a Future FTAA

The two reference agreements on services discussed in the previous sections have been the source of several subregional and bilateral agreements among countries of the Western Hemisphere. Most of them have followed, with slight variations, the framework and the disciplines contained in NAFTA.[22] Some of them have even improved on the original NAFTA text, such as the free trade agreement signed by Mexico and Chile. For example, although this agreement largely reproduces the substance of NAFTA, it includes an additional obligation on "future liberalization."[23] This new provision specifies that, "through future negotiations to be called by the Commission, the Parties shall further the liberalization achieved in the various services sectors, with the aim of eliminating the remaining measures inscribed in conformity with Non-Conforming Measures." This provision does not exist in NAFTA or in the free trade agreement between Chile and Canada. It is included in several of the free trade agreements on services in the Western Hemisphere, namely treaties between Mexico and Bolivia, Mexico and Costa Rica, Mexico and Nicaragua, the Group of Three (Mexico, Colombia, and Venezuela), Chile and Mexico, and Chile and Central America.[24]

However, two groups of countries have chosen to design a framework of services disciplines that differs on some substantial points from the best-known

22. The free trade agreements between Chile and Canada, Chile and Central America, Chile and Mexico, Mexico and Costa Rica, Mexico and Bolivia, and the G-3 (Mexico, Colombia, and Venezuela).
23. Article 10-09 of the free trade agreement between Chile and Mexico.
24. See the chapter by Carlos Piñera González in this volume.

models. Both the Protocol of Montevideo on Trade in Services of MERCOSUR and the General Framework of Principles and Rules for the Liberalization of Services (Decision 439) of the Andean Community can be considered hybrids of the two reference models, even though they differ from each other in their closeness to the other models: MERCOSUR is closer to GATS, whereas Decision 439 of the Andean Community leans more toward NAFTA. But both agreements represent a step forward in the liberalization efforts of intraregional trade by improving on the models from which they drew their inspiration.

The Protocol of Montevideo on Trade in Services in MERCOSUR

On December 15, 1997, the Council of the Southern Cone Common Market approved the Protocol of Montevideo on Trade in Services in MERCOSUR. The protocol established principles and disciplines aimed at promoting free trade in services among the countries that signed the agreement: Argentina, Brazil, Paraguay, and Uruguay. The members agreed to initiate the proceedings for the legislative approval of the protocol "as soon as the Annexes containing specific sectoral rules and the Lists of commitments that form an integral part of [the Protocol] are approved by a Decision of the Common Market."[25]

Although at first glance the MERCOSUR protocol on services seems very similar to GATS, it contains liberalizing elements that make it markedly different. First, the general objective of MERCOSUR on services is distinctly more ambitious than that of GATS. Whereas GATS aims at expanding services trade based on transparency and progressive liberalization, the MERCOSUR protocol aims at promoting free trade or the complete liberalization of trade in services inside the subregion.[26]

Second, the two agreements differ substantially on the issue of most-favored-nation treatment. The absence of any kind of qualification to the MFN principle in the MERCOSUR protocol would indicate that countries have an obligation to repeal, immediately and unconditionally, any measure that discriminates against any party to this agreement and that derives from preexisting preferential sectoral agreements with another party or with third countries. The only exemptions, which are contained in paragraph 2 of Article III, allow "the concession of preferences to adjacent countries, whether or not they are Parties [to the agreement], with the objective of facilitating limited exchanges in the con-

25. Doc. MERCOSUR/CMC/DEC No. 13/97.
26. See the discussion of the MERCOSUR protocol on services in this volume in the chapter by María-Angélica Peña.

tiguous border zones of services that are produced and consumed locally." This obligation represents a substantial improvement over the rules established in GATS and certainly over NAFTA-type agreements, which allow reservations to protect preexisting or future agreements with the current members and with third countries.

But perhaps the most important difference between GATS and the MERCOSUR protocol is that whereas in the WTO agreement the obligations related to market access (Article XVI) and to national treatment (Article XVII) are part of the specific obligations of GATS (that is to say, they are subject to negotiation for each services sector or subsector), under the MERCOSUR protocol both market access (Article IV) and national treatment (Article V) are part of the general obligations and disciplines of the agreement and thus apply to all services. This feature makes the MERCOSUR protocol more similar to the structure of the NAFTA-type agreements. This significant difference has important juridical implications for the liberalizing potential of each type of agreement. Although the MERCOSUR agreement is to follow a liberalizing mechanism similar to GATS based on positive lists for the ten-year transition period, its ultimate objective is to apply Articles IV and V unconditionally to all services at the end of this period, starting from the entry into force of the agreement. On the other hand, while Article IV (Market Access) in the MERCOSUR protocol envisions the possibility of preserving nonconforming measures in accordance with what is specified in the lists of specific commitments, that possibility is not allowed for in the text of Article V (National Treatment). Nonetheless, Article VII (List of Specific Commitments) does authorize the indication of "the terms, limitations, and conditions in what concerns market access and national treatment." This again signals a difference from the language of GATS Article XVII (National Treatment), which allows, within the article, the listing of conditions and limitations to this obligation.

Another remarkable aspect is that paragraph 1 of Article IV (Market Access) of the MERCOSUR protocol includes substantial obligations with respect to financial transfers (cross-border movements of capital and capital transfers) that are similar, albeit less specific, than those contained in Article 1109 of the NAFTA Investment Chapter, yet broader than those of GATS. While GATS allows members to adopt measures related to current and capital transactions that are incompatible with specific acquired commitments, the MERCOSUR agreement states: "The Members commit themselves to allow the cross-border movement of capital that forms an essential part of a market access commitment in cross-border trade, as well as the transfer of capital to their territories when they are related to market access commitments related to commercial presence."

The rules on transparency in the MERCOSUR agreement also reflect an improvement over GATS. Although GATS obliges its members to notify the WTO about new laws and administrative directives that significantly affect trade in services covered by its specific commitments, in the MERCOSUR protocol the obligation is broader, requiring the notification of those measures that significantly affect trade in services in sectors that are included and sectors that are not included in the members' lists of specific commitments.

Concerning commercial practices, it has already been noted that the rules of GATS are extremely weak. By contrast, the MERCOSUR agreement contains in its Article XII (Defense of Competition), the obligation to apply to services trade "the rules of the Protocol on the Defense of Competition of the MERCOSUR." Government procurement (Article XV) and subsidies (Article XVI) receive similar treatment under the MERCOSUR agreement. In both cases, there is specific mention of the obligation to develop disciplines in those areas.

Perhaps the most promising aspect of the MERCOSUR agreement is the liberalization program set up in Part III, specifically in Article XIX (Negotiation of Specific Commitments). Paragraph 1 of this article states:

In complying with the objectives of the present Protocol, the Member States shall conduct successive rounds of negotiations with the purpose of completing, within a time-frame of ten years from the entry into force of this Protocol, the services trade Liberalization Program of MERCOSUR. The negotiating rounds shall be carried out annually and will have as their main objective the progressive incorporation of sectors, subsectors, activities, and modes of service provision into the Liberalization Program of the Protocol, *as well as the reduction or the elimination of the negative effects of measures on trade in services,* as a way of ensuring effective access to markets. [Emphasis added.]

This rule imposes a strong commitment to liberalization, with a time frame of no more than ten years, and encompasses the reduction or elimination of measures that impede services trade. No such provision exists in NAFTA or in GATS, and the wording is more forceful than the language of the free trade agreements negotiated by Mexico and Chile.

The Liberalization of Trade in Services in the Andean Community

On June 11, 1998, the Commission of the Andean Community approved by way of Decision 439 the General Framework of Principles and Rules for the Liberalization of Trade in Services in the Andean Community, which is aimed

at creating a market for the free trade of services no later than 2005. This decision entered into force on June 17, 1998, when it was published in Official
Bulletin No. 347 of the Cartagena Agreement.[27]

Decision 439 of the Andean Community is one of twenty-three decisions
that refer to various services-related areas.[28] The complementary decisions on
services issues address the areas of tourism, transport and communications,
maritime cargo, air and road transportation, telecommunications, satellite systems, and others.[29] Decision 439 is likely the most ambitious of all schemes of
economic integration for services in the Western Hemisphere. Its main objective is to create a market for the free circulation of services in the Andean
Community. An additional goal is to progressively give shape to an Andean
common market in services, as a fundamental component of subregional integration. This objective would require the members to harmonize all the rules,
laws, and regulations that affect the provision of services and to define a common external policy in this area. The establishment of a common market in
services is far from the goals of other subregional or bilateral agreements on
trade in services in the hemisphere. Its only counterpart can be found in the
efforts undertaken by the European Union.

The agreement of the Andean Community employs elements of both GATS
and NAFTA but also introduces improvements that would make possible a
more rapid liberalizing process than that allowed for by its two models. In
Chapter I (Article 1) the framework establishes the general objective of "progressive liberalization in intrasubregional trade in services with the goal of creating an Andean Common Market in Services, by way of the elimination of
restrictive measures inside the Community." The same article calls for the harmonization of "national sectoral policies where necessary." As in GATS and
the MERCOSUR agreement, trade in services is defined by the modes of delivery and includes commercial presence (Chapter II, Article 2).

Chapter III addresses the scope of application of the agreement and stipulates that the acquisition of services by government agencies shall be subject to
the principle of national treatment in accordance with a decision to be adopted
no later than January 1, 2002. If such a decision is not adopted by that date, the
parties shall extend national treatment immediately (Article 4). However, Ar-

27. Legislation and Jurisprudence, Andean Community General Secretariat, Decision 439,
ninety-fourth extraordinary session period, June 11, 1998. (Available only in Spanish)
(www.comunidadandina.org).

28. On Decision 439, see the chapter by María Esperanza Dangond in this volume.

29. See Decisions 171, 185, 224, 277, 288, 290, 297, 314, 320, 331, 360, 361, 390, 393, 395,
398, 399, 429, 440, 462, 463, and 467 of the Andean Community on legislation and jurisprudence (www.comunidadandina.org).

ticle 5 of this chapter indicates that the sectors or subsectors covered by existing sectoral decisions and their modifications are regulated by the rules contained in those decisions. This provision calls into question the degree of compatibility between such regulations and those provided for in Decision 439.

Chapter IV refers to the principles and commitments of the general framework. Articles 6 (Market Access); 7 (Most-Favored Nation); 8 (National Treatment); 9 (Transparency); 10 (Status Quo); 11 (Free Transit and the Temporary Presence of Natural Persons); and 13 (Recognition of Licenses, Certifications, Professional Titles, and Accreditations) define the totality of general obligations applicable to intraregional trade in services. This broad bundle of obligations is significantly more substantial than that covered by other services agreements. However, the wording of certain articles could weaken the liberalizing and nondiscriminatory potential of the agreement.

The language of Article 10 on the status quo places this agreement far ahead of the other services integration schemes in the hemisphere and contains the strongest obligations with respect to transparency and legal certainty in carrying out trade in services. Article 10 states the following: "The Member countries commit themselves to not establish new measures that raise the level of non-conformity contained in Articles 6 and 8 of this General Framework, starting from its entry into force. This commitment shall cover all the measures adopted by Member countries that affect trade in services, those derived from the central, regional, or local public sector, as well as those derived from those entities delegated by the former." This obligation has no precedent in the other regional agreements on services in establishing, in fact, a "status quo" commitment for all the measures that affect trade in services in all modes of delivery. This commitment, together with the inventory of measures called for in Article 14 and the progressive dismantling of nonconforming measures stipulated in Article 15, greatly solidifies the obligations established by this agreement and its ability to achieve the liberalization of trade in services. The actual language of Article 10 does not permit the exemption of any services sectors from the status quo commitment. This is an important difference from NAFTA-type agreements, all of which foresee the possibility of making reservations on the adoption of future measures that raise the nonconformity level of the obligations in some services sectors and subsectors.

Article 7 on most-favored-nation treatment seems to indicate that the Andean agreement does not permit exemptions from obligation, whether between parties to the agreement or with third countries. However, the second paragraph of Article 9 on transparency commitments says: "The international agreements signed with third parties which refer to or affect the functioning of the provisions of the present General Framework, shall be notified to the General Secretariat of the Andean Community, that in turn shall bring them to the knowledge of the other Member countries." This would seem to indicate that by way of a simple notification, it is possible to permanently exempt from MFN treatment those preferential agreements in services signed with third parties. This provision could seriously threaten the goal of reducing the level of discrimination in the treatment accorded to member countries and to third countries and be an insuperable obstacle to the goal of creating an Andean common market in services.

The obligations concerning the movement of natural persons and the procedures for the recognition of licenses, degrees, and certificates are to be subject to rules that will be developed in the future either by the Andean Council of Foreign Ministers (for the movement of natural persons) or by the commission itself in the case of the procedures for the recognition of degrees and certificates.

One of the most remarkable aspects of the Andean agreement addresses the commitments on transparency. In Chapter V, Article 14 stipulates: "In a period not exceeding 31 December 1999, the Commission of the Andean Community shall adopt, by way of a Decision, an inventory of measures that are maintained by each Member country and that run counter to the principles contained in Articles 6 and 8 of the present General Framework." This information is key to progressive liberalization and to efforts aimed at harmonizing the existing regulations in each member country. At the same time, it constitutes an instrument of extraordinary commercial value for the conduct of services trade between Andean countries.

Article 15 envisages annual negotiations that set out to dismantle, gradually and progressively, the measures contained in the inventory referred to in Article 14, reiterating that this process shall culminate no later than 2005 "through the lifting of the measures maintained by each Member country." In addition, the commission shall identify "the sectors that by nature of their characteristics and peculiarities will be subject to a specific sectoral liberalization or harmonization."

Chapter VI includes provisions related to precautionary measures and sanctions for the use of practices that distort competition (Article 17), promotion and incentive measures (Article 18), and international transfers by way of current and capital transactions (Article 19).

Chapter VIII, Article 20, allows for special treatment of Bolivia and Ecuador and gives them more time and temporary exceptions in complying with their obligations. In addition, the competent authorities have been charged with working out specific disciplines in financial services and telecommunications, as well as with elaborating a communitywide regime for the recognition of licenses, certificates, professional degrees, and accreditation in any services activities that require it.

Some Thoughts on a Hemispheric Agreement on Services

It may seem overly optimistic to expect a services agreement under the purview of the FTAA to eliminate all the weaknesses of the main existing agreements. However, taken together, elements from each of them would make it possible to undertake the hemispheric liberalization of services in such a way as to ensure the achievement of mutually advantageous outcomes, with an adequate equilibrium of rights and obligations for all the members.

In order to expand hemispheric production, it may be necessary for the participants to compromise in some areas to accommodate the varied interests in and heterogeneous approaches to services trade. They will need to reach a consensus on itineraries, negotiating spaces, and issue-specific priorities in order to ensure a realistic and acceptable pace of progress.

As some of the agreements, in particular that of the Andean Community, have shown, it is always possible for members with less-developed or smaller economies to move more slowly than others in adopting obligations in order to minimize their costs of restructuring. This differential treatment may include technical support from the other countries to help them develop the institutions and standards that will facilitate their active participation in commerce. Likewise, those countries with more open systems should receive some form of credit for the unilateral liberalizing processes that they have already undertaken. Otherwise, these countries may see few incentives for consolidating their opening levels in exchange for the preservation of protective measures in sectors and markets that are of interest to them. One approach might be to allow countries with higher protection levels to commit themselves to implementing their opening programs at a faster pace than was required for the adoption of commitments by the more open countries.

Finally, the adoption of disciplines should be wide in scope and consistent with the objective of promoting the progressive liberalization of markets. This would not require adopting obligations that go beyond those of market access and national treatment. One way or another, the erosions caused to commitments in these areas by the application of national regulations that undermine such commitments must be confronted in an efficient manner. Particularly with respect to procedures for granting accreditation, licenses, and certificates, it would be desirable to develop "necessity tests" administered by all members in a way that ensures that national regulations adopted to serve legitimate national policy objectives have the slightest possible distortionary effect on services trade.

To the extent that regional spaces allow greater rapprochement between adjacent economies, they also allow a greater depth of reform and a greater commercial opening toward full economic integration. At the same time, the wider these regional areas, the fewer the contradictions in the multilateral system, the better their opportunities for trade creation, and the smaller the distortionary and diversionary trade effects they could generate.

For the countries of the Western Hemisphere, the options are clear and viable. The process set in motion at the Santiago Summit in April 1998 for the negotiation of the Free Trade Area of the Americas ensures that this should be so. The FTAA process offers a unique opportunity for the countries of the hemisphere to position themselves at the vanguard of reform of the multilateral system by developing disciplines that comply with the requirement of being GATS-plus in the area of services and that create the conditions for revitalizing intrahemispheric commerce and thereby raising the levels of income and well-being of their populations.

The countries that form part of the FTAA represented 23.5 percent of worldwide services exports and 22.8 percent of worldwide goods exports in 1994. Even though the average level of hemispheric services and goods exports is similar to the global average (27 percent for the FTAA countries, 26 percent globally), these figures vary substantially *among* the FTAA countries.[30] Twelve of the thirty-four participating countries have services exports that are at least double the size of their merchandise exports (including one, Antigua and Barbuda, where the rate is seven times higher for services); another six have services exports that are between 34 percent and 97 percent of their merchandise exports.

These are some of the reasons for developing a set of hemispheric disciplines in the area of services that could eventually converge with the multilateral system, especially in fields where it will not be possible to initiate the reforms during the next round of multilateral trade negotiations.

---

30. Francisco J. Prieto and Sherry M. Stephenson, "Regional Liberalization of Trade in Services by Countries of the Western Hemisphere," paper prepared for the Conference "Multilateral and Regional Trade Issues" sponsored by Georgetown University and the Organization of American States, Washington, D.C., May 26–27, 1998.

Immediate Priorities for Negotiation of a Hemispheric Agreement on Trade in Services

—Separate the disciplines that apply to cross-border commerce from those that apply to investments in order for the latter to encompass *all* foreign direct investment.

—Include *all* services (including air transport), and organize them in a system of services clusters.

—Develop a negotiating mechanism based on commitments related to the services clusters. This mechanism would allow reservations counter to the obligations of market access and national treatment already in force.

—Develop a methodology that creates greater transparency of the commercial effects of reservations on market access and national treatment. The effects of measures in specific services clusters would be considered individually.

—Develop obligatory guidelines for the harmonization of requirements and procedures for qualification, technical standards, and licensing, including a "necessity test" in such a way that these do not constitute unnecessary barriers to trade in services.

—Develop obligatory guidelines for model agreements on double taxation and double provisional assessment.

—Facilitate, by way of special disciplines, the temporary entry of service providers into the markets of member countries.

—Improve the institutional mechanisms at the international and national levels that allow the markets to function well. The existence of natural monopolies, asymmetries among competitors, and the need to protect the interests and well-being of consumers require the development of norms that will simulate competitive conditions in markets where these do not occur spontaneously.

CHAPTER THIRTEEN

Negotiating Services Agreements:
Challenges Ahead

MARYSE ROBERT

THE CONFERENCE ON SERVICES TRADE AND THE WESTERN HEMISPHERE, held in San José, Costa Rica, in July 1999, brought together services negotiators from governments of the Americas, private sector executives from prominent service industries, representatives of national service coalitions, regulators, and academics. Over two days, participants reviewed the progress achieved in services trade as a result of multilateral and regional rulemaking and unilateral trade liberalization and reform. They assessed the main achievements and shortcomings of the services agreements under the World Trade Organization (WTO) and various trade arrangements in the Western Hemisphere. They also discussed the challenges facing countries at the beginning of the negotiations under the WTO General Agreement on Trade in Services (GATS) and the Free Trade Area of the Americas (FTAA). This chapter summarizes the key issues addressed during that conference.

The Growth and Importance of Services Trade

In the 1990s services grew significantly as a share of international trade. According to the WTO, on a balance-of-payments basis, the growth of world services trade outstripped the growth of merchandise trade by 1 to 3 percent each year during the decade. As a whole, the Western Hemisphere accounts for almost a quarter of total world exports of services. Rolf Adlung of the WTO Secretariat mentioned, however, that Latin America is the only large region in the world where exports have grown more rapidly in goods than in services. From 1990 to 1997, services exports grew at an annual rate of 8 percent, whereas merchandise exports increased by 10 percent annually.[1] Adlung suggested that the shift away from import substitution in the area of services may partially explain higher growth in merchandise trade in Latin America. He also noted that this phenomenon may reflect the fact that services embodied in the export of goods are not counted as such because of the poor quality of services statistics. Data from 1994 show that eleven FTAA countries, nine of which are in the Caribbean, have a ratio of service to merchandise export higher than 100 percent, indicating that they are very dependent on services for export earnings.[2]

Services are critical inputs for the production of a wide range of goods and other services, commented Jeffrey Schott of the Institute for International Economics. Service outputs may also be the result of a combination of certain goods and services. In tourism, for instance, a country needs an efficient transportation network, advanced telecommunications, marketing services, and hotel facilities in order to be competitive.

Growth in services trade has greatly benefited from rulemaking, regulatory changes, and technological innovations. Adlung observed that these factors are intertwined. It was technology that first pushed services onto the domestic regulatory agenda and later into the international arena.

Improving GATS

Negotiated during the Uruguay Round, GATS is the first multilateral framework to be developed in the area of trade in services. Efforts to bring trade in services into the multilateral arena started in the early 1980s. The 1982 Ministerial Declaration of the General Agreement on Tariffs and Trade (GATT) included a recommendation to study services trade and to consider whether multilateral action was appropriate or desirable. At the beginning of the Uruguay Round in 1986, the matter was contentious. Several developing countries feared that proposals on services would favor industrialized countries because of their comparative advantage in know-how and technology. As a result, services discussions were put on a separate track. In the end, though, GATS became one of

1. On trade in services, see Guy Karsenti, "How Significant Are the Barriers? Measuring Impediments to Trade in Services," paper prepared for the World Services Congress, Atlanta, Georgia, Nov. 1–3, 1999.
2. Francisco J. Prieto and Sherry M. Stephenson, "Multilateral and Regional Liberalization of Trade in Services," in Miguel Rodriguez Mendoza, Patrick Low, and Barbara Kotschwar, eds., *Trade Rules in the Making: Challenges in Regional and Multilateral Negotiations* (Washington: Organization of American States/Brookings Institution Press, 1999), pp. 238–39.

the annexes to the agreement that established the WTO. It has twenty-nine articles supplemented by various protocols, annexes, and ministerial decisions. Since GATS might have been a free-standing agreement, it covers all the issues pertaining to trade in services. As underlined by William Yue of the U.S. Department of Commerce, GATS is therefore much more self-contained than most services agreements in the Western Hemisphere. In the North American Free Trade Agreement (NAFTA), for example, cross-border services, investment, temporary entry of business persons, government procurement, safeguards, dispute settlement, and other relevant issues are covered in different chapters.

At the San José conference, discussions about how to improve GATS centered on the exemptions to most-favored-nation (MFN) treatment and especially on the implications of GATS Article V, the need to revisit GATS Articles XVI (Market Access) and XVII (National Treatment) in order to separate non-discriminatory quantitative restrictions from discriminatory measures, and how to reconcile trade and regulatory objectives, liberalization modalities, service sector classification, and mutually exclusive definitions of modes of supply.

MFN Exemptions

The MFN provision of GATS set out in Article II applies across the board to all members and all service sectors. Temporary exemptions are allowed if listed in an annex at the time of the entry into force of the agreement; any exemptions are subject to multilateral review. Francisco Prieto of the University of Chile and consultant to the Ministry of Foreign Affairs in Chile noted, however, that several of the 380 exempted measures listed by seventy WTO members have an indefinite duration, even if, in principle, they should not exceed ten years. Geza Feketekuty of the Monterey Institute of International Studies and former U.S. services negotiator in the Uruguay Round, pointed out that, in addition to the exemptions taken to the obligations under Article II, there are three other types of MFN exceptions: those allowed under certain conditions in GATS Article V on economic integration agreements (see section below); those permitted under the agreements on mutual recognition built into GATS Article VII; and those included in the agreements on recognition of prudential systems in the Financial Services Annex. Feketekuty explained that the MFN principle is not simple to apply in services. He noted that MFN is meaningless in numerous service industries because the regulatory systems of different countries vary so greatly. This is the case, for example, in professional services with respect to experience and education obtained and in financial services with regard to prudential matters. GATS allows for the negotiation of mutual-recognition agreements (MRAs) to address these regulatory issues. Such agreements are generally negotiated bilaterally and therefore constitute a de facto departure from MFN treatment. Feketekuty concluded that model instruments with regard to MRAs should be developed to deal with regulatory matters. This would encourage third-party accessions.

Implications of GATS Article V

Regional trading arrangements violate the MFN principle in GATS Article II because they give their members preferential treatment. Such violations are allowed under GATS Article V if the economic integration agreements have substantial sectoral coverage, eliminate substantially all discrimination as called for in Article XVII (National Treatment), and do not raise the overall level of barriers to services trade for third parties. In San José, Sherry Stephenson of the Organization of American States (OAS) argued that GATS Article V lacks clarity and suffers from having inherited most of the concepts of GATT Article XXIV, which applies to goods only. In particular, Stephenson pointed out that the requirement on "substantial sectoral coverage" is difficult to assess. The lack of disaggregated data in the area of services makes it almost impossible to measure services trade by sector.

The second requirement under GATS Article V, to eliminate substantially all discrimination, is also challenging because services trade barriers are not present at the border. They are contained in the form of laws, decrees, regulations, and regulatory practices of individual countries. Bernard Hoekman of the World Bank noted that it is appropriate to ask whether it makes a difference if liberalization takes place at the multilateral or regional level in services. The transformation of regulatory structures, which is the basis of much of the liberalization in trade in services, is almost impossible to apply on a preferential basis, and therefore any liberalization is good liberalization. However, the manner in which liberalization is achieved may have a substantial impact on third parties.

Stephenson addressed the issue of determining whether the overall level of barriers to services trade for third parties has increased. She underlined the data and methodological difficulties inherent in calculating the price equivalent of the trade-restrictive effects of national laws and regulations. She also raised two other issues: countries' low compliance with the requirement that they notify the WTO of their regional agreements, and the application of GATS Article V to the FTAA.

Revisiting Articles XVI (Market Access) and XVII (National Treatment)

The GATS provisions regarding market access in Article XVI and national treatment in Article XVII are conditional in the sense that they reflect the specific sectoral and mode-of-supply commitments listed in each member's schedule of obligations. Geza Feketekuty suggested that these two articles need to be revisited. Article XVI covers two types of quantitative limitations on the delivery of services: those that apply to any services or service providers and those that apply only to foreigners (and are thus discriminatory). Since there is an overlap between the terms of GATS Articles XVI and XVII when quantitative limitations are placed on foreign services or service providers, Article XX(2) of GATS provides that a measure that is inconsistent with both articles should be listed under the market-access column in a country's schedule. But Feketekuty underlined that "the entry in the market-access column is limiting on national treatment only if it represents a specific quantitative limitation on foreigners. However, some countries have a different interpretation of Article XX(2)."[3] In fact, these countries assume that they are not fully committed on national treatment when they have taken no commitment (that is, they are "unbound") in their market-access column, even if they have made no restrictions under national treatment. To solve this problem, Feketekuty proposes putting all forms of discriminatory barriers, be they qualitative or quantitative, into the national-treatment column (Article XVII), and renaming GATS Article XVI "Nondiscriminatory Quantitative Restrictions on Services." He suggests that this would allow countries to highlight progress on trade liberalization by scheduling commitments under the national-treatment column and progress on domestic regulatory reform by scheduling commitments under the market-access column.

How to Reconcile Trade and Regulatory Objectives

The trade-impeding aspects of national regulatory measures are covered by GATS in the transparency commitments, the obligations under Article VI(5), and the national scheduling commitments under Articles XVI and XVII. GATS Article VI(4) requires that the Council for Trade in Services develop standards to ensure that technical standards, licensing requirements, and other types of regulatory measures are based on objective and transparent criteria, such as competence and the ability to supply the service; are not more burdensome than necessary to ensure the quality of the service; and are, in the case of licensing procedures, not in themselves a restriction on the supply of the service. Pending the entry into force of disciplines to be negotiated under GATS Article VI(4), GATS Article VI(5) provides that, in sectors where it has undertaken commitments, a WTO member must not apply licensing and qualification re-

---

3. This and other quotations in this chapter are taken from notes made by the chapter author at the July 1999 conference in San José, Costa Rica.

quirements and technical standards that nullify or impair such specific commitments in a manner that does not comply with the criteria outlined in GATS Article VI(4), and that could not reasonably have been expected of that member at the time the specific commitments in those sectors were made. In San José, Joel Trachtman of the Fletcher School of Law and Diplomacy at Tufts University argued that the GATS provisions on the matter are not as strong as those of the Agreement on the Application of Sanitary and Phytosanitary Measures and those of the Agreement on Technical Barriers to Trade. Those two WTO agreements do not incorporate a nullification or impairment requirement, which means, commented Trachtman, that "in the case of trade in goods, determination of a violation of a provision of a covered agreement results in prima facie nullification or impairment under Article 3(8) of the Dispute Settlement Understanding, whereas under Article VI(5) of GATS, if there is no nullification or impairment, there is no violation."

Trachtman explained that several options are available to GATS negotiators for imposing stronger disciplines on nondiscriminatory domestic regulation. WTO members may choose to "laisser régler"—that is, to give countries the freedom to regulate as they already do. They may opt for enhanced policed regulation by providing stronger standards for application to domestic regulation in dispute resolution, such as in the "Disciplines on Domestic Regulation in the Accountancy Sector" developed by the WTO Working Party on Professional Services. Alternatively, they may favor "rules of harmonization and/or rules of recognition negotiated and enforced multilaterally." Geza Feketekuty pointed out that WTO members should prioritize negotiations called for under GATS Article VI(4) and adopt the objectives listed in that article. He suggests the inclusion of four additional principles in GATS Article VI(4): transparency of regulatory objectives, appropriate use of market mechanisms, minimizing the scope of regulations, and use of international regulatory standards.

Liberalization: Where Do We Go from Here?

The Uruguay Round produced only modest commitments to liberalization. There are large gaps in the GATS schedules of commitments across members, sectors, and modes. GATS makes use of what is known as a "positive list," a list on which each member identifies the sectors covered by the agreement. In the mode-of-supply context, the agreement uses a "negative list" approach. Once a sector is listed in a member's schedule, that member is bound in full by the market-access and national-treatment obligations for the four modes of supply, unless a limitation to that treatment is specified. The level of policy commitments in most sectors has not, however, gone beyond the status quo, except in basic telecommunications and financial services. As pointed out by Rolf Adlung, large, economically important sectors such as air and maritime transport have eluded any significant inclusion. Adlung also noted that the focus of the first round of multilateral negotiations on services was on rulemaking, not on liberalization: "There is no requirement regarding the breadth or depth of individual countries' commitments. GATS requires each member to submit a schedule of concessions, but it does not define its sectoral scope." Therefore, small participating countries with nonlucrative markets found it relatively easy to avoid economically meaningful commitments.

Adlung explained that, of the 160 subsectors included in the GATS classification list, one-third of all WTO members undertook commitments in fewer than twenty-one subsectors; another third included in their schedules between twenty-one and eighty subsectors, and the remaining third made commitments in up to 145 subsectors. The composition of these groups reflects their level of development: industrialized countries generally have broader coverage.[4] These 160 subsectors are classified in eleven broad sectors, including tourism, which has the highest number of binding commitments. More than 120 of the 135 WTO members have made some form of commitment in one or more of the subsectors in that area. Finally, the majority of commitments have been made subject to limitations. For others, the entry into force may be phased in over time. This instrument, known as "pre-commitments," has been used quite frequently in basic telecommunications.

There is a striking contrast among the commitments made under each of the individual modes of supply. Mode 2, consumption abroad, has been scheduled for full liberalization (without limitations) by about half of the WTO members for both market access and national treatment; mode 1, cross-border services, by about 25 to 30 percent; mode 3, commercial presence, by 20 percent; and mode 4, movement of natural persons, by less than 1 percent. Moreover, it is worth noting that the negative list approach has been turned on its head in the modal context. Most schedules include a number of "unbound" entries. Commercial presence, as underlined by Francisco Prieto, is "the mode with the lowest percentage of unbound commitments." This observation led Sherry Stephenson to question whether the structure of commitments in GATS favors the development of services trade along the lines of comparative advantage for small and medium-sized economies (in modes 1 and 2). Pierre Sauvé of Harvard University's Kennedy School of Government argued that local-presence disciplines or the right of nonestablishment as in NAFTA promote cross-border

---

4. However, Adlung mentioned that one least-developed country has made commitments in eighty-five subsectors.

services: "They encourage regulators to start thinking about alternative ways of satisfying legitimate concerns, which otherwise prompt them to require establishment as a precondition for delivery."

The imbalances in commitments under GATS among members, sectors, and modes define the starting line of the new round of trade talks. GATS Article XIX requires WTO members to launch services negotiations no later than the year 2000. It provides for successive rounds of services negotiations with the aim of achieving progressively greater liberalization. Francisco Prieto noted that the main shortcoming of GATS Article XIX is that it does not provide for a ratchet mechanism similar to the one included in several free trade agreements in the Western Hemisphere. Such a mechanism would allow unilateral liberalization between negotiating rounds to be automatically incorporated into a country's commitments. Pierre Sauvé suggested that FTAA countries have the opportunity to go beyond GATS by adopting such an instrument.

However, the main problem in negotiating liberalization commitments is that GATS has relied in the past on the request-offer approach. Since services barriers cannot be converted into tariff equivalents that could then be made subject to reduction formulas, the formula or model approach has had a limited role so far in services negotiations. But the request-offer approach has its own limitations. One participant in the conference noted that the larger traders tend to pursue the export agenda of their economically strong sectors and that the request-offer approach does little to promote liberalization in economically weak and peripheral markets. The idea of the formula approach is not to impose rigid solutions across countries and ask WTO members to override the developmental objectives contained in the agreement, but to encourage them to consider greater liberalization. One "soft formula" proposed during the conference would be to require all members to undertake commitments in at least one subsector in each of the eleven services areas classified under GATS.[5]

Sector Classification and Mutually Exclusive Definitions of Modes of Supply

Several speakers and participants identified two other issues related to national schedules and liberalization commitments that should be improved in the next round of multilateral negotiations. First, Francisco Prieto raised the problem of incomplete coverage and ambiguous definitions in the GATS sector

---

5. For an excellent article on formula approaches, see Rachel Thompson, "Formula Approaches to Improving the GATS Commitments: Some Options for Negotiators," paper prepared for the World Services Congress, Nov. 1–3, 1999.

classification system. Bonnie Richardson of the Motion Picture Association of America (MPAA) and former U.S. negotiator in the Uruguay Round gave a vivid example of major sectors falling between the cracks because the GATS classification system does not mention them: two highly traded services, investment in cable infrastructure and investment in service provision by satellite-delivered television services, are nowhere listed in the GATS classification list. Roberto Echandi of Costa Rica's Ministry of Foreign Trade noted the additional problem of services incorporated into goods, such as magazines. In the periodicals case between Canada and the United States, the question became which of the GATT or GATS classification systems should apply.[6] It was finally decided that both systems apply simultaneously. Pierre Sauvé observed that the negative list approach, as used in NAFTA, does not entail the need for such a classification support because the focus is on the nature of the measure that has discriminatory or market access–impairing effects, regardless of the sector in which it falls. Sauvé also emphasized that "the nature of services is so dynamic that new services are emerging all the time. Classification will always be a moving target and will always be behind negotiations." Another important issue is the arbitrary separation of the four modes of supply. For example, during the next round of negotiations, WTO members will have to decide which mode(s) covers electronic transactions. In what circumstances do they fall under mode 1 or mode 2? Whatever decisions are made could affect the schedules of countries that had a different interpretation in mind when they made commitments under GATS in the Uruguay Round.

Negotiating Services Agreements: The Challenges Ahead

Participants in the San José conference identified numerous challenges facing countries in the negotiation of a services agreement. First, as in any negotiation, to make the process work, each state needs to have a clear strategy, commented Bernard Hoekman. Information is the key to determining domestic objectives. Data on the effects of policies on domestic industries are crucial. So is information about barriers imposed by other countries that may inhibit access to their markets.

Luis Abugattas of the Economic and Social Research Institute of the National Society of Industries in Peru noted that such information is usually not available. He emphasized that expanding empirical work in the area of services

6. On the periodicals case, see World Trade Organization, "Canada—Certain Measures Concerning Periodicals: Report of the Panel," WT/DS31/R, October 14, 1997; and World Trade Organization, "Canada—Certain Measures Concerning Periodicals: Report of the Appellate Body," WT/DS31/AB/R, October 30, 1997.

trade will be necessary if countries are to be convinced to embrace liberalization. Geza Feketekuty concurred. He emphasized the need for a thorough analysis of the implications of making commitments for the regulatory process and for being able to meet regulatory objectives. He observed that most schedules in GATS say "unbound" because countries were unsure, for lack of information, of the real implications of making commitments. Eduardo Lizano, president of the Central Bank of Costa Rica, mentioned that the lack of information has allowed a few key sociopolitical groups in developing countries to slow down the liberalization process. For instance, local service providers may worry that if their services are less technologically advanced they will not be able to compete in the new economy. In many countries, these services are in the hands of state enterprises with monopoly power and a strong trade-union component. Moreover, regulators often resist opening services markets because they fear losing some of their discretionary power, a situation also prevalent in industrialized countries. Better information would allow local groups to develop their comparative advantages and would support market opening.

To increase transparency and provide additional information on the entire domain of service industries, Bernard Hoekman argued that the multilateral trading system could be of great help. He suggested that the mandate of the WTO Trade Policy Review Mechanism (TPRM) be expanded by having governments report on their regulatory regimes as they apply to different sectors. This exercise would not be a scheduling commitment but would increase transparency by providing information about discriminatory and nondiscriminatory barriers. Hoekman noted that this mechanism could also apply regionally. The adoption of the negative list approach in several trade arrangements in the Western Hemisphere offers more transparency than the positive list approach of GATS because all sectors are covered except those that are specifically exempted. However, he reiterated what Sherry Stephenson had previously noted: in practice, the members of many of the free trade agreements negotiated among Latin American countries have not made public their list of reservations. Therefore, transparency is also needed at the regional level.

Hoekman reminded the participants that there is much to be gained by participating in international trade negotiations. He emphasized that countries should use negotiations as an opportunity to lock in policies and to signal to the international financial community that the negotiated agreement provides legal security with respect to these policies. Pierre Sauvé added that trade negotiations and trade liberalization are not ends in themselves. Rather, they are means of promoting efficiency and generating growth and development. Sauvé argued that unilateral liberalization, particularly for a small country, is always a good idea. He pointed out that most countries in the region have "embraced the need to promote privatization of key service industries, enforce competition policy more actively, and develop procompetitive and market access–friendly regulatory regimes." Sauvé noted, however, that the signaling effect of unilateral liberalization is more powerful when bound in international agreements. He particularly underscored the need for the Western Hemisphere to gain credibility by narrowing the gap between bound and applied commitments to market openness. Although he cautioned countries to maintain a rational degree of expectations regarding likely negotiating outcomes, Sauvé observed that "one should never discount the considerable confidence-building value of locking in the regulatory status quo."

Robert Vastine, president of the U.S. Coalition of Service Industries, ended the conference by emphasizing that countries must have a stake in trade liberalization: "There has to be a goal, a reason, a motivation to undertake the pain of opening up markets, of loosening up entrenched monopolies. Negotiators need to reflect on what will motivate the body politic to undertake the steps necessary to bite the bullet." Geza Feketekuty reiterated that countries first have to identify the domestic and foreign barriers in each of their key sectors, and then analyze the implications and effects of liberalization commitments on their export opportunities and on the modernization and development of their domestic economies.

Contributors

María Esperanza Dangond is responsible for services negotiations in the General Secretariat of the Andean Community in Lima, Peru.

Geza Feketekuty is distinguished professor of commercial diplomacy, Monterey Institute of International Studies, and president of International Commercial Diplomacy Project, Inc.

Pamela Coke Hamilton is a trade lawyer on secondment from the government of Jamaica to the Caribbean Regional Negotiating Machinery (RNM).

Eduardo Lizano is president of the Central Bank of Costa Rica.

Hector A. Millán Smitmans is an attorney and senior counselor in the WTO Secretariat in Geneva, Switzerland. During the Uruguay Round he was responsible for the Negotiating Group on Institutions, which negotiated the Marrakesh agreement that established the World Trade Organization and the Understanding on Rules and Procedures Governing the Settlement of Disputes (DSU).

Kalypso Nicolaïdis is associate professor at the John F. Kennedy School of Government, Harvard University, and a fellow of St. Anthony's College, Oxford University.

María-Angélica Peña is a specialist in services and director of the Department of Trade Policy, Office of Planning and Budget, Uruguay.

Carlos Piñera González is director general of negotiations on services of the Secretariat of Commerce and Industrial Development, government of Mexico.

Francisco Javier Prieto is former chair of the FTAA Working Group on Services and a consultant on services to the Ministry of Foreign Affairs, Chile.

Maryse Robert is a senior trade specialist with the Trade Unit of the Organization of American States.

Alvaro R. Sarmiento is coordinator of the Project of Support to the Participation of Central America (PROALCA) in the Free Trade Area of the Americas (FTAA), a project of the U.S. Agency for International Development (USAID) and the Secretaria de Integración Economía Centroamericana (SIECA).

Pierre Sauvé teaches at Harvard University's John F. Kennedy School of Government and is a fellow of its Center for Business and Government. He is also nonresident senior fellow at the Brookings Institution while on leave from the Organization for Economic Cooperation and Development (OECD) in Paris.

Sherry M. Stephenson is deputy director of the Trade Unit of the Organization of American States (OAS).

Joel P. Trachtman is professor of international law and academic dean at the Fletcher School of Law and Diplomacy, Tufts University.

Index